KT-153-129

THE CHILDHOOD BIPOLAR DISORDER

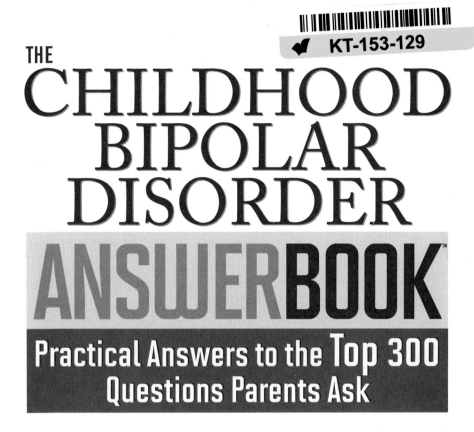

ANSWERBOOK™

Practical Answers to the Top 300 Questions Parents Ask

TRACY ANGLADA AND SHERYL M. HAKALA, MD

SOURCEBOOKS, INC.®
NAPERVILLE, ILLINOIS

Copyright © 2008 by Tracy Anglada and Sheryl M. Hakala, MD
Cover and internal design © 2008 by Sourcebooks, Inc.
Cover photo © iStockphoto.com/Jani Bryson
Sourcebooks and the colophon are registered trademarks of Sourcebooks, Inc.

All rights reserved. No part of this book may be reproduced in any form or by any electronic or mechanical means including information storage and retrieval systems—except in the case of brief quotations embodied in critical articles or reviews—without permission in writing from its publisher, Sourcebooks, Inc.

This publication is designed to provide accurate and authoritative information in regard to the subject matter covered. It is sold with the understanding that the publisher is not engaged in rendering legal, accounting, or other professional service. If legal advice or other expert assistance is required, the services of a competent professional person should be sought.—*From a Declaration of Principles Jointly Adopted by a Committee of the American Bar Association and a Committee of Publishers and Associations*

This book is not intended as a substitute for medical advice from a qualified physician. The intent of this book is to provide accurate general information in regard to the subject matter covered. If medical advice or other expert help is needed, the services of an appropriate medical professional should be sought. This book does not establish a doctor-patient relationship.

All brand names and product names used in this book are trademarks, registered trademarks, or trade names of their respective holders. Sourcebooks, Inc., is not associated with any product or vendor in this book.

Published by Sourcebooks, Inc.
P.O. Box 4410, Naperville, Illinois 60567–4410
(630) 961–3900
Fax: (630) 961–2168
www.sourcebooks.com

Library of Congress Cataloging-in-Publication Data

Anglada, Tracy.
  The childhood bipolar disorder answer book : practical answers to the top 300 questions parents ask / by Tracy Anglada and Sheryl Hakala.
      p. cm.
  Includes bibliographical references.
  1. Manic-depressive illness in children—Miscellanea. 2. Manic-depressive illness in children—Popular works. I. Hakala, Sheryl. II. Title.
  RJ506.D4A54 2008
  618.92'895--dc22
                                            2008022928
            Printed and bound in the United States of America.
                       BG 10 9 8 7 6 5 4 3 2 1

Contents

Acknowledgments

This book was the result of collaboration between a dedicated physician and an advocate mother. We would like to join in giving thanks to our families and friends who support and inspire us. We would also like to thank our publisher, Sourcebooks, Inc., for printing this important information. Thank you to Shana Drehs for bringing this project to us. Thank you to Peter Lynch for his efforts to make it a reality. Thank you to our editor, Erin Nevius, for smoothing out the rough edges, and to our proofreaders for their wonderful suggestions. Finally, we would like to thank our readers, who make it all worthwhile.

Introduction

Bipolar disorder has long been recognized in the adult population; and yet, more than half of these adult sufferers report the onset of symptoms before age eighteen. Despite this recognition, childhood bipolar disorder continues to be hotly debated, and it can be hard to find real, helpful answers. Whether you are worrying that your child may have bipolar disorder, are dealing with a newly diagnosed child, are worried about misdiagnosis, or are an old hand at the disorder who is simply looking for some fresh ideas, you have tough issues and questions that deserve straightforward, no-nonsense answers.

This book has been written to give you those answers based on the most up-to-date information the field has to offer. The questions and answers were a joint effort by a mother who has been in nearly every parenting stage of bipolar disorder, from very young children to teenagers, and a medical doctor who treats the condition and sees a wide variety of patients with the illness. This combination of personal experience and medical expertise has resulted in a medically accurate picture with a first-hand intimate knowledge of what parents really want and need to know. Each author adds a unique perspective and a wealth of usable information to the book. If you have ever wanted to sit with an experienced mother and a physician side by side, to ask them endless questions, and to get real answers for your everyday life, this is the book for you. It will serve as a reference for years to come as you go through various stages of your child's life and illness. Whenever possible, the authors have sought to give you tips, suggestions, and advice that have been proven to work for others. Please note that for ease of reading and writing, pronouns in the book are in the male gender but apply equally to females. No discrimination is intended by this usage. Please refer to Appendix A and the References section for more information on books, studies, and journals mentioned throughout the text.

The book contains plans to assist you in taking what you have learned and moving your child toward success. The authors recognize that each plan is very individual, but the goal should always be for the personal assessments to help you examine your own child's situation and put into place both short-term and long-term goals to help your family.

The answers in this book were written with the recognition that your time is precious. We know you may be reading in between dealing with difficult situations. In respect for this, we have tried to be extremely concise and to the point. The book may be read from cover to cover, but it has been designed so that you can pick it up, read an answer to any question that concerns you, and have immediate access to the specific information you need. It is our hope that this book will prove to be a constant resource for you.

Chapter 1

UNDERSTANDING CHILDHOOD BIPOLAR DISORDER

- What is childhood bipolar disorder?
- How does it differ from adult onset?
- How is onset in late teens different?
- How might my child exhibit mania?
- How might my child exhibit depression?
- How might my child exhibit a mixed state?
- Is my child hallucinating or imagining?
- Why does my child draw gory pictures?
- Why is my child fearful?
- Why is my child so irritable?
- Why is my child angry?
- What is a "rage"?
- Do rages and temper tantrums differ?
- Why does my child have trouble getting out of bed in the morning?
- Is suicide a real risk?

Q. What is childhood bipolar disorder?

A. Childhood bipolar disorder is a chronic illness that affects the most complex organ of the body: the brain. The impact of bipolar disorder on the brain is thought to include abnormal structures, abnormal levels of neurotransmitters (the chemical messengers of the brain), abnormal cellular function, and abnormal metabolic function. Thoughts, memories, movements, moods, energy, behaviors, learning, and sensory processing are all based in the brain's amazing network of interconnected cells and neurons. It is not surprising, then, that when an illness impacts such a complex organ in multiple ways, it can have far-reaching consequences. Such is the case with bipolar disorder in children. There is little in their lives that is not touched by their illness.

Children with bipolar disorder are subject to extreme mood swings, ranging from the highs of mania to the depths of depression and despair. They suffer from extreme irritability, abrupt changes in energy levels, low tolerance for frustration, sudden changes in thinking, and odd or oppositional behaviors. Children with bipolar disorder also have some perceptual differences. Studies have shown that they incorrectly process facial expressions and may misinterpret social cues as a result. It is also common for executive functioning, sensory processing, attentional abilities, and cognitive functioning to be impaired. At the same time, these unique children may be gifted, articulate, engaging, artistic, poetic, and precocious for their age.

Bipolar disorder was once thought to be an "adult" illness, meaning that people thought it could not express itself in children. Studies are now showing that half of the patients who suffer from bipolar disorder had their onset before the age of eighteen. The misconception about its prevalence in childhood led to long delays in treatment that resulted in decades of suffering for those affected. The good news is that the illness is treatable. Identifying the symptoms early and providing treatment can give children who suffer from bipolar disorder a better quality of life.

Q. How does it differ from adult onset?

A. The onset of bipolar disorder can come at any age, but when it occurs during childhood, it presents some unusual difficulties that differ from its adult counterpart. Children are still growing and reaching developmental milestones. They are establishing their identity and discovering their place in the world. When bipolar disorder strikes during this time period, it interrupts this normal developmental process. They face difficulties unique to the pediatric population as they attend school and try to make social connections and to handle the already difficult transition to puberty. Their illness can turn all these steps into monumental tasks.

Children with bipolar disorder are generally more volatile in their mood swings than their adult-onset counterparts. Adults with bipolar disorder may spend weeks or months in one mood phase before switching to another; they also experience periods of wellness in between. However, children with bipolar disorder experience very few periods of wellness, and their moods swing rapidly between the extremes. The pediatric population is much more likely to experience chronic irritability than the "high" feelings of euphoria that accompany mania. Children spend more time in a "mixed" state, meaning that they are experiencing symptoms of both mania and depression at the same time. They are also more prone to experiencing a co-occurring condition, such as an anxiety disorder, attention deficit hyperactivity disorder (ADHD), obsessive-compulsive disorder, learning disabilities, and so on.

Not unlike other illnesses that onset during youth, childhood bipolar disorder is considered more chronic and more ever-present than its adult counterpart. Some believe these differences constitute a completely different illness altogether. Hopefully, current ongoing research will clarify the degree of difference in the expression of the illness between adults and children.

Q. How is onset in late teens different?

A. No matter when the onset of bipolar disorder occurs, it can be devastating to the individual suffering the ill effects, but when the first symptoms of the disorder occur in late adolescence, they can differ somewhat from a younger childhood onset. The late-teen onset is more likely to mimic the adult onset characteristics of the disorder, including longer periods of time spent in one mood state before switching to another. The development of older teens may be less affected by the symptoms of the illness simply because they have already reached certain developmental milestones before the onset of symptoms.

At the same time, these teens may be overlooked and undiagnosed—the symptoms of their illness may be attributed to "teenage rebelliousness." If undiagnosed and untreated, this age group is at particular risk for abusing drugs, dropping out of school, and attempting suicide. Many parents may feel that these adolescents are simply struggling to get through the difficult teen years and may not even consider the possibility that the onset of an illness has occurred. Normal teenage events such as breaking up with a girlfriend, moving into a new apartment, starting a job, or going away to college may be blamed for an increase in mood symptoms. While these factors should not be dismissed, they also should not be used to excuse extreme behavior that may indicate bipolar disorder. Parents should know that these normal, stressful events can trigger an onset of the illness in those who are at risk for the development of the disorder. It should also be noted that drug use may unmask symptoms of the illness, while, conversely, symptoms of the illness may drive the teen to experiment with self-medication through drugs.

If you suspect your teenager may be suffering from bipolar disorder—even if you are not 100 percent sure—it is important to take him to a doctor for an evaluation. It could prevent your teen from getting into some serious trouble.

Q. How might my child exhibit mania?

A. The following symptoms may indicate that your child is experiencing mania. Periods of mania may alternate with depressive symptoms within short periods of time or may persist over longer periods. Manic symptoms may be more pronounced in spring and summer months. Be aware of changes in patterns of sleep, behavior, energy level, thought, and routine, especially when these differ from your child's normal functioning or personality.

- **Overtalkativeness:** Your child may feel a strong pressure or need to talk. You may notice that your child speaks loudly and rapidly.

- **Elation or giddiness:** Your child's mood may be unusually and inappropriately elevated without reason. Your child may laugh hysterically or sing and dance during what might otherwise be a sobering event. For instance, while being punished, your child may be unable to do anything but laugh.

- **Irritability:** Your child may have a chronic irritable mood instead of an elated mood. Your child may be argumentative, easily agitated, and generally irritated by everything.

- **Decreased need for sleep:** Your child may appear to have boundless energy, as if he is driven by a motor, or may have great difficulty falling asleep and require less sleep than usual.

- **Grandiosity:** Your child may feel advanced, superior, and gifted with special knowledge that is beyond what other humans could understand or comprehend.

- **Hypersexuality:** Your child may have a strong sexual impulse and desire. Young children may make inappropriate comments, gestures, and advances of a sexual nature. Preteens may dress provocatively and engage in sexual activity beyond their years. Teens may engage in risky sexual behaviors with multiple partners.

- **Racing thoughts:** Your child may have thoughts and ideas that race through his brain; he might jump from topic to topic as his speech tries to keep up with the swirl of thoughts.

- **Increased goal-directed activity:** Your child may hyperfocus on a particular need, goal, or project to the exclusion of other things. Your child may begin multiple projects with much enthusiasm.

Q. How might my child exhibit depression?

A. The following symptoms may indicate that your child is experiencing depression. Depressive symptoms may last over an extended period of time or may alternate with manic symptoms throughout the day. Depressive symptoms may be more pronounced in fall and winter months.

- **Lack of motivation:** Your child may lose the desire to do things that would normally be appealing. Incentives are meaningless. Your child may say things like, "Who cares?" or "Why bother?"

- **Reduced energy:** Your child may feel heavy or weighed down. Playing may feel like too much work. You may hear comments like, "I'm too tired!" or "I can't do it."

- **Difficulty concentrating:** Your child may not be able to focus on the task at hand. Homework that used to be manageable now takes hours. He may appear to be constantly daydreaming.

- **Thoughts of death:** Your child may focus on death or give away precious possessions in preparation for death. You might hear things like, "My family would be better off without me."

- **Self-harm or risk taking:** Your child may lose regard for personal safety. You may find him sitting in the middle of the road or engaging in other daredevil acts. Your child may scratch, hit, cut, or otherwise cause harm to his body.

- **Crying spells:** Your child may cry easily and for no apparent reason. A small incident can cause your child to cry for a prolonged amount of time.

- **Anger or irritability:** The smallest event may cause an angry outburst and yelling from your child. You may feel as if you are walking on eggshells around him.

- **Altered sleeping and eating patterns:** Your child may have difficulty falling asleep, staying asleep, or waking up in the morning. Dinnertime may find your child staring aimlessly at the plate. Any change in these patterns from what is normal for your child may be a warning sign.

Q. How might my child exhibit a mixed state?

A. A mixed state occurs when your child is experiencing symptoms of both mania and depression at the same time. This may seem impossible because the symptoms are opposite extremes, but in reality, this state is experienced frequently by young people with bipolar disorder. There can be many variations or mixtures of symptoms. Often children in a mixed state remain in a depressed frame of mind but have energy. This produces an agitation in the mood. Mixed states are especially dangerous—your child may use his energy and motivation brought on by the mania to carry out plans of self-harm caused by the depression. Here are a few ways your child may exhibit symptoms of a mixed state:

- **Agitated pacing:** Your child may have extra energy but no positive outlet for this energy due to underlying depression. The result may be an agitated pacing back and forth. If approached, your child may become more agitated or upset.

- **Projects with a dark twist:** Your child's manic energy may be put into projects that take on a depressive or dark twist. He may create a large amount of artwork focusing on death, weapons, suffering, blood, and gore or may write a great deal of poetry that focuses on negative feelings.

- **Running away:** Your child may feel strongly pushed by negative feelings and intense energy. He may start feeling desperate to get away and might even run away from home.

- **Impulsive self-harm:** Your child may be experiencing racing thoughts that center on suicide or self-harm. He may impulsively act on any one of these thoughts. His mood may also seem out of place with his actions. For instance, he may laugh while deliberately scratching or cutting himself.

Q. Is my child hallucinating or imagining?

A. Imagination in children is harmless; however, hallucinations should be carefully monitored. It is possible that your child with bipolar disorder could experience symptoms related to psychosis, such as hallucinations. Other signs of psychosis include loss of touch with reality, paranoid or false beliefs, illusions, or false perceptions. Psychosis can be present in both manic and depressive states. The illness is considered more severe when psychosis is present.

A hallucination can involve seeing, hearing, tasting, smelling, or feeling something that is not there. It involves experiencing these things and believing them to be real without any outward stimuli and with the sense that the experience is out of the person's control. In contrast, imagination is vivid imagery that is deliberately called up by the person and *thought about* versus *experienced*. Distinguishing between the two can be difficult for parents because both occur privately in the child's own mind. Here are some examples that may help you differentiate between the two. Your child's doctor will be able to factor in the appropriate developmental stage of your child and also consider other symptoms being displayed that may give clues as to the origin of the event.

Imagination	Psychosis
A young child talks to stuffed animals and creates interactions that mirror life. Examples may include having tea parties or playing school or house.	A young child reports that stuffed animals are giving orders or commands that must be obeyed. The commands may be harmful in nature. The child feels that something bad will happen if he fails to comply.
A child has an imaginary friend.	A child sees scary people or objects that are not there and asks if they are real.
A child watches a scary movie, thinks that a monster is in the closet or under the bed, and needs a light on to sleep.	A child strongly believes that people are trying to kill or hurt him. The child feels that his food is being poisoned.

Q. Why does my child draw gory pictures?

A. It is a joy for most parents to gaze upon the artwork of their children. But what if your child draws knives, guns, blood, and gory scenes? Many children with bipolar disorder depict violent scenes in their artwork, and parents are often confused and embarrassed by such expressions. In some cases, these children have never been allowed to view violent programs on television, and the fixation on blood and gore is a mystery and is very disturbing to parents. Why is it that children with bipolar disorder can have such a fixation on dark and scary artwork?

These drawings can be a reflection of the child's inner turmoil and feelings. Other times, the drawings may reflect the child's dreams, fears, or obsessive thoughts. While your first reaction may be to scold your child for such drawings or to hide them away, this would be a mistake. Take the time to compliment your child on his skill and talent. Artwork can be an important way to draw out your child's inner feelings. It may serve as a vehicle through which your child can express scary thoughts to you before these thoughts can be verbalized. Scolding your child could send him the message that he is bad or shameful and that scary feelings should be kept a secret. On the contrary, you want to send just the opposite message. It is very brave for your child to express these feelings. Your child is to be commended for being able to express such scary and difficult emotions. View artwork as a way to open communication into areas that are very private. Never shut an entryway into your child's emotions.

Q. Why is my child fearful?

A. Your child may be terrified to go outside, to go to the bathroom, or to sleep alone. Additionally, your child may react to nonthreatening situations with an unusual amount of fear. This fear is persistent and may be present even into the teenage years. There are several underlying causes of this fear in children with bipolar disorder.

- **Separation anxiety:** Early on, many children with bipolar disorder exhibit separation anxiety. These children attach themselves to their parents and will not let go.

- **Psychosis:** Your child may be having persistent feelings that someone is endangering them, trying to poison them, or attempting to harm them in some way. He may also be seeing and hearing things that are not there, which can cause an unusual amount of fear.

- **Nightmares:** Children with bipolar disorder frequently experience nightmares that are explicitly gory, bloody, and violent. They may see themselves or the ones they love being killed in these nightmares. These images make nighttime difficult and also carry over into daytime worries and thoughts that can make the child constantly fearful.

- **Obsessive thoughts:** Your child may have obsessive, intrusive, and repetitive thoughts. These thoughts may center on the child causing harm to himself even when he has no desire to do so. The child may fear that these intrusive thoughts will come true.

- **Fear reactions:** Children with bipolar disorder can falsely interpret nonthreatening situations as real threats. Your child may react to normal situations as if his life were endangered.

Telling your child not to worry or be fearful will not reduce the fear. You may need to accompany your child outside, allow him to leave the bathroom door open, and perhaps even allow him to sleep in your room for a time until treatment can address these symptoms. The important thing is that you recognize this fear as a symptom of his disorder and seek help for it.

Q. Why is my child so irritable?

A. Children with bipolar disorder can be chronically irritable. Irritability is a symptom of both mania and depression, so it is perpetuated by every mood state in bipolar disorder. In addition, irritability can be associated with anxiety, faulty sensory processing, and a low tolerance for frustration, all of which are common problems for kids with bipolar disorder.

There is another frequently overlooked cause of irritability in children with bipolar disorder. Many children with bipolar disorder complain of headaches, backaches, and stomachaches. Your child may have difficulty verbalizing this discomfort, but it certainly can add to the irritability factor. Because your child is expending a great deal of energy to try to keep his moods in check, there may not be any more resources left to deal with these additional aches and pains.

This constant state of irritability is like a match waiting to ignite. When your child is exposed to stresses or triggers, an explosion is difficult to escape—and while the result is an angry outburst, the cause may be irritability. In addition to experiencing the irritability related to his illness, your child is still subject to the normal causes of ill temper in childhood. Being aware that this is a symptom of bipolar disorder that can be addressed with treatment can help you to be understanding when your child is irritable. Additionally, identifying the specific factors that contribute to your child's irritability can help you to reduce this problem. Reducing sensory input and minimizing frustrations may help your child feel less irritable. Giving a pain reliever for aches and physical pain may also decrease irritability.

Causes of normal childhood irritability	Causes of irritability in bipolar disorder	
Lack of sleep	Mania	Depression
Hunger	Additional aches and pains	Low frustration tolerance
Sickness	Sensory overload	Anxiety

Q. Why is my child angry?

A. Anger is a normal human emotion—all of us get angry, sometimes for good reason, sometimes not. Anger can be an outward expression of other emotions, such as anxiety, frustration, disappointment, embarrassment, guilt, fear, and betrayal, or it can result from a traumatic experience. However, many children with bipolar disorder experience anger as a general state of being. Some children report waking up angry, experiencing anger during what would normally be a pleasant experience, or having anger sweep over them in a sudden and overpowering manner. In this context, anger is a symptom of the child's illness. It can be an expression of depression, agitated mania, mixed states, or the child's extreme irritability.

In addition to anger as a symptom of bipolar disorder, anger may also exist as a reaction to having an illness. How do these two things differ? Anger as a symptom of bipolar disorder is caused by the moods of the disorder and is an expression of the illness itself. But anger may also be evoked by the injustice of having a chronic illness. Your child may feel that it is unfair that he must struggle with bipolar disorder. He may be angry at himself for his inability to manage moods. He may be angry when the illness causes him to lose friends or to become the target of bullying.

Anger is a complicated part of bipolar disorder. The anger that is a symptom of the illness will subside with treatment, but other expressions of anger may need to be addressed with a therapist who can help your child come to grips with having such a serious illness. A therapist may also help your child learn to repair friendships and to deal with the stigmatizing reaction of others.

Q. What is a "rage"?

A. An extreme expression of anger and instability displayed in an intense and destructive manner is commonly referred to as a "rage." Many children with bipolar disorder will have a rage at some point in their illness. For some children, this turns into a daily event. The instability inherent in bipolar disorder sets the stage for a rage, which can then be triggered by any minor event. If your child is experiencing the altered thinking of psychosis, he may be especially susceptible to raging. An explosive rage is characterized by both its intensity and length. Once triggered, the child's rage may remain out of control for an extended period of time. He may hit, kick, punch, and spit at whomever is the target of this rage. Additionally, furniture and other objects nearby may suffer damage.

Some children will not recall what transpired during a rage. Others report remembering the rage but experiencing it as if they were a third party watching the activity and being unable to stop the event. All of them report a loss of control. After the event, response can vary from shame, depression, and sorrow to indifference and a seeming lack of regret depending on the prevailing mood state. For example, a child who experiences rage while in a state of depression may feel very guilty afterward. However, if a child is manic and grandiose when a rage occurs, the child may feel as if the rage was justified because of an elevated view of himself. His illness may cause him to feel as if those around him are lesser beings and somehow deserve his wrath.

Rages generally lessen or subside completely with treatment. Until this happens, minimize situations that are likely to result in rages. By observing your child's rage response, you may identify triggers—such as sensory overload or frustration—that inevitably lead to a rage. Minimizing such triggers can prevent a rage. For instance, if homework is routinely a trigger for rage, then reduce or eliminate homework until your child is closer to stability. (For suggestions on working with the school, consult Chapter 10.)

Q. Do rages and temper tantrums differ?

A. It is very common for preschool-age children to have what is known as a temper tantrum. Young children may lie on the ground, cry, and flail about wildly to express their anger, disappointment, or frustration. Young children lack the skills to manage these emotions, so they express themselves with a tantrum. However, as children mature, so does their ability to deal with emotions. Generally, by the time children reach school age, temper tantrums are infrequent. How can parents differentiate between a developmentally appropriate temper tantrum and a rage? Here are a few telltale signs:

- **Intensity:** While both tantrums and rages may start as a reaction to frustration or emotion, a rage goes to the extreme and may involve injury to the child or others.
- **Length:** A temper tantrum may vary in length from a few seconds to a few minutes. A rage, on the other hand, can be prolonged. The child may remain out of control for more than forty-five minutes and sometimes even for hours.
- **Age:** Temper tantrums are a frequent occurrence in young children and are considered a part of normal childhood development. A rage is never developmentally appropriate and can occur at any age.

Rages are physically and mentally exhausting for both you and your child. If your child is having a rage, make sure other children in the household have a place of safety to which they can retreat. Do not prolong a rage by yelling, screaming, or losing your cool. This throws fuel on the fire. Reduce all sensory input. Speak in a calm, low, soothing voice. The goal is to end the rage as quickly as possible. It is not the time to lecture, shout, or threaten—it is doubtful that your child will even hear your words in the midst of a rage. Your job is to help your child regain control.

Q. Why does my child have trouble getting out of bed in the morning?

A. The overwhelming majority of children with bipolar disorder have problems with sleep, including difficulty falling asleep, trouble staying asleep, difficulty waking up, nightmares, morning headaches, reduced REM sleep, and an increased amount of time in non-REM sleep. Some of these difficulties can be directly related to mood states. Depressive states not only can cause the child to have difficulty falling asleep but also can increase the need for sleep. Manic states can render the child unable to sleep. Difficulty with sleep, then, can change depending on the child's prevailing mood state. Children whose moods have stabilized may still exhibit a pattern of disturbance in their sleep/wake cycle.

With all these sleep difficulties, you may feel that waking your child is like trying to wake the dead. Even after your child is out of bed, it may be hours before he truly wakes up. The reverse is true at bedtime. Parents are frustrated; they can lead a child to bed, but they can't make him sleep. It may be hours before he can settle down and fall asleep. School days can be incredibly stressful when trying to combat this difficult scenario.

It is important to maintain regular patterns of sleep for your child. Reducing the temperature before bedtime can help; cold may slow down his natural functions and make him sleepy. Having your child wear amber-tinted lenses in the evening may also help set regular sleep patterns by blocking the blue light waves that tell the body that it is daytime. With these light waves blocked, the body starts preparing for a state of sleep; natural melatonin production increases, which is vital to the sleep cycle. Additionally, morning transitions may be easier with a dawn simulator, a device that imitates a natural sunrise.

Q. Is suicide a real risk?

A. Suicide is an uncomfortable topic for most people. It is even more uncomfortable to speak of suicide and young people. No one likes to think of this as a possibility. But reality demands that we take notice of this very real risk to young people with bipolar disorder. More than four hundred children and adolescents with bipolar disorder participated in a study on suicide conducted at the Western Psychiatric Institute and Clinic (Goldstein et al. 2005). The results revealed that nearly one-third of them had attempted suicide. Those children in the study whose illness presented with psychosis and mixed states were at higher risk for a suicide attempt. Adolescents were more likely to attempt suicide than younger children, although suicide attempts can occur in the very young as well.

Suicide rates in young people with bipolar disorder are sobering. Bipolar disorder will prove fatal in approximately 15 to 20 percent of all cases. The risk is far greater to these young people than to healthy youths. What can you do to minimize the risk in your child? First, recognize that suicidal impulses are a symptom of bipolar disorder. Identifying the illness and seeking treatment can greatly reduce this risk. Make sure that dangerous items such as guns, medications, and large kitchen knives and other sharp household items are locked away and inaccessible to your child. Be aware that young children do not have the same vocabulary that you do to express suicidal thoughts. A preoccupation with death or dying should be taken as a warning sign. Giving away important possessions can also indicate a desire to die. Keep communication open. If you suspect that your child is having suicidal thoughts, talk to him about it and contact a doctor immediately.

Chapter 2

SPOTTING THE SYMPTOMS

- What are the early symptoms of bipolar disorder?
- Are there levels of symptom severity?
- At what age can a child be diagnosed with bipolar disorder?
- How do symptoms differ from normal mood variation?
- Is this a fad diagnosis?
- Is this illness genetic?
- Why does it strike at different ages?
- Will my child grow out of bipolar disorder?
- Will my child lead a normal life?
- Do all children with bipolar disorder act the same?
- How do boys and girls with bipolar disorder differ?
- What should I do if I suspect my child has bipolar disorder?
- What risks come with bipolar disorder?
- Do I have reason to hope for my child's future?

Q. What are the early symptoms of bipolar disorder?

A. In some cases, bipolar disorder has a sudden onset with clear symptoms that differ significantly from your child's previous functioning. A child's first full-blown episode could be depressive, manic, or mixed. A sudden onset of mania is accompanied by erratic behavior. Your child may go days without sleep, may not make sense when he talks, and could appear very agitated. A sudden onset of depression is accompanied by a loss of desire to participate in regular activities and may be mistaken for major depression. Your child may not want to get out of bed for days. A severe and sudden depression can culminate with a suicide attempt. Sudden onset may also bring psychosis, including delusions and hallucinations. If onset is sudden, your child may end up being hospitalized and treated immediately.

More often than not, however, there is a more gradual display of symptoms—and this can be deceiving. Parents may mistake these symptoms as a "phase" or something the child will "grow out of." As parents become accustomed to more and more unusual or alarming symptoms, these behaviors might not seem as shocking. Parents can be lulled into a false sense of security. In other cases, parents may have been reporting concerns and worries for years in a desperate attempt to get help for their child, only to be met with parenting advice from well-meaning relatives and shrugs from physicians who tell them not to worry.

The earliest manifestations of the illness are referred to as prodromal or subsyndromal symptoms. For children, these include anxiety, poor attention spans, excitability, changing moods, physical complaints—such as headaches and stomachaches—without obvious cause, and difficulty in school. While the child may not go on to develop bipolar disorder, parents would do well to be aware of these early warning signs, especially if family history suggests that the child is at increased risk for bipolar disorder. If you do notice early warning signs, don't panic but do be watchful in case symptoms progress.

Q. Are there levels of symptom severity?

A. There is variance from child to child in the severity of the symptoms that are displayed with bipolar disorder, and there can also be variance from episode to episode. Two children with bipolar disorder may seem very different from each other in the ways and degree that their symptoms are manifest. News media sources generally tend to use extreme cases and sensationalize their coverage of children with bipolar disorder. Unfortunately, a parent could mistakenly conclude from such coverage that a child with less severe symptoms might not have the disorder. In reality, the symptoms can range from mild forms to severely impairing forms of the illness.

The difference might be compared with a child who has a high fever with convulsions versus a child who has a low-grade but chronic fever that doesn't go away. Both children are sick and need medical attention, but their symptoms and presentations are very different and could be misleading. The child with the high fever may seem as though he needs the most attention, but it also doesn't make sense to ignore the child whose symptoms are at a lower level but are still serious enough to indicate a problem. Similarly, bipolar disorder can have a huge impact on your child's life even in its mildest forms. Symptoms are severe enough to seek treatment if your child's life is being negatively impacted. Ask yourself a few questions about your child's moods:

- Do they interfere with his functioning in school?
- Do they prevent him from maintaining friendships?
- Do they interfere with his ability to function in the family?
- Do they negatively affect his self-perception?
- Do they cause him to have impaired judgment and make poor choices?
- Do they interfere with his interaction with authority figures?

Q. At what age can a child be diagnosed with bipolar disorder?

A. Many parents of children with bipolar disorder report that there was something different about their child from infancy. Some of these babies were easily overstimulated, difficult to calm or soothe, and had difficulty separating from the parent. Other babies who were diagnosed with bipolar disorder as children did not show any difficulties as infants. There are no infant markers as of yet that can conclusively point to bipolar disorder. Some babies who never develop an illness may be difficult to calm or soothe for a variety of reasons. Figuring out what is wrong and how to address it is a challenge with very young children.

Research in the field of autism has given doctors the ability to diagnose this disorder early and start intensive interventions to curb the effects of the disorder. This early intervention gives the child better functioning than would have been achieved otherwise. The same is hoped for further research in the area of childhood bipolar disorder. Being able to definitively identify the illness as soon as it manifests could potentially allow for early and intensive intervention, giving the child the best chance to achieve wellness.

Until researchers are able to make progress in this area, there will remain controversy over the age at which children can be diagnosed and treated for bipolar disorder. Currently, there is an average ten-year gap between first symptom manifestation and correct diagnosis. This delay in diagnosis shows that some children start manifesting symptoms long before doctors and parents are able to understand what those symptoms mean. If your child is manifesting symptoms and is not being correctly diagnosed as having bipolar disorder, don't give up in your search for answers. A correct diagnosis can make all the difference in your child's future.

Q. How do symptoms differ from normal mood variation?

A. All children go through changes as they age, and the mood swings that come along with them. Telling the difference between behaviors that are part of a child's existing mood disorder and those that are just part of growing up becomes a particularly common concern during the transition to the teen years. Failure to recognize normal mood changes could lead to frustration and unnecessary medication adjustments. On the other hand, failure to recognize symptoms early enough could lead to an extended period of instability. Clearly then, a balanced and educated approach is needed.

As a parent, you already have a very good awareness of your child's nature and personality. In addition to knowing your child well, it will be helpful to become familiar with the various developmental stages of children and what is normal for each stage. If you have concerns about a particular set of changes in your child, talk to your child's physician. This could quickly either resolve or validate your worries—but either way, you'll know how to handle the situation.

Also recognize that your child with bipolar disorder may have trouble adjusting and adapting to the various changes and stages of maturing. So while the changes may be normal and appropriate, your child's ability to handle these changes may not be. Healthy children and teens find growing up to be challenging; bipolar disorder will magnify these challenges. Be prepared to give your child extra support through all these changing needs.

Q. Is this a fad diagnosis?

A. There has been a forty-fold increase in the number of children diagnosed and treated for bipolar disorder in recent years. However, this increase alone does not indicate that somehow the disorder has become glamorous, popular, and sought after, as the term "fad" would indicate. The pitiful lack of recognition of the illness in children during previous decades has strongly contributed to the current increase. Bipolar disorder remains somewhat stigmatized, and children are still more likely to go undiagnosed and untreated than to receive the help they need.

According to the Centers for Disease Control, reporting of serious emotional and behavioral difficulties by parents has remained at a constant 5 percent in the under-eighteen population for the past five years. Since parental reports are one of the first indicators of the illness, it does not appear that the recent increase in diagnosis is related to a huge rise in the illness itself but rather an appropriate recognition of the illness by medical professionals. Currently, bipolar disorder is diagnosed in approximately 1 percent of children—which was the estimated occurrence rate published over a decade ago (Geller and Luby 1997). Results from the National Comorbidity Survey Replication indicates the prevalence of adults with bipolar spectrum disorder to be 4.4 percent. Approximately 50 percent of adult onset happens before age eighteen; this means that expected childhood rates would fall nearer to 2 percent, making the current diagnosed cases about half of the actual occurrence of the illness. This indicates that the rates will continue to increase as more children with bipolar disorder are correctly identified and properly treated.

Using language such as "fad" or "latest craze" only serves to discourage families from seeking help and widens the gap to treatment. Through education and early identification efforts, improved recognition of the illness will continue. This in turn will make rates of childhood diagnosis increase, not decrease. These ever-increasing numbers are not because it is glamorous and popular, but because people are finally becoming aware of the warning signs and the potential hazards of not heeding them.

Q. Is this illness genetic?

A. Genetic factors can put people at a greater risk for developing an illness or can reduce the risk of illness. Bipolar disorder clearly has underlying genetic factors—the disorder has a tendency to run in families. When one parent has bipolar disorder, children have up to a 30 percent chance of developing the illness. When both parents have it, the risk jumps as high as 75 percent. When a child has bipolar disorder, the risk to siblings is up to 25 percent. The risk for an identical twin is up to 70 percent. The genetics involved in bipolar disorder are complicated, and the illness does not seem to pass through one identifiable gene—a combination of genetic factors interacting with environmental factors may be responsible for the disorder. Genetic factors also play a role in how a person reacts to treatment for illness. Further identifying the role of genetics in bipolar disorder can lead to advances in both the treatment and prevention of the illness.

This complex subject is being pursued by a number of researchers in all areas of disease and illness. The National Institute of Mental Health Genetics Initiative has made advances in researching the human genome for genetic variations in people with bipolar disorder—their research indicates that bipolar disorder is most likely a polygenic illness. This means that small variations of several genes are involved in the expression of the illness, some of which influence production of proteins or enzymes that are involved in brain-cell functioning. Other polygenic illnesses include autism, heart disease, diabetes, and cancer.

Q. Why does it strike at different ages?

A. It is disturbing to parents when an otherwise healthy child is struck with illness. Even armed with the understanding that the illness has a genetic base, many parents wonder why the onset occurs when it does. Why does an otherwise healthy teen abruptly begin to show symptoms? Why does a first grader have an emergence of the illness? Why do others advance well into adulthood before the illness manifests? And why do some seem to have symptoms from infancy?

All humans are unique, and there are a number of variants in our backgrounds and experiences that may cause symptom onset at a given age. The amount of genetic predisposition for the illness alone may be enough for some people to have an early expression of the illness, whereas for others a mixture of environmental factors along with genetics can bring on symptom onset later in life. Environmental factors can include a stressful life event, like the death of a loved one, or something as seemingly simple as changing schools.

Another theory under investigation is the possibility that exposure to infectious agents, either during gestation or later in life, can serve as a trigger to developing the illness in people genetically predisposed. Infections currently under suspicion for playing a role in symptom expression of bipolar disorder and schizophrenia include *Toxoplasma gondii*, herpes simplex viruses 1 and 2, and cytomegalovirus. Research currently underway with Stanley Medical Research Institute includes the use of antibiotic and antiviral agents as adjunctive treatment in bipolar disorder and schizophrenia. Additionally, it is not known how exposure to environmental toxins and waste may affect symptom presentation and onset.

Progress in all these areas is important for both treatment and prevention of illness. Conclusively identifying such areas could lead to different treatment approaches as well as future development of immunizations that could prevent infectious triggers. We cannot yet determine why a person might develop the illness at a certain age, but hopefully we'll soon be able to—and possibly even prevent or at least delay it.

Q. Will my child grow out of bipolar disorder?

A. When children struggle with a psychiatric disorder (or with anything, really), parents can't help but hope that these challenges will diminish as the child reaches adulthood. Children change quickly as they grow; does this mean that children can grow out of bipolar disorder? Unfortunately, this has not been shown to be the case. Adults with childhood onset of the illness continue to manifest symptoms of the illness throughout their adult lives.

However, the expression of specific symptoms of bipolar disorder can change over time. Indeed, symptoms switch from one extreme to another so rapidly that many have noted that change is one of the constants about this illness. Other related factors involved in childhood may also change and interact with how the illness is expressed. For example, some children with bipolar disorder lag behind in other areas of development such as social skills. As these children grow into adults, some developmental concerns may even out. Also, during adolescence there is a mixture of normal hormonal changes that can make dealing with bipolar disorder more difficult. Naturally there will be changes in the individual as he passes through this momentous time of life. Even with these variables, researchers note that adults with the childhood onset form of the illness generally continue the pattern of chronic symptom expression into their adult years.

Q. Will my child lead a normal life?

A. There is no doubt that people with bipolar disorder have more than the usual amount of challenges to face and overcome throughout their lives. None of us can know what the future will hold for our children. Especially during periods of extreme instability, parents worry about what life holds in store for their children—and rightly so, since this illness can be fatal. The following factors will play a role in the kind of life your child will have:

- Severity of your child's illness
- Ability to manage the illness
- Compliance with treatment
- Response to medication
- Skill of the treatment team
- Family support system
- School support system
- Your child's resiliency

Children with bipolar disorder can grow up to lead happy successful lives. However, this happy and successful life may or may not coincide with a parent's preconceived idea of normal. Forcing your child into a specific mold of normalcy could hamper his chances of being happy and successful. When a child has a disability of any kind, his future is changed. Sometimes these changes contribute to the creation of an amazing person who learns to overcome and succeed in spite of difficulties.

If you feel that happiness and success can only be achieved by erasing bipolar disorder from you child's life, you will be disappointed. If your view of the future is one that includes how your child can be happy while successfully dealing with the illness and handling the setbacks it will bring, then you are more likely to see all the possibilities that await him. (For information on dealing with parental emotions, please see Chapter 14.)

Q. Do all children with bipolar disorder act the same?

A. If you compare your child to another child with bipolar disorder you will likely see some similarities in symptoms, but it can also be misleading. Every child is different, and there are varying ways of expressing symptoms. Concluding that your child doesn't have bipolar disorder because he doesn't exactly fit the mold of another child with the illness would be a mistake. This mistake could prevent you from getting the help that your child needs. Even two children with the disorder in the same family may have unique presentations. We have already noted that there are varying degrees of the illness, and co-occurring conditions can also affect how your child manifests symptoms.

In addition, each child's own personality will play into how symptoms are expressed. Some children are very open, and symptoms are expressed in an outward manner. It may be difficult to overlook the types of symptoms that these children manifest. Other children are not openly expressive. These children may be more difficult to diagnose, as they may keep their feelings and symptoms to themselves.

When there are other people in the family who have been diagnosed, such as a parent or a sibling, some children attempt to hide their own symptoms so as not to add to the family burden. If there is a known genetic predisposition in the family, brain health should be an open topic so that children know they can share freely. Asking direct questions or having your child complete a questionnaire can open the way to identifying warning factors early, which could prevent tragedy later.

Q. How do boys and girls with bipolar disorder differ?

A. Bipolar disorder is present in boys and girls at approximately the same rates. While there are reports of symptom differences between the genders in adult bipolar disorder, there does not appear to be a significant difference in the way boys and girls display most symptoms of the illness—though, one study did indicate that girls may have higher rates of depressive moods, whereas boys may have higher rates of manic moods. There does not seem to be a difference in functioning at home or in school for girls and boys. However, one specific area of concern for girls with bipolar disorder is menstruation. Symptoms can worsen before the monthly cycle. Higher incidence of menstrual irregularities during adolescence has been reported by women with bipolar disorder. Also, a gender difference has been reported in the area of suicidal thoughts. Girls with bipolar disorder have more suicidal thoughts and are more likely to attempt suicide. However, boys who attempt suicide are more likely to result in fatality (Dilsaver et al. 2005).

Differences between genders are also being discovered in the brain. A study from the University of Texas Health Science Center examined the orbitofrontal cortex, the front part of the brain located just behind the eyes. This part of the brain is thought to be involved in decision making, sensory integration, and sensitivity to reward and punishment. Both boys and girls with bipolar disorder have abnormalities in this part of the brain—boys had a reduction in gray-matter volume, whereas girls had larger gray-matter volume. Another part of the brain that shows some variation between boys and girls with bipolar disorder is the hippocampus, which is thought to play a part in emotion and memory. A study published in the July 2005 issue of the *American Journal of Psychiatry* (162[7]: 1256–65) noted that girls with bipolar disorder, more than boys, have a smaller volume of the hippocampus when compared to healthy children. (More information on brain abnormalities can be found in Chapter 9.)

Q. What should I do if I suspect my child has bipolar disorder?

A. If you are seeing signs and symptoms that make you think your child might have bipolar disorder, it warrants a doctor's appointment regardless of the final diagnosis. A complete physical examination with your child's pediatrician is an excellent place to start. Communicate honestly and openly regarding your child's symptoms so that the pediatrician can rule out other conditions that could contribute to these symptoms. If he suspects bipolar disorder, ask for a recommendation to a doctor who specializes in child and adolescent psychiatry. Finding the right psychiatrist is vital and can make a huge difference in the outcome of your child.

While this may seem overwhelming, you don't have to go through it alone! Parents who have gone before you have forged the way, making support and guidance available to you. The Juvenile Bipolar Research Foundation (http://www.jbrf.org) features a questionnaire that can help your child communicate what symptoms he may be experiencing. This is vital information to bring to your doctor and psychiatrist. The Child and Adolescent Bipolar Foundation (http://www.bpkids.org) is an invaluable resource for support on this difficult journey and also has a "Find a Doctor" directory, which can help you locate a reputable psychiatrist. BPChildren (http://www.bpchildren.com) has tools, including books, mood charts, posters, coloring pages, and newsletters to help your child understand and deal with the illness. The Bipolar Child website (http://www.bipolarchild.com) features an invaluable newsletter for parents. The STARFISH Advocacy Association (http://www.starfishadvocacy.org) can help you understand what supports your child will need in school. There are other online communities of parents, including Brainstorm (http://www.bpinfo.net), which features an "Ask the Doctor" segment. But talking to your pediatrician is the important first step to getting treatment and support for you and your family. Then, be sure to find a supporting community and learn from those with experience in dealing with this disorder.

Q. What risks come with bipolar disorder?

A. Children with bipolar disorder face a number of increased risks as they navigate through childhood, adolescence, and into their adult years. We have already discussed the greater risk of suicide, which is the most serious of all risks related to bipolar disorder. Additionally, alcoholism and substance abuse rates are very high in youths with bipolar disorder who are attempting to self-medicate. Teens and adolescents with bipolar disorder frequently exhibit lack of impulse control, which can lead to addictive behaviors such as cutting, smoking, binge eating, and shoplifting. And they are very likely to experience multiple-symptom relapse, misdiagnosis, medication noncompliance, and lack of appropriate mental-health care.

Untreated symptoms of the illness also put the young person at an increased risk of being victimized. Young girls who are experiencing hypersexuality in a manic state may become a target for rape. In school, symptomatic children may be the target of bullying and are at risk for school failure. Conversely, they may bully others and be at greater risk of arrest and incarceration. Future risks that cross over into adulthood include financial distress, divorce, job loss, postpartum depression, or psychosis, as well as the development of other health issues such as diabetes, cardiovascular disease, thyroid disease, and obesity. Without the appropriate medical, therapeutic, and educational interventions, these risks are even greater. While these realities are quite sobering, being aware of them and acting accordingly can help to possibly prevent or minimize poor outcomes for your child.

Q. Do I have reason to hope for my child's future?

A. The future for children with bipolar disorder is not guaranteed to have a fairy tale ending. As a parent, you know that the road is difficult and long. But while you travel this road, there are very real, very solid reasons to have hope for your child's future. Consider a few of the following:

- There has been no better time than now to have a child with bipolar disorder. Right now, we have more knowledge, more research, and more treatment options than ever before for children with this illness.

- There are no less than forty new studies under way to further the present level of knowledge on bipolar disorder in children. These studies include medication safety, therapeutic interventions, alternative and complementary approaches, prevention of the illness, and brain-scan studies. Studies are being completed and new studies are being added continuously.
- There are many physicians and researchers who are committing their entire careers to helping your child's future. These dedicated individuals are transforming the face of psychiatry today.
- New discoveries have led researchers to look toward new approaches to develop more targeted medications, which in turn could lead to more effective control of symptoms with fewer side effects. You can expect to see new medicines developed in your child's lifetime.
- There is more information and support for families now than ever before. Never in history have there been so many other parents reaching out to support those new to this journey.
- Genetic studies are giving more insight into the physical nature of the illness and helping to reduce stigma.
- Increased recognition in society is leading to increased awareness and understanding.

So while the road may feel long and hard, know that there is strength in numbers. Wherever you go, whatever you do, there is an entire network concerned with one thing: improving your child's future!

Chapter 3

EVALUATION AND DIAGNOSIS

- How is bipolar disorder diagnosed?
- What are mania and hypomania?
- What are depression and mixed episodes?
- What are the categories of bipolar disorder?
- What constitutes a thorough evaluation?
- Can I prevent misdiagnosis?
- Can the illness be treated?
- Can other illnesses mimic bipolar disorder?
- Will my child be stigmatized?
- Can my child be treated without a diagnosis?
- Should all family members be evaluated?
- Can children have co-occurring conditions?
- How do additional conditions complicate things?
- How can I pay for medical bills?
- What if the medical experts disagree?
- When should I tell my child about the diagnosis?
- Should I tell other people about the diagnosis?

Q. How is bipolar disorder diagnosed?

A. Bipolar disorder is diagnosed if your child experiences a manic or mixed episode or recurring episodes of both mania and depression that cannot be accounted for by other causes. Risk factors for developing the illness are also taken into consideration when examining a child who may have the illness or be in the early stages of expressing symptoms. If a child doesn't qualify for a bipolar diagnosis but is showing symptoms and there's history of the illness in the family, doctors should recognize that this may be an early expression of the illness and monitor it closely for progression.

There is not currently a widely accepted blood test or brain scan used to diagnose bipolar disorder at the clinical level, though a few doctors are using Single Photon Emission Computed Tomography (SPECT) scans to aid in diagnosis. Doctors use the American Psychiatric Association's *Diagnostic and Statistical Manual of Mental Disorders (DSM-IV)* as a guideline for diagnosing bipolar disorder. In many countries, the World Health Organization's *International Statistical Classification of Diseases and Related Health Problems* is the preferred manual. Currently, neither of these books has a category that reflects the unique presentation of bipolar disorder in children, though the guidelines listed do not prohibit using the criteria to diagnose children. Children generally do not display the same clearly defined episodes as adults; instead, they display a constant state of volatile moods with much irritability. In addition to using these manuals as guides, the doctor's personal knowledge, training, clinical experience, and interaction with the patient are all critical components of the diagnostic procedure.

There are four basic mood states related to bipolar disorder as recognized by the current diagnostic criteria for the illness: mania, hypomania, depressive, and mixed. In addition to the four basic mood states, there may be periods of euthymic moods—"good" or stable moods—though these are less common in children with bipolar disorder. The diagnosis of the illness is divided into categories or types of bipolar disorder based on how your child experiences these various mood states. Each mood state involves changes in mood, energy levels, thinking, and behavior.

Q. What are mania and hypomania?

A. Here is an overview of the diagnostic requirements for mania and hypomania. To qualify for a diagnosis, moods cannot be caused by another illness, drug use, or a side effect from a medication.

Mania is an unusually euphoric or irritable mood lasting at least one week. If a patient's manic symptoms are severe enough that they can no longer be managed safely at home and result in hospitalization, then no time period is required. (For more information on hospitalization, see Chapter 11.) To be diagnosed with bipolar disorder, these symptoms must cause significant problems in relationships and normal functioning. There may be psychotic features present, including irrational beliefs, hallucinations, and paranoia. During the period of heightened mood, three or more of the following symptoms must be present. If the mood is irritable versus elevated, then four of the following symptoms are required:

- **Inflated self-esteem:** Your child views himself as extremely important and possibly even more powerful than others.

- **Overtalkativeness**: Your child talks more and louder than usual and feels an intense need or pressure to keep talking.

- **Racing thoughts:** Your child has too many thoughts swirling through his brain at one time.

- **Decreased need for sleep:** Your child may be wide awake after a few hours of sleep or may find it very difficult to fall asleep.

- **Distraction**: Your child has difficulty focusing on one thing and can't filter out unimportant information.

- **Risky behavior:** Your child is excessively involved in activities that are high risk and has little regard for consequences.

- **Agitated movement:** Your child is physically restless or hyperfocused on specific activities.

Hypomania is a milder version of mania. Hypomania includes almost all the requirements of full-blown mania, with just a few exceptions. To be diagnosed with hypomania, your child's symptoms only need to last four days instead of a week. And while the impact of the symptoms would be noticeable and your child would show a change in functioning, it would be less severe than mania. Additionally, psychosis would not be present, and hypomania would not be severe enough to require a hospital stay.

Q. What are depression and mixed episodes?

A. Here is an overview of the diagnostic requirements for depression and mixed states. To qualify for a diagnosis, depression cannot be caused by another illness, drug use, or a side effect from a medication.

Depression is a depressed mood lasting at least two weeks and causing significant problems in the person's ability to function. Symptoms are not caused by normal grief. To meet the diagnostic criteria for depression, your child must have five or more of the following symptoms nearly daily for the duration of the mood. At least one of the symptoms must be the first or second one listed:

- **Depressed mood most of the day:** Your child has overwhelming feelings of sadness or emptiness and a tendency to cry easily. This may be demonstrated as irritability in children.

- **Loss of interest:** Your child no longer finds pleasure in activities he once enjoyed.

- **Fatigue:** Your child experiences a loss of energy.

- **Weight changes:** Your child loses or gains weight when not trying. Children may not meet normal weight development.

- **Lack of concentration:** Your child has difficulty making decisions and thinking clearly.

- **Sleep changes:** Your child can't sleep or sleeps way too much.

- **Changes in physical activity level:** Your child experiences either increased restless movements or heavy, slowed movements.

- **Guilt/worthlessness:** Your child has decreased feelings of self-worth and feels guilty about everything.

- **Thoughts of dying:** Your child has ideas about suicide or makes a suicide plan or attempt.

Mixed states occur when your child is having the symptoms of both mania and depression together. The normal time requirements of depressive and manic episodes are not applicable if they are occurring at the same time. Instead, a mixed state requires that the patient experience these symptoms together for one week.

Q. What are the categories of bipolar disorder?

A. While bipolar disorder is one illness, it can be displayed in a variety of ways. How particular patients experience shifts in mood states will determine their specific diagnosis. According to the *DSM-IV*, there are four standard categories of bipolar disorder that a patient may fall into. Each category represents a unique illness presentation. Here are the four categories and their requirements:

- **Bipolar I disorder:** This diagnosis can be made if an individual experiences one manic or mixed episode. This category does not technically require that a depressive episode has also been experienced, but with this diagnosis there will generally be recurring episodes of both mania and depression.

- **Bipolar II disorder:** This requires recurring episodes of depression with at least one hypomanic episode. Full manic episodes do not occur in this category of the illness.

- **Cyclothymic disorder:** This diagnosis requires many recurring hypomanic episodes alternating with depressive symptoms that do not meet the full criteria for a depressive episode. This is the mildest presentation of the illness, but it is chronic and continuous in nature.

- **Bipolar disorder NOS (not otherwise specified):** If the patient is displaying bipolar disorder symptoms but does not neatly fit into one of the above categories, he may be classified with bipolar disorder NOS. Many children are put into this category since they may not meet the time requirements for displaying symptoms.

In addition to these categories, you may hear unofficial terms such as "soft bipolar" or "childhood bipolar." These are not diagnostic categories but are common descriptions of certain groups who display symptoms of bipolar disorder. It should also be noted that a bipolar classification can change over time. A person classified as cyclothymic may later have a full-blown manic episode and be reclassified as bipolar I. A person classified as bipolar disorder NOS may later show more symptoms specific to a different classification.

Q. What constitutes a thorough evaluation?

A. Ideally, a thorough evaluation would be conducted by a psychiatrist who specializes in child and adolescent psychiatry. Evaluations may vary somewhat from doctor to doctor, but a thorough evaluation will share some basic components:

- **Sufficient time:** A thorough evaluation is more than a quick screening. It generally requires at least forty-five minutes of time.

- **Complete information** including the following:
  - ❏ *Medical history:* A thorough evaluation will carefully consider the past history of both the patient and the patient's family members. Expect to fill out several forms regarding health matters.
  - ❏ *Current symptom presentation:* Current symptoms will be discussed as well as any possible contributing environmental factors. Severity and duration of mood symptoms will be examined.
  - ❏ *Functioning in various situations:* Questions regarding functioning in several environments, including home and school, will be considered.

- **Interaction with people:** Your child's ability to interact appropriately with other people, including family members and authority figures, will be discussed.

- **Elimination of other causes:** A thorough evaluation will rule out other causes of symptoms. This step may have already been done by your child's regular doctor. If not, tests may be ordered to rule out other conditions.

- **Observation:** The doctor will closely observe the patient during an evaluation and note any symptoms that are present and observable.

It is important to recognize that even after a thorough evaluation it may not be possible to give a diagnosis immediately. The doctor may need to interact with and view the patient over a period of time to come to an accurate diagnosis.

Q. Can I prevent misdiagnosis?

A. Before your child is diagnosed with bipolar disorder, he may already have been diagnosed with any number of other psychiatric illnesses. This can happen for a variety of reasons. Your child may have more than one condition, his symptoms may have changed over time, or he could have been misdiagnosed.

A diagnosis depends on a number of factors, including the thoroughness of the evaluation, the skill of the doctor, and the accuracy in reporting symptoms. While a diagnosis can look at past history and current functioning, it cannot consider symptoms that have not yet occurred. If your child begins displaying new symptoms, an additional diagnosis may need to be added or the initial diagnosis may need to be changed. Here are some things you can do to increase the likelihood that your child will be given a correct diagnosis:

- **Have your child evaluated:** A large number of children are never correctly diagnosed because they are never evaluated.

- **Give complete information:** Don't hide embarrassing symptoms from your child's physician. Even if you think a symptom is not important, it may help the doctor give a correct diagnosis.

- **Ask questions:** Find out why your doctor feels this diagnosis is correct, and ask if any other condition could be contributing to symptoms.

- **See a specialist:** There is less likelihood that a condition will be misdiagnosed or overlooked if you take your child to a specialist.

- **Get a second opinion:** Sometimes two heads are better than one. If you have doubts about the diagnosis or feel that you need to confirm it, then take your child for a second opinion.

Q. Can the illness be treated?

A. Bipolar disorder does not have to be a hopeless illness or a death sentence—it is actually very treatable. Not only are there medications currently available to curtail the symptoms and prevent future episodes but also there are new medications being researched and developed for more effective treatment down the road. Additionally, therapy along with medication can improve your child's ability to function and stay well for longer periods of time. Despite this fact, there are children and families who suffer every day without help or hope due to lack of treatment.

One of the biggest obstacles to treatment is convincing people to seek it out. Most children and adults with the disorder go undiagnosed and untreated. This happens for a variety of reasons. Lack of knowledge regarding the symptoms of the illness, fear of being stigmatized, financial constraints, lack of qualified physicians to treat children with bipolar disorder, and denial are some of the biggest roadblocks to receiving treatment.

Children with bipolar disorder must rely on the adults in their lives to seek out treatment for them. Parents and guardians are vital to this process—they are generally the first people to suspect a problem. Pediatricians are also in a key position to identify symptoms and refer children to a specialist for evaluation. But what if no one takes the child for an evaluation? What if the pediatrician misses the early warning signs? What if parents are discouraged from using medication for this serious illness? Treatment can only assist a child if it is received. Childhood bipolar disorder can be treated. Whether or not it will be treated is an entirely different matter.

Q. Can other illnesses mimic bipolar disorder?

A. Treatment for any illness will only be effective if that illness has been properly diagnosed, and the symptoms of bipolar disorder can be easily mistaken for other conditions. A good evaluation will rule out other causes of symptoms or identify conditions that exist along with bipolar disorder. Here are some conditions that can mimic the symptoms of bipolar disorder:

- **Hyperthyroidism** is an overproduction of thyroid hormones, which are responsible for the body's metabolism. The patient may become irritable or easily upset, have difficulty sleeping, and become depressed. A blood test can help doctors rule out or diagnose hyperthyroidism.

- **Temporal lobe seizures** are epileptic seizures that involve abnormal electrical activity specific to the temporal lobes of the brain. The patient may experience hallucinations and intense emotions, which can range from joy to agitation. Repetitive motor movements may also be present. An electroencephalogram (EEG) may be used to help diagnose the condition.

- **Wilson's disease** is a rare disease that inhibits the body's ability to eliminate copper. This buildup of copper damages the liver and other organs. Symptoms can include mood swings, suicidal thoughts, irritability, anxiety, and depression. Blood and urine tests can check copper levels, and a special eye test can look for evidence of the disease.

- **Fetal alcohol syndrome** is caused by exposure to alcohol while in the womb, which causes abnormal development and can manifest in poor impulse control, short attention span, learning difficulties, hyperactivity, and poor judgment skills.

Additionally, other illnesses such as lupus and multiple sclerosis can cause symptoms of depression. Head injuries, trauma, illicit drug use, and reactions to prescribed medications such as steroids may also result in symptoms of those like bipolar disorder. Finally, other psychiatric illnesses may have symptoms that overlap with bipolar disorder. The key is to get an accurate evaluation, which will eliminate other possible conditions before a diagnosis is given.

Q. Will my child be stigmatized?

A. You may be concerned that a bipolar disorder diagnosis could lead to your child being ostracized or stigmatized. It is a sad fact that society in general is still not very accepting of people who suffer from brain disorders. While this trend is slowly changing with newer generations, these changes take time. But it's not the act of diagnosing or labeling the illness that creates the problem.

Many times it is the illness itself and untreated symptoms of the illness that cause a negative reaction from others. Withholding a label does not mean your child will somehow stop having symptoms of the illness and that others won't be aware of his difficulties. In fact, if your child is diagnosed and successfully treated, he is less likely to have the extreme symptoms that might lead others to shun him. Diagnosis and treatment will give him the best shot at having a childhood closer to that of his peers.

Additionally, your reaction to the illness is likely to affect how your child feels about the condition. If you view the illness as shameful, your child will pick up on that shame. Be open to entering counseling and therapy to combat any lingering guilt or shame that you may associate with this serious illness. Therapy of this sort may enable you to be a stronger positive force in helping your child. It is true that your child may have to deal with the stigma of the illness from time to time, but if you view the illness as any other medical condition that merely needs treatment, then your child will not grow up feeling overwhelmingly stigmatized.

Q. Can my child be treated without a diagnosis?

A. Treating a condition without a diagnosis is like playing darts while blind-folded—you might hit the target or you might not. Treatment is most effective when there is a clear diagnosis. Additionally, most insurance companies will require a diagnosis of some kind before they will pay for treatment. What if the diagnosis is uncertain? A doctor may need to evaluate the patient over a period of time before being able to make any diagnostic determination. In that case, should treatment still be started?

If your child's symptoms are severe and require immediate attention, he may be given a working diagnosis based on the most prominent symptoms and be prescribed medication to alleviate these symptoms. However, use caution with this approach. If symptoms of depression, anxiety, or attention difficulties are addressed independently, the medications used for these symptoms could possibly worsen the expression of bipolar disorder. Bipolar disorder should be ruled out before beginning medications for these other symptoms.

If the doctor suspects that your child is in the early stages of manifesting bipolar disorder, the diagnosis may at first be more generically stated, reflecting both the uncertainty and the caution that must be exercised in diagnosing a young child. As your child grows, his diagnosis may become more apparent. If medications are deemed necessary at a young age, extreme care should be taken to ensure proper treatment. Both antidepressant and stimulant medications given without a mood stabilizer can wreak havoc on a child who has bipolar disorder. Taking a child you suspect might be bipolar immediately for an evaluation will help ensure a proper diagnosis and correct treatment.

Q. Should all family members be evaluated?

A. When bipolar disorder strikes one member of a family, everyone is affected. It's natural for the person who was diagnosed to take up a great deal of your attention, worry, and time, but there may be other family members who are also suffering with symptoms. Sometimes it is only after the most symptomatic person is treated that the family starts seeing the symptoms in another child or a parent.

Due to the genetic nature of bipolar disorder, every family member is at increased risk for having the illness if one member is diagnosed. Additionally, there is a higher rate of other related conditions such as depression or anxiety in family members of patients with bipolar disorder. The stress of dealing with an unstable child or sibling can cause additional difficulties. It would be wise for each member to at least be screened for these conditions. A complete evaluation should be scheduled for any family member who is displaying warning signs or symptoms of an illness.

It's also a good idea for each family member to educate themselves about the illness. This can be accomplished through therapy or through education classes such as the Family to Family courses given through the National Alliance on Mental Illness (http://www.nami.org/). Creating an atmosphere of education and understanding can go a long way in helping the child who is suffering from bipolar disorder and each member of the family who is struggling to cope.

Q. Can children have co-occurring conditions?

A. Other conditions can and do co-occur with childhood bipolar disorder. A co-occurring condition is diagnosed if the symptoms can't be explained by the bipolar disorder and if they are present as a unique and distinct illness. Diagnosis of co-occurring conditions can be tricky since there is symptom overlap in several of these conditions. The best way to correctly diagnose each disorder is to be completely honest with your doctor about your child's symptoms and to allow the doctor to observe him for as long as is necessary.

Co-occurring condition	Symptoms may include	How often does it occur with childhood bipolar disorder?
Attention deficit-hyperactivity disorder (ADHD)	Hyperactivity, impulsiveness, distractibility	Up to 90 percent in childhood onset and up to 40 percent in teenage onset.
Anxiety disorders (obsessive compulsive, post-traumatic stress, general anxiety, social anxiety, and panic disorders)	Excessive worry, anticipating disaster, startling easily, obsessions, compulsions, panic attacks	Up to 56 percent. Anxiety disorders are more common in patients with bipolar II.

Asperger's syndrome	Avoidance of eye contact, sensitivity to sensory stimulation, inability to read social cues, preoccupation with a favorite topic	Up to 11 percent have Asperger's syndrome. Others may have more severe forms of developmental disorders, including autism.
Conduct disorders	Physical aggression toward people and animals, serious violation of rules, destruction of property, lying and stealing	Up to 37 percent. Conduct disorders are more frequent in patients with bipolar I.
Oppositional defiant disorder	Refusal to follow rules, arguing with adults, being easily annoyed, purposeful annoyance of others, loss of temper	Up to 75 percent of children with bipolar disorder also have oppositional defiant disorder.
Tourette's syndrome	Involuntary movements or sounds (tics), may also include obsessions and compulsions	Tourette's syndrome patients are four times more likely to also have bipolar disorder, which indicates a co-occurring link.
Learning disabilities	Difficulty with basic educational tasks such as reading, writing, and math	It is estimated that 50 percent of children with bipolar disorder have a learning disorder in the area of writing.
Substance abuse	Dependence on drugs, drug craving, withdrawal effects, denial	Up to 40 percent of children with bipolar disorder have a co-occurring substance abuse disorder. Teens are nearly nine times more likely to experience this than preteens.

Q. How do additional conditions complicate things?

A. Some parents find that when their child has a correct diagnosis and treatment, other symptoms that look like a co-occurring condition disappear. Other children, however, have strong lingering symptoms that are suggestive of another condition along with bipolar disorder. This complicates many areas:

- **Clouded diagnosis:** Additional conditions can make initial evaluations more difficult. The doctor must tease out the overlapping symptoms and the root cause of each. Sometimes an initial co-occurring condition is more readily observable and may become the first target of treatment. It may be after these symptoms are under control that the bipolar disorder diagnosis becomes apparent.

- **Conflicting treatments:** Once bipolar disorder with a co-occurring condition is diagnosed, it can be difficult to treat. Some medications that are good for a co-occurring condition may actually make bipolar disorder symptoms worse. Treatments must be chosen very carefully and monitored closely. Addressing additional symptoms through therapy can be a good option with more than one condition because the treatment will not aggravate bipolar disorder symptoms.

- **Additional symptoms:** Along with the complications in diagnosis and treatment are the parenting complications. You are dealing not only with the set of symptoms that come from bipolar disorder but also with a whole other disorder and its symptoms and requirements. You will have to educate yourself on two disorders and the best treatment options for both—as well as how those treatments will interact with each other.

However, there actually can be at least some benefits to having certain co-occurring conditions. For example, patients with bipolar disorder and obsessive compulsive disorder or social phobia actually exhibit a greater insight and awareness into their own symptoms, illness, and response to treatment. This can be a definite advantage for treatment compliance and reporting of symptoms, but it may come at a high price if these other symptoms are severe. No matter what conditions your child is suffering from, the best way to make them less complicated is to understand as much about them as possible.

Q. How can I pay for medical bills?

A. As you focus on how to get your child the appropriate help, the issue of how to pay for this help is unavoidable. If you have good medical coverage, try to access providers within your coverage to minimize costs. If you do not have insurance, here are some possible options to find coverage and minimize out-of-pocket expenses:

- **Parental coverage:** In the case of separation or divorce, an ex-spouse may be able to add a child onto his or her existing insurance plan.

- **State insurance:** Every state offers a health insurance program for children. This insurance is available either free or at low cost to eligible families. Check http://www.insurekidsnow.gov to see if your child qualifies.

- **Medicaid coverage:** Families with limited income and means may qualify for free medical coverage under the Medicaid program. To find your state's Medicaid information, visit http://64.82.65.67/medicaid/states.html.

- **Medicaid waiver:** A child may qualify for Medicaid coverage through a Medicaid waiver such as the Katie Beckett waiver. This allows children with severe medical conditions to be covered even when their family's income surpasses normal income eligibility requirements.

- **Social Security disability program:** If your child's condition is severe and persistent, he may qualify for medical coverage under the Social Security disability program. To see if your child qualifies, visit http://www.ssa.gov/disability/.

- **Patient assistance programs:** Pharmaceutical companies have established programs for needy patients; in some cases, medications can be received at no charge. For more information, go to http://www.needymeds.com.

- **Medication samples:** While waiting to qualify for one of these programs, check with your child's psychiatrist and pediatrician to see if medication samples are available.

- **Local charity groups:** Local charity groups may offer to pay for some medical bills or prescriptions. The St. Vincent de Paul Pharmacy offers free medications in some areas to families who are in desperate need. They also offer advocate assistance to access other programs of care. Learn more about this charity at http://svdpusa.org/, or look in your local white pages under "Society of St. Vincent de Paul."

Q. What if the medical experts disagree?

A. There may be times when the medical experts who evaluate your child disagree on the diagnosis or treatment. This can be frustrating when you are searching for answers, but it can also be a relief if you felt the original evaluation was not competent.

The best way to deal with a disagreement in expert opinion is to become an informed consumer. To make a decision regarding who to trust with your child's health, you need to have a basic understanding of your child's symptoms, what they mean, and how they are generally treated. If your gut instinct is telling you to choose one doctor's evaluation over another, ask yourself why. After careful examination you may realize what factors are leading you to this conclusion, and once you recognize these factors you can evaluate the usefulness of this inclination. While it may be helpful to talk to others who have been in your position, be wary of well-meaning advice from friends who may not be educated about your child's medical condition.

In the end, the decision about who to trust and what route to take may be very clear to you. If not, perhaps more time or an additional evaluation can help. Unfortunately, most parents in this position do not have the luxury of time and endless evaluations. You will then need to make the best decision that you can based on the facts at hand. Realize also that you may need to step back from time to time to reevaluate the situation in light of your growing knowledge and experience.

Q. When should I tell my child about the diagnosis?

A. If your child is diagnosed with bipolar disorder, it is likely that he already knows something is wrong, and he may have been longing for answers just as much as you have been. You may decide that it would be a kindness to give him those answers, along with an understanding of the illness based on his age level. After all, he will ultimately grow into the responsibility of managing this illness. To help you when talking to your child, think of bipolar disorder in terms of other illnesses. If your child was diagnosed with diabetes, wouldn't you talk to him about why he is seeing a doctor, what is going wrong in his body, and how he will need to manage the illness?

However, some parents feel very conflicted about when to tell a child about the diagnosis of bipolar disorder. Talk it over with your child's doctor or therapist. You may also find that your fears about this conversation will subside as you become more comfortable with your child's diagnosis. As with all education, this is a process that will take place over time. A very simplistic explanation may suffice for young patients, and more detailed information will be given over time as the child naturally progresses. Adolescents, on the other hand, will need to be given more detailed information, possibly straight from the psychiatrist. There are books, brochures, and tools available to help start conversations about bipolar disorder with both young children and teens. Check out http://www.bpchildren.com for these resources.

Q. Should I tell other people about the diagnosis?

A. For some people, health conditions are a very private topic not to be discussed outside the family. Other people are open and talkative about health concerns. Either way, there will be some situations in which medical safety will warrant sharing information regarding your child's diagnosis. Certainly, all medical professionals who are involved in the care of your child should be made aware of the diagnosis and any treatment being administered. All information shared with medical personnel is protected by privacy laws. Additionally, those who share the responsibility of caring for your child should be aware of important health issues.

However, what you choose to share with friends and acquaintances about your child's diagnosis is up to you. When addressing this topic, you should also bear in mind the feelings of your child; teenagers in particular may have strong feelings one way or another. Some children are naturally more private and don't wish personal information to be shared. Others are expressive and feel very comfortable talking to others about their illness. Indeed, two children in the same family may take alternate approaches to this topic. There is no blanket right or wrong answer on this—just do whatever makes you and your family feel comfortable.

Whatever your choice in the matter, it should not be made based on shame or guilt. That's not beneficial for anyone; you'll end up making the family member with bipolar disorder feel stigmatized within his own family. Some parents and teens find that when they are able to openly speak about the illness they no longer feel trapped and alone. Others feel that such openness helps to minimize the illness's stigma. Still others find enrichment in reaching out to help other families who are beginning this difficult journey.

Chapter 4 WORKING WITH DOCTORS

Q. What is the role of the psychiatrist?

A. A psychiatrist is a physician who has specialized training to identify and treat various disorders of the brain. A child and adolescent psychiatrist has additional training to identify and treat these illnesses in children, and a child psychiatrist who specializes in mood disorders would be the most qualified doctor to diagnose bipolar disorder in young people.

A diagnosis of bipolar disorder can be complicated and may require observation over time. It may not initially be apparent if the child is experiencing bipolar disorder or another condition with similar symptoms, such as an anxiety disorder, ADHD, a reaction to trauma, or a recurring depression. The psychiatrist must look at all factors in determining a diagnosis—however, his role goes well beyond identification of the illness. It is the psychiatrist who prescribes medications, makes adjustments in treatment, and refers the patient to other supportive care services.

If your child has bipolar disorder, you will want to build a treatment team consisting of your child's pediatrician, psychiatrist, therapist, pharmacist, and other specific medical professionals as needed. Your role as the parent is to manage your child's overall health. You can hire and fire team members depending on their benefit to your child. And if you're the manager of the treatment team, a psychiatrist could be viewed as the star quarterback. His ability to accurately view a situation and make decisions can help your child gain ground. Of course, no one is perfect, and sometimes a treatment decision leads to losing ground. When this happens, a good psychiatrist will reevaluate the game plan and adjust as necessary. Carefully consider your choices before deciding on this important part of the treatment team.

Q. What is the role of the therapist?

A. As you build your child's treatment team, you will find that there are several members of the team who can help support and complement the treatment provided by the psychiatrist. A therapist is one of these support members who can play an important role. Research has demonstrated that children with bipolar disorder who have intensive therapy along with medication have better outcomes than those who do not. There are many kinds of therapists and many different therapeutic techniques. Your child's psychiatrist may be best suited to recommend a particular therapist and kind of therapy for your child. The goals of therapy may include the following:

- **Education:** A therapist can work with you and your child to help you both understand and deal with his illness in a healthy way.

- **Compliance:** Many patients don't stick to the treatment plan outlined by the psychiatrist. A therapist can help young people learn the importance of compliance.

- **Brain health:** A therapist can teach overall brain health to promote better functioning. Brain health includes a regular sleep schedule, healthy eating, and exercise. It also includes avoiding such things as violent entertainment.

- **Identification of triggers:** Identifying situations that can increase symptoms can help your child recognize and avoid problem areas such as overstimulation.

- **Calming strategies:** Your child's therapist may work with him on using calming strategies both as part of an ongoing daily brain health program and as a way to be aware of his mood states.

- **Stress reduction:** Teaching your child what stress is, how it can affect his illness, and how to reduce it is a wonderful way that the therapist can make a lasting impact.

- **Special concerns:** The therapist should also help address any additional concerns specific to your child, such as learning difficulties.

The key to success with therapy is choosing a skilled therapist and working intensively with him. Whatever the chosen therapy, make sure that it is frequent enough and lasts long enough to really make a difference for your child. Intensive therapy would occur one to two times a week over a period of six to nine months or longer if required. These factors matter more than the actual type of therapy chosen.

Q. What is the role of the pharmacist?

A. In this age of long pharmacy waiting lines and mail-order prescriptions, you may not think of your local pharmacist as part of your child's treatment team. But a good pharmacist can be an invaluable resource when medication has been prescribed. The pharmacist can alert you to special instructions for new medications and can warn you about possible medication interactions with both prescription and over-the-counter medicine. Additionally, your pharmacist can be a good source of information regarding medication side effects. Here are some questions to consider when choosing a pharmacy:

- **Are the hours of operation convenient?** A pharmacy with weekend and evening hours can be a lifesaver.

- **Does the pharmacy accept your insurance?** Using a pharmacy that accepts your insurance and files the claim electronically will save you money and effort.

- **Is the pharmacist easily accessible to discuss medication concerns?** Your pharmacist should be available to talk with you in person or on the phone.

- **If you travel out of state, will you have access to medication refills?** Nationwide chain stores can give the benefit of making prescriptions available no matter where you travel.

- **Are customers treated respectfully?** You have the right to be treated with respect when dealing with the pharmacist and pharmacy staff. Pharmacy staff should not treat you differently if you fill a medication for bipolar disorder or a medication for allergies.

- **Will the pharmacy special order items that they don't normally carry?** Your pharmacist should be willing to stock the items that the psychiatrist prescribes.

- **Does the pharmacy work well with your psychiatrist's office?** Your pharmacist should have a good working relationship with local offices.

- **How long is the typical wait before medications can be picked up?**
  Your pharmacy should be staffed sufficiently so that lengthy wait times are minimized.

Q. What is a developmental pediatrician?

A. Your child may be referred to a developmental pediatrician at some point during the course of treatment. This specialized pediatrician works with children who have various developmental issues or delays. While bipolar disorder would generally be out of his scope of specialty as far as treatment is concerned, the related developmental issues that come with the illness can be addressed by this type of doctor. Depending on your child's needs, this member of the team may take a very active role or more of a consultative role. You may never need to consult a developmental pediatrician at all. Work closely with your child's psychiatrist to make sure you get a recommendation to a trusted specialist who understands the specific needs of children with bipolar disorder. Because these specialized pediatricians sometimes prescribe medications similar to those prescribed by psychiatrists, these two doctors will want to work together in case of any treatment additions or changes.

Developmental pediatricians may help identify and address learning disabilities and delays in development. These types of doctors may want to review any and all educational testing and perform additional testing. They will also want a history of your child's progression, growth, and development. They may be able to help you as a parent understand your child's special needs in this area and could also provide comprehensive educational recommendations to your child's school and provide recommendations for therapeutic intervention for appropriate development.

Because of the specialized nature of this doctor, there may not be one close to you. If you have to drive a long way for this visit, you may well wonder if the trip is worthwhile. If your child's learning and development is not being adversely impacted, then this is probably a step you can skip.

Q. Will my child see a neurologist?

A. Neurology and psychiatry are closely related medical fields. A neurologist is a physician who specializes in illnesses of the central nervous system, which includes the brain and spinal cord. Neurologists and psychiatrists often see some of the same patients, since both specialties deal at least in part with the brain. For instance, both specialties may be involved in treating patients with tic disorders like Tourette's syndrome. However, each specialty has its unique patients. While neurologists generally don't treat bipolar disorder, they may treat conditions that can be present along with bipolar disorder.

There is a higher occurrence of bipolar disorder in patients with seizures, so it is good to be aware of the possibility of having both conditions. And if it is suspected that your child with bipolar disorder also has seizures, a referral to a neurologist would be in order. The neurologist may order tests such as an EEG to detect seizures. If it is determined that your child does have an additional condition, then it will be important for all the specialists involved in your child's treatment to work together.

If medications are prescribed by both a psychiatrist and a neurologist, it will be important for the doctors to consult with each other. Medications can be dangerous when mixed, and any medication used to treat one condition should not aggravate the other. If possible, choosing a medication that can help both conditions would be ideal. For instance, symptoms of both seizure disorders and bipolar disorder can sometimes be managed by the same medication, such as Depakote (valproic acid), Lamictal (lamotrigine), or Equetro (carbamazepine).

Q. What other specialists might be necessary?

A. It may be overwhelming to think about your child needing any additional specialists. However, keep in mind that if different specialists are necessary, this will likely be over the course of years, not all at once. These specialists probably are not involved in the day-to-day needs of your child but are consulted as necessary. Each specialist may address unique needs of your child and contribute to an overall improvement in functioning. How many specialists are necessary will depend on your child's specific needs. Here are some of the specialty areas that may benefit your child over time and in conjunction with your child's psychiatrist:

- **Endocrinologist:** This medical specialist deals with imbalances of hormones that may affect growth and metabolism. An imbalance in these hormones may also impact moods. Additionally, some medications can cause a hormonal imbalance that may need to be addressed by this specialist. Your child with bipolar disorder may have difficulty stabilizing if there is an additional endocrine problem.

- **Sleep specialist:** This specialist deals with sleep disorders such as sleep apnea, narcolepsy, sleepwalking, and night terrors.

- **Occupational therapist:** An occupational therapist helps your child overcome various limiting factors in day-to-day functioning. Occupational therapy may be recommended to help with sensory issues and writing difficulties.

- **Physical therapist:** If your child has additional physical challenges, these can be addressed through physical therapy.

- **Speech therapist:** Issues with speech and language may be present when bipolar disorder co-occurs with learning disabilities or developmental disabilities.

Q. How can I find a good psychiatrist?

A. The decision to take your child to a psychiatrist may come with feelings of failure, fear, and uncertainty. This decision may even be discouraged by well-meaning family and friends. However, seeking out help for your child is the right thing to do when you suspect your child has bipolar disorder. You are also faced with choosing the right psychiatrist, which may make you feel lost and alone. But you are not alone! There are others in your state, your county, and even your town who have had to do the same thing. There is no reason for you to go it alone. Here are some good places to start looking for a qualified psychiatrist for your child:

- **Pediatrician:** Your child's pediatrician can be an excellent source of information in finding a psychiatrist. Ideally, you have already brought your child for a physical and told the pediatrician about your concerns over symptoms related to bipolar disorder. Your pediatrician may be familiar with qualified psychiatrists in your area.

- **Local support groups:** Attending a local support group is a terrific way to network and to hear firsthand about the skills of local psychiatrists. Several organizations sponsor support groups, including the National Alliance on Mental Illness and the Depression and Bipolar Support Alliance. Check your local paper and the internet for times and locations near you.

- **Internet support groups:** If there are no local support groups or you wish to have more anonymity, try an internet support group. The Child and Adolescent Bipolar Foundation (http://www.bpkids.org) is a great place to sign up for an internet support group and to search listings for a good psychiatrist. There are several other groups available on the internet with people who are willing to help.

Q. What should I look for in a psychiatrist?

A. As a parent, you want the best possible care for your child, and a good psychiatrist will be an indispensable asset to the treatment team. Here are some important qualities to look for in a psychiatrist:

- **Knowledge:** Physicians who are board certified in child and adolescent psychiatry have passed a national exam demonstrating mastery of knowledge in their specialty. This is not a guarantee that a specific psychiatrist will be a good choice; however, it can be one indication of a competent level of knowledge in this field. More important, knowledge comes from the everyday experience of treating children with bipolar disorder.

- **Experience:** If you were taking your child for heart surgery, would you pick the surgeon who had performed two or two hundred successful operations? Experience adds confidence.

- **Compassion:** A doctor could be both knowledgeable and experienced but lack the important element of compassion. While doctors may need to distance themselves from the emotions of their patients so as not to become drained, they should speak to you and your child with respect, retain a caring attitude, and be responsive to patient needs.

- **Experience with children:** Children are not just little adults. Their symptoms, reaction to medications, and life issues may be very different from those of adult bipolar disorder sufferers. An ideal psychiatrist not only is willing to treat children but also is trained and experienced in treating children.

- **Skill in psychopharmacology:** Managing medications is a very large part of treating children with bipolar disorder; having a psychiatrist who is skilled at psychopharmacology is crucial.

What if your psychiatrist fits some but not all of the above descriptions? You have to decide which of the above skills most closely meets the needs of your child. Also recognize that the needs of your child may change over time, and a combination of psychiatrists may help your child over the years.

Q. How often should my child see the psychiatrist?

A. After your child is initially evaluated, follow-up visits will be important to monitor your child's condition, response to treatment, and changing needs. At first these visits will need to be frequent, especially if your child is unstable or if a new medication has been started. You can expect to return every few weeks for these first visits. After your child has been stabilized, follow-up visits may be scheduled every month or every few months; you'll want to work closely with the psychiatrist to determine what is best for your child.

If your child's follow-up visit is still far off and your child's symptoms begin to worsen, don't try to wait it out. If the psychiatrist doesn't hear from you, then he will assume that all is well. It is up to you to let the physician know if your child is not improving or is getting worse. A call to the office may result in an earlier appointment, but no matter what, always leave a message for your child's psychiatrist. He may not be able to return your call immediately, but a responsive physician will take care of phone calls by the end of the day.

When scheduling follow-up appointments, keep in mind events that may affect your child. It may be helpful to make sure your child has an appointment a few weeks before school begins in case a small adjustment in treatment needs to be made. A follow-up appointment a month or so after school begins could also be helpful to review how the additional stress of school is affecting your child's functioning. A psychiatrist is an important ally for your child in the fight against bipolar disorder; you should involve them as much as is necessary.

Q. Why does it take so long to get an appointment?

A. Perhaps you've identified your child's needs and gotten a referral to an excellent psychiatrist, but when you call for an appointment, there is a three-month wait for a new patient to be seen. This is a common scenario and one that can be incredibly disheartening. However, before you call another office, consider making the appointment. Having this appointment set up won't prevent you from seeking help elsewhere, and if you do find another psychiatrist who can see your child sooner, he may not be a good fit, or you may want a second opinion. No matter what, it is much easier to cancel an existing appointment than it is to get a new one.

This lapse in child psychiatric services is a nationwide crisis. Many child psychiatrists are unable to take new patients because they can hardly care for their current patient load. It is not uncommon for parents, especially in rural areas, to drive two or more hours to see a qualified psychiatrist. Sometimes these families are able to arrange a consult with an expert who is willing to send recommendations to a local physician for follow-up treatment.

It can be challenging for a psychiatrist to find time in his schedule for a new patient because of the time needed to establish a rapport with that patient. Some doctors also put a limit on how many new patients can be seen in a week to ensure that they can adequately care for them. Once your child is established as a patient, it should be much easier to schedule follow-up appointments.

Q. How should I prepare for my child's first visit?

A. There is some information you will want to have handy at your child's first visit to a psychiatrist. Initial visits generally include an extensive medical and family history, a review of current physical complaints, a discussion of sleeping and eating patterns, and a discussion of mood and behavior patterns. It can be somewhat disconcerting to try to remember all the information you need, especially as your child will be with you and may require much of your attention. You may be able to pick up new patient forms ahead of time or download them from your doctor's website. Being able to fill these out in advance will help on the day of the visit.

It will also help if you have been keeping a record of your child's difficulties. If you haven't started charting your child's mood symptoms, you may want to do so in advance of your first visit to the psychiatrist. Make sure to record sleeping patterns, changes in energy levels, and comments made while depressed or in periods of heightened activity. While the psychiatrist may not look over all your personal notes, it helps to have it all written down so that you can mentally review your concerns in advance. No symptom should be too odd or embarrassing to report to the doctor.

Also bring along the results of any previous evaluations that have been done. This could include any psychological testing, occupational therapy, speech therapy, blood work, or other medical tests that have been performed. This additional information will help the psychiatrist get a complete picture and properly evaluate your child. Finally, make a list of your biggest concerns, and write down any specific questions you want to ask. Without having this written guide, it is quite likely that you will remember what you wanted to say only as you are traveling home, and your important questions may be left unanswered.

Q. How should I prepare my child for his first visit?

A. Before taking him to the psychiatrist, you might tell your young child that he will be seeing a doctor who likes to talk with kids and help them with how they feel and act. Reassure your child that it's okay to talk to the doctor—even about scary feelings. It may take time for your child to feel comfortable with a new doctor, and if your child tends to hyperfocus or worry excessively, you might not want to tell him about the appointment too far in advance.

Your approach will change if your child is older. The reaction of adolescents to an initial visit may range from relief to refusal. How you handle your adolescent's concern will vary greatly according to the child. Be open and honest about why the visit is necessary. Reassure your teen that you want to help. Turn statements that place blame into positive statements:

Negative	Positive
"If you could control yourself, you wouldn't need to see a doctor!"	"This doctor may be able to help you feel more in control."
"It's your anger that has landed you in this position."	"I'm concerned that anger seems to be overtaking you."
"Get yourself together and maybe you won't need to see a shrink."	"It's time to see a specialist who can help you get rid of this depression."

Your teen may be relieved that you are seeking help for him even if he outwardly objects. If he doesn't want to go for an evaluation or treatment, let him know that his health is nonnegotiable. Just as you wouldn't let a teen with diabetes avoid seeing a doctor to monitor his condition, neither should you allow a teen with a mood disorder avoid seeing a specialist. Hopefully, at some point in the future, your teen will be able to understand the benefit.

Q. Will the psychiatrist order any blood tests?

A. Your child's psychiatrist may need to order lab work. If you already have recent lab work from your child's pediatrician, bring a copy of these results so that tests are not unnecessarily duplicated. Results of blood work may be used to rule out other causes of symptoms. Also, baseline functioning of the kidneys and liver may be checked before any medication is initiated.

A prescription for blood work can strike fear into your child's heart, but there are a few things you can do to help ease the pain. First, call the lab beforehand and ask which technician specializes in drawing blood from children. Also, if your child has sensory issues, make sure the lab is skilled at addressing these. Getting the right lab tech may mean the difference between a good experience and a disaster. Ask the lab if they use a topical analgesic such as Eutectic Mixture of Local Anesthetics (EMLA) cream to deaden the site where the needle is inserted. If you cannot find a lab that uses a topical analgesic, your doctor can prescribe EMLA cream for your child. You can also request a butterfly needle, which is the smallest needle and is usually used on young children. Butterfly needles can be a little less intimidating. Make sure to ask the doctor if there are any special instructions about the blood test. Some tests require no food or drink beforehand; others need to be performed twelve hours after the previous dose of medication or at certain times of the day. If there are no restrictions, then have your child drink plenty of water right before the test. This generally makes it easier to draw blood. And finally, give your child a big reward afterward. A trip to the ice cream shop helps make a bad experience better. (For more information regarding blood tests, please see Chapter 6.)

Q. What if the doctor doesn't listen to me?

A. Whether you are taking your child for the first appointment or for the hundredth appointment, you want your doctor to listen to you and to respond to the unique needs of your child. The person who will be treating your child should be someone with whom you are comfortable and someone you can talk to and trust.

You may not find this doctor on your first attempt. If you have a poor experience with a new doctor, you may want to look for another physician instead of holding on. Not everyone will be a good fit for you and your child. If it is obvious that this first doctor is not the one for you, then move on. If you have a good relationship with a skilled doctor, you may still come away from an appointment feeling disappointed. It may be that the doctor's interpretation of symptoms differs from yours, or you may feel like the doctor is overlooking something that is important and is not listening to your input. If this happens, don't give up immediately.

To improve communication with your doctor, write out your thoughts in advance. Don't minimize symptoms in an effort to stay positive or exaggerate symptoms due to frustration. Stay open to ideas that differ from your own. Finally, you may wish to take your spouse along to help during the appointment. In the end, a glitch in communication should be a small bump in the road. If it turns out to be a permanent roadblock, then it's time to find a new path.

Q. What if I disagree with the evaluation?

A. More and more parents are becoming educated consumers when it comes to health care. By the time you take your child to his first doctor's visit, you may already have a strong suspicion that your child has bipolar disorder. This may or may not turn out to be the case. What if the doctor's evaluation leads to another conclusion? The important thing is that your child receives the correct treatment no matter what the diagnosis. If you disagree with the doctor's evaluation, ask yourself the following questions:

- Was the evaluation thorough?
- Was family history considered?
- Were other health conditions ruled out?
- Did the doctor fully understand your child's symptoms?
- Was a careful history taken to show symptoms over time?
- Were you given enough time to convey information to the doctor?
- Did the doctor seem prejudiced against any particular diagnosis?
- Was the doctor able to explain why this diagnosis is appropriate?

It is important to keep an open mind to diagnoses other than bipolar disorder. There are crossover symptoms with several other illnesses. At the same time, it does not hurt to be cautious and to seek a second opinion. If you feel the evaluation was inadequate, seek a more comprehensive evaluation from a specialist. Also keep in mind that it may take several visits and observation over time before the doctor is able to make a correct diagnosis.

Q. Should I videotape my child?

A. It can be frustrating when specialists do not see the mood swings and difficult behaviors that your child exhibits through the course of a day. Your child may be quite angelic and charming during an office visit, leaving you to wonder how a physician will understand the gravity of the extreme behaviors you witness each day. Videotaping or audiotaping a child during normal activities can give the physician a window into your child's life and can validate reports of behaviors. However, a number of factors should be considered before you decide to turn on the camera.

First, does the physician feel this is necessary? Many physicians who are familiar with mood disorders realize that your child will have great variation in functioning. They will rely on a number of methods in addition to direct observation to treat your child. Some physicians would prefer that you don't make a recording of your child. A second factor to consider is what effect videotaping will have on your child. If your child is crying or upset, it is likely that turning on a camera will escalate difficult behaviors. Your child may feel betrayed or insulted by such an act. If you feel you must record your child, do so very discreetly. Audiotaping may be somewhat easier and less intrusive.

Finally, video or audio devices should never be used as a shaming tool. Your child may already feel embarrassed and ashamed of behaviors that are out of his control. Viewing or listening to an episode at a later time does not give your child any additional ability to control mood swings, but it may contribute to low self-worth. If a recording is made, keep it confidential and only share it with medical personnel for the purpose of gaining better treatment.

Q. What emergency services are available?

A. There are emergency situations in which you should not wait for a doctor's appointment to seek help for your child. Such emergencies may include a child raging out of control or making an attempt to harm himself or a family member. Since emergencies can happen in an instant, it is wise to prepare in advance for this possibility. Familiarize yourself with the specific mental health facilities in your area and in surrounding areas before these services are needed. The availability of emergency services and the quality of care can vary dramatically by area. If your child already has a psychiatrist, make sure you have discussed an emergency crisis plan with him in advance. Check to see if your local police have been trained to deal with a mental health crisis. Know which of the following emergency care providers you will call upon first:

- **911 call:** Critical emergencies of all varieties are handled through 911 operators, who dispatch the appropriate personnel. When an emergency involves a mental health crisis, an ambulance may be dispatched to transport a patient to a mental health facility. Be aware that a 911 call of this nature will likely bring both the ambulance and police. Once authorities are on the scene, the outcome will likely be out of your hands.

- **Crisis stabilization unit:** The general goal of a stabilization unit is to safely monitor suicidal patients and to get them through a short-term crisis period. Admission may be voluntary or mandated by authorities if it is deemed in the best interest of the patient. The patient may be released without any change or initiation of treatment if he is no longer considered suicidal.

- **Psychiatric hospital:** A psychiatric hospital is better equipped for longer stays. Admission to a psychiatric hospital may be made from another facility or emergency room that does not specialize in psychiatric care. Not all psychiatric hospitals are suited to treat children. A hospital stay would be appropriate if your child has not stabilized at home and needs more intensive intervention than can be given at home or in a short crisis stabilization stay.

Q. How can I make a crisis plan for my child?

A. Having a child with bipolar disorder makes it likely that you will have to deal with a crisis situation at some point. Nobody likes to think of worst-case scenario situations, but when they do happen, it can be hard to think clearly. Making a crisis plan ahead of time will help you to be ready to act quickly and decisively during a crisis.

To start making a crisis plan, first consult with your child's psychiatrist. He may already have clear guidelines for you to include in your plan. At the very least, you will need to record the doctor's contact information, including office phone numbers and after-hours emergency contact information. It will also be useful to have the doctor's fax number in case an emergency facility needs to fax over permissions or a request for records. In addition to this information, you will want to gather relevant insurance documents. While you likely have most of this information somewhere, you don't want to go hunting for it in the middle of an emergency. Having a crisis plan requires you to put all relevant information in one place. It also requires you to record important information that you might forget to report if you are under stress, such as information about allergies or medications that have caused a bad reaction in the past.

Once you have a crisis plan, remember to update the information if you change doctors, change insurance plans, move to a new city, or change your preference of treatment centers. The crisis plan will only be helpful if you keep it up to date. Consider reviewing your crisis plan yearly.

Q. What is an example of a crisis plan?

A. This is an example crisis plan; a template can be found in Appendix D. Your crisis plan should be tailored with information relevant to your child, and it is important to fill out the three steps with instructions from your child's psychiatrist. Along with giving you steps to follow in a heated situation, this plan gives you pertinent information for quick referral should you need to admit your child for treatment. If you have to fill out a hospital admission form when completely drained from an emotional experience, this crisis plan will be a relief.

Crisis Plan

Child's name: *Jane Doe*
Child's date of birth: *dd/mm/yyyy*
Child's diagnosis: *Bipolar with Obsessive Compulsive Disorder and Anxiety*

In a crisis, my doctor has advised us to follow these steps (If crisis is severe, call 911):

1. *Administer a prescribed fast-acting medication in the manner instructed by the doctor* (describe manner here).
2. *If #1 fails to bring crisis under control, call doctor emergency contact.*
3. *Call 911 or report to the hospital emergency room.*

Current medications: *Mood stabilizer XX mg daily; secondary mood stabilizer XX mg daily; antipsychotic medication XX mg daily; complementary supplement*

Allergies to medication: *penicillin*
Bad reaction to these meds: *Antidepressant XYZ, antianxiety med A,*
                                   stimulant C
Pediatrician: *Dr. Helpful*   Office number: *111–111–1111*
Psychiatrist: *Dr. Kares*   Office number: *222–222–2222*
Emergency number: *999–999–9999*
Fax number: *555–555–5555*
Preferred hospital: *Peaceful Stability Valley*
Insurance: *Managed Care HMO*
Primary insured: *Breadwinner*
Insurance ID#:   *VT987654321*
Group #:   *ID 2654*
Insurance pre-authorization   *Prior authorization not required for ER.*
requirements: *Must call within 24 hours of admittance.*
Insurance phone number
for authorizations: *123–456–7878*

Chapter 5

MEDICATION TRIALS AND TRIBULATIONS

- Will medication help my child?
- What else can be done?
- What types of medications are used?
- Are most medications used to treat bipolar disorder approved by the Food and Drug Administration (FDA) for children?
- Are the medications used to treat bipolar disorder safe for children?
- What is a mood stabilizer?
- What are atypical antipsychotics?
- How many medications will my child take?
- What are common medication side effects?
- What are serious medication side effects?
- What are side effects of antipsychotics?
- How can I minimize side effects?
- What about stimulants and antidepressants?
- What is a PRN medication?
- Should I adjust medication dosages?
- Is over-the-counter medicine safe for my child?
- When will the medicine start working?

Q. Will medication help my child?

A. If your child is diagnosed with bipolar disorder, recommended treatment generally includes medication to minimize current symptoms and prevent future episodes. The decision to give medication to a child can be a difficult one for parents. It involves first recognizing and accepting that your child has a lifelong illness. This is not easy to face. At the same time, it can feel like a welcome relief to know that there are medications that can help ease the symptoms experienced by your child.

While there are medications available for the treatment of bipolar disorder, you will not know if a specific medication will help your child until he tries it. When a new medication is tried, it will take time to see the full effects, good or bad. Medications must be started at low levels and raised over time to help minimize the possibility of negative reactions and overmedication. Trials of new medication take a lot of patience. Initially, your child may experience side effects such as sleepiness. These side effects may go away as your child's body adjusts to the medication, so it's important not to abandon a medication in the early stages of the trial period. You may notice positive results in the first few days and then become discouraged when symptoms reappear. This is a common effect. It is not unusual to take a few steps forward and a few backward when your child begins a medication. While this may be disheartening, it is a process that happens as the medication builds to therapeutic levels in your child's body. And once it reaches therapeutic levels, it will still take a few weeks to see the full effect of any given medication.

Q. What else can be done?

A. Medication can go a long way to stabilize moods and is the cornerstone of treatment for bipolar disorder. However, helping your child with bipolar disorder create a happy, successful life involves much more than medication. Stability is a delicate balance that can change with stress in the environment, growth spurts, and the progression of the illness. To effectively treat childhood bipolar disorder and maintain a measure of wellness, there must be a multifaceted approach. This approach will be specific to each child's needs but should include the following interventions:

- **Therapeutic intervention:** While therapy alone has not been found to effectively treat bipolar disorder, it is an important part of an overall treatment plan. Therapy along with medication will give your child a better chance of reaching stability and of staying stable longer. It may reduce the need for additional medication and can increase your child's functionality.

- **Family intervention:** You may have to learn to parent your child with bipolar disorder in a completely different way than you had before diagnosis or parent them differently than you parent your other children. Medication will not change the fact that your child may still have some unique needs that must be addressed through a modified parenting style. (See Chapter 12, Intense Parenting.) Because this illness is genetic, make sure that each family member has an evaluation and treatment if necessary. This will help the whole family move forward to achieve wellness.

- **School intervention:** Interventions in the school environment should support your child's treatment. This intervention should include education on bipolar disorder and its treatment for all who work with your child. Being aware of symptoms and how these interact with your child's learning can enable educators to create a more welcoming and less stressful learning environment.

Q. What types of medications are used?

A. In centuries past, patients suffering from bipolar disorder were often considered possessed—they were sometimes subjected to exorcisms or were the target of witch hunts. When the medical community did start to recognize and treat the illness, treatment options were limited to such procedures as bloodletting, primitive electric shock therapy, and experimental surgeries. Medical understanding of the illness was very limited, and medication to relieve symptoms was not available. Only the most severe cases were identified, and these frequently ended in early death or permanent institutionalization in horrific conditions.

Of course, the psychiatric medical scene has changed over time. One of the major milestones came when Australian doctor John Cade discovered the therapeutic value of lithium in 1949. Lithium proved to be effective in calming manic moods and preventing suicidal behaviors.

However, it would take some twenty years before lithium was routinely used to treat people with bipolar disorder. It is still used today.

Though lithium was effective for some people, not everyone could tolerate it or benefit from its use. Thankfully, modern medicine has given us a variety of medications that can be used to successfully treat bipolar disorder, such as anticonvulsants and antipsychotics. Many of these medications were originally developed to treat other conditions, such as seizures and schizophrenia. Later it was discovered that they are also beneficial for people with bipolar disorder. While each medication may affect overall stability, different medications are more effective in treating either the depressive or manic phase of the illness. Your child's psychiatrist will choose the appropriate medication based on a number of factors, including safety information for your child's age, predominant symptoms, side effect profiles, and the results he's seen with other children on this particular medication.

Q. Are most medications used to treat bipolar disorder approved by the Food and Drug Administration (FDA) for children?

A. Medications for most illnesses are tested and approved for use in adults with little information available on their use in children. Medication trials in children, which are needed to gain approval for the drugs from the FDA, have moved forward very slowly due to the ethical concerns surrounding testing on children. This has been a problem for pediatricians. When a medication is not specifically approved by the FDA for children, a doctor may still prescribe it to a child. This is called "off label" use. Nearly 80 percent of all children who have a hospital stay receive a medication that has not been specifically approved for children.

The medications frequently prescribed to treat bipolar disorder in children have been tested and proven effective in treating adults with the condition. Some have also been specifically approved for children with bipolar disorder or other conditions. The FDA has approved lithium for children as young as twelve and may approve it for even younger children after current clinical trials are completed. Risperdal (risperidone) has been FDA-approved for children with bipolar disorder who are as young as ten and for autism in children as young as five. Several of the anticonvulsants used as mood stabilizers are approved to treat even very young children who have seizures. Abilify (aripiprazole) was approved by the FDA in 2008 for the treatment of bipolar disorder in children as young as ten years old. Some older antipsychotics are approved in children for tic disorders, psychosis, and behavioral problems.

Your child's psychiatrist will use information from clinical trials and his own clinical experience to choose a medication that will be appropriate for your child. Having an experienced psychiatrist will help you feel comfortable with his treatment choices even if these are off label. As a parent, become an active part of these treatment decisions. Don't be afraid to research new medication recommendations and discuss the pros and cons with your child's psychiatrist.

Q. Are the medications used to treat bipolar disorder safe for children?

A. All medications, whether over-the-counter or prescription, bring a measure of risk—no medication can be guaranteed to come without side effects or be accurately billed as 100 percent safe. Then why do we take medications? Generally, the decision to take a medication is made with your physician and based on a ratio of risk to benefit. For example, an infant might undergo surgery to correct a heart defect; although a surgery involves possible fatal risks, the risks involved with not correcting the defect are greater than the risk of the surgery. A young child might take medication for asthma when the risk of an asthma attack and resulting complications outweighs the potential risk of the medication. The same is true with bipolar disorder in children. Medication is considered when the risk of leaving the child untreated is stronger than the risk of the medication.

Your child's psychiatrist may have much clinical experience in which medications are most effective in children. Still, each person is different and may react to medications in a unique way. There is always some trial and error no matter how experienced your doctor is. Here are some questions to ask your doctor when a medication is recommended:

- Why do you feel this is the best medication for my child?
- What effect will this medication have on my child?

- How long will it take for this medication to work?
- What are the possible side effects?
- Are there any long-term effects of using this medication?
- Have you had good results using this medication with other children?
- Does this medication interact with any other medication?
- Does this medication require periodic lab work, and if so, why?
- Are there any medications that are as effective but have fewer side effects?

Q. What is a mood stabilizer?

A. The term "mood stabilizer" refers to a medication that can even out the extreme moods of bipolar disorder and return your child to a more normal pattern of mood variation. In addition, these medications help prevent the recurrence of mood episodes, which are the time periods that your child stays in depression, mania, or mixed states. Many mood stabilizers were first developed to calm seizure activity in the brain but have also been shown to improve mood stability in people with bipolar disorder.

- **Eskalith, Lithobid (lithium carbonate):** Lithium is a mineral that occurs naturally in the earth. It has the longest track record in successfully treating patients with bipolar disorder. It helps calm manic episodes and lowers the risk of suicide. Some researchers also believe that lithium helps maintain the health of neurons in the brain. Periodic blood tests are required to monitor levels of this medication.

- **Depakote (valproic acid):** Depakote works on the manic symptoms of bipolar disorder. Although not FDA approved for depression, it sometimes seems to help with depressive symptoms as well. Depakote comes in a variety of formulas, including liquid and sprinkle capsules, which can be opened and sprinkled over food, making it easy for very young children to take. Depakote causes an increased occurrence of polycystic ovary disease. Periodic blood tests are required to monitor levels of this medication.

- **Lamictal (lamotrigine):** Lamictal is frequently prescribed for bipolar II patients and those who have rapid mood swings. It has a low side effect profile, but a serious rash can develop. This risk is higher if used in conjunction with Depakote. Lamictal must be started at a low dose and raised slowly to minimize the risk.

- **Equetro (carbamazepine-ER):** Equetro is an extended-release formulation of carbamazepine, which has been proven effective for acute mania and mixed states. Carbamazepine is also available without extended release as the brand name Tegretol and can be taken as a chewable tablet. If your child is of Asian descent, the FDA recommends a genetic test to rule out a specific gene mutation that could cause a serious skin reaction. Blood tests are required to monitor a patient's white blood cell count while on this medication.

- **Trileptal (oxcarbazepine):** Trileptal is closely related to Tegretol but does not require frequent blood tests. It works primarily on the manic symptoms but may have a milder effect on moods than Tegretol. While Trileptal is frequently prescribed for bipolar disorder, it has not yet been FDA approved for that purpose.

Q. What are atypical antipsychotics?

A. Newer antipsychotic medications are called "second generation" or "atypical" antipsychotics. They work differently than older antipsychotic medications, which have largely fallen out of favor due to their side effects. Antipsychotic medications are used to control hallucinations and the altered thinking of psychosis. In addition, some of the newer antipsychotic medications are considered mood stabilizers because they can help control moods and prevent future episodes. Here are some of the atypical antipsychotics often prescribed to treat bipolar disorder:

- **Seroquel (quetiapine):** Seroquel works on both the manic and depressive states of bipolar disorder. It may also exert an effect on anxiety.

- **Risperdal (risperidone):** Risperdal works on manic and mixed states. It has also been FDA approved for treating bipolar disorder in children as young as ten and for treating irritability in children and adolescents with autism. Risperdal is also available in liquid form and in a dissolvable tablet form.

- **Abilify (aripiprazole):** Abilify is sometimes called a "third generation" antipsychotic because it works through a different mechanism than other atypical antipsychotics. Instead of blocking dopamine, it balances dopamine in the brain. It is used for manic and mixed states and has been approved for maintenance use in adults and treatment in children as young as ten. Abilify is also available in liquid form and dissolvable tablets.

- **Zyprexa (olanzapine):** Zyprexa is used to control manic episodes and mixed states. It is available in dissolvable wafers. Although it is approved for maintenance use in adults, Zyprexa has been shown to cause significant weight gain and blood sugar problems.

- **Geodon (ziprasidone):** Geodon is used for manic and mixed episodes. It has less risk of weight gain and hand tremors when compared to the other antipsychotics.

- **Clozaril (clozapine):** Clozaril is a very potent medication that is generally only used in treatment when other medications fail. It is FDA approved to reduce the risk of suicidal behavior in patients with schizophrenia or schizoaffective disorder, but it is sometimes used off label for patients with bipolar disorder. Clozaril requires weekly blood tests to monitor for a serious medical complication that lowers the white blood cell count.

- **Invega (paliperidone):** This is an extended-release formulation of Risperdal. Extended-release formulations help maintain consistent levels of medication in the body, which promotes a more even mood and minimizes side effects.

- **Symbyax (olanzapine and fluoxetine HCl):** This medication combines the active ingredients of Zyprexa and Prozac. It is FDA approved to treat depressive episodes in adults with bipolar disorder; however, because it includes an antidepressant, the FDA has issued a warning that it may increase suicidal thoughts in children and adolescents.

Q. How many medications will my child take?
A. Monotherapy, or using one medication, is preferred by many physicians when initiating treatment. The doctor will choose this medication based on current medical literature and medication safety information as well as the age and prominent symptoms of your child. For many doctors, lithium and Depakote are first choices for monotherapy in both adults and children.

Your child may have a good response to the first medication used. However, if your child has too many side effects or a poor response at therapeutic levels, then your doctor may change to another monotherapy treatment. If your child has a "partial response," meaning that the medication does improve some of your child's symptoms but not others or may not improve symptoms enough for your child to function properly, the doctor may switch to what is called polypharmacy or polypharmacology. These terms mean that the doctor will use more than one medication to control symptoms. The add-on medication will depend on what specific symptoms are still being experienced. After reaching a therapeutic dose—the right medication(s) or amount needed to control bipolar disorder symptoms—your child's symptoms will be reevaluated, and decisions will be made as to staying with the current treatment, switching medications, or adding another into the mix. As your child moves out of acute symptoms and into maintenance treatment, the medications and dosages will be reevaluated.

When a child has psychosis with his mood states, this changes the treatment approach. If monotherapy is still used, then it is likely that the medication chosen will be an antipsychotic. Another treatment option would be to start polypharmacy immediately, with one of the medications being an antipsychotic. Starting two medications at once may be necessary due to symptom severity, but it is harder to evaluate the effectiveness and side effects of each medication individually when this is the case. Most doctors prefer to start with one medication and gauge its effects before adding another.

Q. What are common medication side effects?

A. All medications have a side effect profile. It can be very overwhelming to read all the side effects of any given medication, but it is better to go into a medication trial knowing the possible side effects. One child may experience many of these effects, while another child may not have any at all. Some are bothersome but may not be worth stopping a medication over, while with others it's best to stop the medication. You will need to check with your doctor before stopping a medication, as some medications must be tapered down slowly. Initial side effects may go away after a few weeks. If symptoms persist or are severe, your child's psychiatrist should be notified. Here are some of the most common side effects when beginning a new medication:

- **Headache:** Your child may have a headache the first few days after starting a new medication. Before giving your child a pain reliever, make sure that it won't interfere with the new medication. For instance, ibuprofen can increase lithium levels.

- **Stomachache:** Stomachaches can range from bothersome to very painful. The risk of stomachache may be minimized by giving the medication with food if directed.

- **Sleepiness:** Taking the medication before bedtime can help make this effect less of a problem. Sleepiness may be most pronounced during the first few weeks of a new medication.

- **Insomnia:** If medication makes it difficult for your child to fall asleep, you may want to talk to the doctor about changing the dosage time to the morning hours.

- **Dizziness:** Some medications may cause your child to experience periods of dizziness for the first several days. Talk to your child's doctor if this side effect persists.

- **Dry mouth:** If your child complains of dry mouth, you may want to let him suck on mints or chew gum to increase saliva. Also, make sure your child drinks plenty of water to avoid dehydration.

- **Constipation or diarrhea:** Have your child drink plenty of water. Report this symptom to the doctor if it persists more than a few days.

Q. What are serious medication side effects?

A. Some side effects to medications are extremely serious and will warrant discontinuation of the medication or an immediate change in dosage. While many of these side effects are rare or dose related, they are serious enough that a parent should be informed of these possible reactions. All these reactions require contacting your doctor immediately and possibly using emergency services.

- **Medication toxicity:** Medications can prove deadly when an overdose occurs. Parents should be especially cautious that all medications are kept out of the reach of children, even if they are medications prescribed for the child. Medications such as lithium have a small range between an effective dose and a toxic dose. Symptoms of toxicity may include vomiting, diarrhea, loss of coordination, weakness, slurred speech, confusion, and blurred vision.

- **Stevens-Johnson syndrome:** This is a serious adverse medication reaction that can be caused by antibiotics, over-the-counter medications, anticonvulsants, and anti-inflammatory medications. Signs include a rash and blisters in the mucous areas of the body such as the eyes, nose, and mouth; fever; and swelling of the eyelids.

- **Paradoxical reactions:** This is a reaction that creates or worsens the very symptoms that the medication is intended to treat. It is important to chart your child's response to medication so you can realize if your child is having a paradoxical reaction.

- **Serotonin syndrome:** This is a mild to severe reaction resulting from too much serotonin in the system. This condition is generally from a combination of several agents that have a combined effect on serotonin. Illegal drugs, over-the-counter medications, and natural products all may affect serotonin. Symptom onset is usually sudden and may include fever, agitation, confusion, muscle twitches, sweating, and nausea.

- **Lower seizure threshold:** Some medications lower the body's threshold for seizures. Make sure your doctor is aware of any past history of seizures so that these medications may be avoided.

Q. What are side effects of antipsychotics?

A. While antipsychotic medications can be very beneficial in controlling symptoms, they also come with some specific side effects. Some of these side effects will require immediate discontinuation of the medication; others will warrant a medication reduction or a temporary medication to stop the reaction.

- **Neuroleptic malignant syndrome:** This rare but potentially lethal reaction includes muscle rigidity, fever, racing heart, fluctuations in blood pressure, and confusion. It is most common in the first few weeks of starting or increasing a medication. This reaction may be more likely to happen when dosage is started higher than recommended or is raised rapidly. Immediate medical attention is required.

- **Tardive dyskinesia:** Tardive dyskinesia involves involuntary movements, especially of the mouth, lips, and tongue. It may include facial tics, tongue rolling, and lip licking.

- **Extrapyramidal symptoms (EPS):** The extrapyramidal system is the part of the nervous system that controls muscle reflexes. When a side effect from medication has a bad effect on this part of the nervous system, it is classified as an EPS. The following are some types of EPS:

  - **Parkinsonism:** Tremor, slowed movement, rigidity, shuffling movements, stiffness, and decreased facial expression.

  - **Akathisia:** Extreme inner restlessness marked by pacing and the inability to sit still.

- **Dystonia:** Sudden muscle contractions or painful spasms occurring after the very first dose or within the first few days of starting or increasing medication.

- **Bradykinesia/bradyphrenia:** Abnormally slow or sluggish movements and thoughts.

- **Oculogyric crisis:** Movement of the eye into a fixed position, usually upward, for a few minutes or hours.

- **Neuroleptic dysphoria:** Unusual feeling of unwellness and discontent. This is difficult to distinguish from the symptoms of the illness but would coincide with the start of a new antipsychotic medication or a dosage increase.

- **Hormonal imbalances:** There may be an increase or decrease in the hormone prolactin. An increased level can cause production of breast milk. It is not fully known how a decrease in this hormone affects the body.

- **Substantial weight gain:** Antipsychotics may cause substantial weight gain, and some may be associated with the development of diabetes.

Q. How can I minimize side effects?

A. As a parent, you likely want to maximize the best results and minimize any negative side effects from medication. One of the best things you can do at the beginning of treatment is to keep a record. As your child tries new medications, note his response and any side effects. Over time, this record can provide invaluable information and show response and side effect trends. Believe it or not, after years of treatment, it can be difficult to remember what medications were tried and your child's response. It is easier to keep these notes handy in a chart than to dig through a medical record each time you need details on a medication.

The general rule of thumb with medications is "start low and go slow." Many side effects can be avoided by starting at a low dose of the medication and raising it slowly. So while it may be frustrating to see your child still experiencing symptoms as you wait for the next medication increase, this slower approach may be better in the long run—you want the least amount of medication possible that controls symptoms, and this is the way to find it. If a medication is raised prematurely, the optimal dose may be overshot and your child may end up on too much medication. Only when symptoms are dangerous or extreme would a quicker approach to medication increases be desirable.

Also, understanding the medication side effects will help you quickly discern when a medication is having a negative effect. Reporting these promptly to the doctor, who may adjust the medication accordingly or alter treatment, is another way to minimize the overall side effects that your child will experience.

Q. What about stimulants and antidepressants?

A. Your child with bipolar disorder also may have been diagnosed with other conditions, such as depression, anxiety, or ADHD. When this is the case, sometimes your child has already tried such medications as stimulants, antidepressants, and antianxiety medications. There is a group of children with bipolar disorder who may be able to tolerate low doses of these medications while on a mood stabilizer. In fact, some children need these add-on medications to properly function. However, extreme caution is necessary here. Many children with bipolar disorder cannot tolerate these medications at all. One mother jokingly said that her son couldn't even look at a bottle of antidepressants without becoming manic! These medications can in fact induce manic symptoms in children prone to them. Also, antidepressant medication currently carries strong warnings from the FDA regarding their use in children due to the possibility of increased suicidal thoughts.

When there is a diagnosis in addition to bipolar disorder or if bipolar disorder is suspected, the safest course is first to use the medications recommended to treat bipolar disorder. Many times symptoms that would be addressed separately by these other medications are brought under control, and there is no longer a need to even consider them. If residual symptoms do remain that would warrant using a risky medication, then parents must proceed with great caution. It would be even more important to start low and watch for any negative effects. Also realize that sometimes it can take six to eight weeks for you to notice the ill effects of a medication, while other times they will become apparent in two weeks or even a day.

Q. What is a PRN medication?

A. Sometimes doctors will prescribe an additional medication on a PRN or "as needed" basis. This means that the medication isn't taken regularly but only when necessary. This is common for children who occasionally have trouble sleeping or have an aggressive outburst.

Before giving a medication on a PRN basis, the doctor will first analyze the situation to see if your child is stable overall. If your child is not stable, it may be more desirable to raise an existing medication than to prescribe a PRN medication. If your doctor determines that the existing medications are adequate but that your child just needs some occasional help with a specific difficulty, he might suggest a PRN medication. There are a few things you should ask your doctor in this situation:

- What symptoms would warrant the use of this medication?
- How often should this medication be given?
- How many doses of the PRN medication can be given, and how close together can the doses be administered?
- What should I do if my child doesn't respond to the PRN medication?
- What are the safety considerations of this medication?

If you find that the PRN medication is no longer effective, be sure to report this to your child's doctor. He may wish to adjust another medication or to prescribe the PRN medication as a regular medication. PRN medications are sometimes given to girls with bipolar disorder whose mood symptoms become extremely aggravated in connection with their menstrual cycle. Other medication may be necessary on a temporary basis. For instance, children who tend to suffer from seasonal depression may take a medication in late fall and winter that addresses these symptoms. Once spring and summer arrive, this medication may not be necessary.

Q. Should I adjust medication dosages?

A. When your child is having a difficult time, it may be tempting to adjust or discontinue your child's medication without consulting his physician. If you have this urge, pick up the phone and call the doctor's office. Even if it's after office hours, you can leave a message or talk to the on-call physician. Even if a medication needs to be stopped, there may be specific instructions on how this should be done. Discontinuing a medication abruptly could cause a seizure or other ill effects. If your child needs a medication increase, this can only be accomplished through the physician because a prescription is necessary. Additionally, giving too much of a medication can have potentially deadly consequences. Always follow the doctor's instructions when it comes to medication—never adjust a dosage on your own.

If you have established a working relationship with a trusted doctor, he may give you instructions on increasing dosages when starting a new medication. Or he may give you instructions on what to do if you see certain negative effects. This is different from adjusting a medication on your own. If you are concerned about the possibility of needing to increase or decrease a medication, then check with your doctor in advance to see if there are guidelines that he wants you to follow.

If you disagree with your doctor's approach and you are convinced that his treatment protocol is indeed worsening your child's condition, then it would be advisable to switch to a physician whose treatment approach more closely matches the needs of your child. But again, you always want to be working in conjunction with a doctor when it comes to medication.

Q. Is over-the-counter medicine safe for my child?

A. You may be used to giving your child certain over-the-counter medications without a second thought—because they're available over the counter, they seem totally harmless. However, the fact is that these medications can sometimes cause unfavorable reactions when mixed with prescriptions. Some over-the-counter medications may hinder a prescription medication from being absorbed into your child's system. Others may increase the concentration of the medication in your child's body. When your child is given a new prescription for a psychiatric medication, ask the following questions:

- If my child needs a fever reducer or a medicine for headache, which one is safe to give with this medication?
- Will any cold medications interact with this medication?
- Are antacids safe to take with this prescription?
- Will antibiotics interfere with the effectiveness of this medication?

You may also wish to check with your child's pharmacist about these possible medication interactions. Additionally, you can refer to the information insert given along with the prescription medication. If you can't find this insert, many are available online through the drug company's website.

Generally, if there is a nonmedical approach to relieving your child's discomfort, you should try it first; for instance, crackers and ginger ale may settle an upset stomach and not risk medication interaction. However, even natural things can interfere with medications—grapefruit juice is listed as a possible interfering agent. You can also check for possible negative drug interactions online at http://www.drugdigest.org.

Q. When will the medicine start working?

A. If your child is experiencing very difficult symptoms, you probably feel like medication can't start working fast enough. It is indeed painful to watch a child suffer the severe effects of depression or mania. While you may see some symptom relief with the first few doses, it takes time for a medication to reach a full therapeutic dose. It usually requires raising the dosage over weeks and perhaps months before seeing the full benefit. Additionally, a medication may work on some symptoms but leave other symptoms untreated.

While trying a new medication for your child, it is important to remember not to rush through this process. Some people may equate higher doses of medication with greater symptom relief. This is not always the case. It is important to reach a therapeutic dose—the dose that most effectively treats the symptoms—but the dosage may differ from individual to individual. Higher doses of medication are generally associated with more side effects, and some medications are just as effective in smaller doses.

As you go through this process, you may see a certain amount of symptom relief and then a return of symptoms. Don't get discouraged. This is part of the process. Usually this happens before reaching a therapeutic dose. If a medication doesn't seem to be working, the doctor may check the level of that medication through blood work. This can give your doctor important information that may lead him to increase or decrease the dosage. You won't fully know if a medication will work for your child unless you give it adequate time.

Chapter 6

LIVING WITH MEDS

- Will medicine alter who my child is as a person?
- What if the first medication doesn't work?
- Will symptoms get worse after treatment?
- Why is charting my child's moods important?
- How are blood tests beneficial?
- What blood tests will need to be performed?
- Do medications have long-term effects?
- Will medication cure my child?
- How does metabolism affect medications?
- Should my child have genetic testing to determine his metabolic rate?
- What if my child still has residual symptoms even after treatment?
- How does growth affect treatment?
- Is my child ready to swallow pills?
- How can I teach my child to swallow medicine?
- What if my child refuses to take medicine?
- How do I explain the need for medicine to my child?
- Will treating my child rob him of his gift?
- What will happen if the illness is left untreated?

Q. Will medicine alter who my child is as a person?

A. You are not alone in worrying about this—even when parents realize that medication is necessary, they wrestle with the thought that somehow they are altering their child's core personality. While parents of other ill children may worry about this to some extent, it especially hits home with parents of children with psychiatric disorders because the medications work within the brain.

No doubt you have loved and nurtured this child, and, as with all family members, we accept the good and the bad aspects of their personalities. Keep in mind, however, that medication is not given to make a child "good" or to control a child's free will. The goal of treatment is to ease the suffering of the child and to erase both manic symptoms and depressive symptoms. When these symptoms are removed, it allows your child to express his personality without the heavy burden of his illness. Just as a child freed from asthmatic symptoms may now be able to run without losing his breath, a child freed from bipolar disorder symptoms may now be able to enjoy life in an entirely new way. He will still make both good and bad choices, but these choices will not be based on symptoms that are out of his control.

If medications start to rob your child of his personality or "spark," perhaps it's time to reevaluate those medications. This could happen if your child is overly sedated or on too many medications. In cases where your child is experiencing severe and possibly psychotic symptoms, it may take a strong medication to bring symptom relief. But as this acute period passes and your child enters into a maintenance phase, the medications and their effects—both good and bad—should be reviewed. At this stage, you may be able to have the dosage lessened or get a new prescription for a milder drug, which should help return your child to a more normal state.

Q. What if the first medication doesn't work?

A. After weeks or even months of trying a new medication, it can be extremely disheartening to have the medication fail to work effectively. It is especially difficult if the medication was working but produced a side effect that was intolerable. It may seem as if a gift that was given is now taken away. If this is the case, don't consider the experience a total loss. If a medication produced too many side effects at a higher dose, it may still be somewhat helpful at a lower dose or as a secondary medication. Some researchers are investigating the possibility that lithium and Depakote prevent cellular loss and increase intercellular connections and gray matter in the brain. Lithium's positive results in animal laboratory tests are leading researchers to also study its possible protective qualities for stroke, Huntington's disease, Alzheimer's, and Parkinson's. So, even if it doesn't seem like a medication is working, there still could be unseen positive effects of taking a low dose of that medication over time. Your doctor will advise if it is beneficial for your child to continue on a low dose of a particular medication.

Trying a medicine that does not work out can also give you important information about what medication may work more effectively for your child. Different medications work through different pathways in the brain. A failed medication trial may lead your doctor to choose a medication that takes a different path. Continue to chart your child's response to medications. Also be aware that sometimes medication responses can run in families. If another family member had a good response to a specific medication, this can provide clues to what may work for your child. As the fields of science and medicine advance, it may be possible to know through testing which medications will be the most effective for any given person, but until then, medication trial and error is the best way to find out.

Q. Will symptoms get worse after treatment?

A. Once your child has been evaluated and diagnosed and treatment has begun, the one thing you really don't want to happen is for his symptoms to worsen. Unfortunately, this can and sometimes does happen. Worsening symptoms can occur anytime through the course of the illness. There are several reasons:

- **Progression of the illness:** Bipolar disorder can worsen over time. This worsening may cause your child to experience more symptoms despite the treatment.

- **Episodic breakthroughs:** Because bipolar disorder is an episodic illness, your child may experience symptoms during an episode that break through the treatment. While medication minimizes symptoms and the number and severity of episodes, your child may still experience breakthrough symptoms.

- **Environmental factors:** Changes or stress in the environment can trigger a worsening of symptoms in your child. Even good stress such as a family vacation can trigger an increase in symptoms.

- **Growth spurts:** If your child has a sudden growth spurt, you may notice an increase in symptoms. This may be because the previous dosage is no longer adequate for your child's size.

- **Other sickness:** If your child is sick with the flu or another illness, he may have an increase in symptoms. This would especially be true if he is unable to hold down his medications.

- **High-risk medications:** There are some medications that are high-risk for people with bipolar disorder because these medications have the tendency to cause increased cycling through moods. Stimulants, antidepressants (including natural antidepressants such as St. John's Wort), antianxiety medication, and corticosteroids all hold the possibility of increasing mood symptoms.

- **Paradoxical medication reaction:** Your child may have a bad reaction to a medication that is typically good for treating bipolar disorder.

If your child's symptoms worsen after treatment, contact your child's psychiatrist. Also try to identify any factors that could be contributing to this worsening. Until your child stabilizes, reduce stress, chart mood changes, and document any negative medication reactions.

Q. Why is charting my child's moods important?

A. Charting your child's moods and response to medications is an important tool that can give you and your doctor invaluable information. Record any medications your child currently takes, sleeping patterns, and symptoms of depression, mania, and mixed states. Also record any problems at school and with friends. If your child complains of anything out of the ordinary, including headaches and other physical complaints, make a note of it. Also, any comments about death, blood, or gore should be recorded. In addition, any side effects from medication should be noted.

It's important to rate the severity of your child's symptoms, and even brief symptoms should be noted. Sometimes parents feel overwhelmed at the thought of charting moods. The key is to find a system that works for you and to set aside a few minutes at the end of each day to record important information. These few minutes can make a huge impact on your child's overall treatment course. Charting can also help you realize when your child has made progress. You may wish to make your own chart, or there are several free mood charts to choose from online. A variety of mood charts can be found at http://www.bpkids.org.

In addition to charting your child's moods, it is a good idea to help your child learn how to chart his own moods. This is important for several reasons. Charting moods can help your child start to recognize mood states and how to manage them. It may help your child become aware of how environmental factors such as stress or seasonal depression affect his moods. It also gives your child the chance to express thoughts and feelings that may otherwise go unspoken and that you might have no way of knowing about. Charting moods is your child's first step toward learning how to manage the care of his illness. Children's mood charts can be found at http://www.bpchildren.com.

Q. How are blood tests beneficial?

A. There are several blood tests that will be recommended throughout your child's diagnosis and treatment process. These tests give your child's doctor specific information. Each test is used in a different way. Some tests may be recommended to rule out other conditions before diagnosis. Other tests will measure the "baseline," which tells the doctor how well your child's body is functioning before starting medication. Periodic checks will see if medication is having any negative effect on your child's body and if medication is at a therapeutic level. When checking medication levels, bear in mind that the blood should usually be drawn twelve hours after the last medication dose to get an accurate result.

The blood work will only be beneficial if your doctor has timely access to the results of these tests. It is frustrating to show up for a doctor's appointment only to find out that they do not have results yet. You'll want to check prior to your child's appointment to verify that the doctor's office received results from the lab. If your doctor has not received the results, ask the lab to fax them to the doctor. If you wish to pick up the lab results yourself and take them to your doctor, then have your child's blood drawn at a hospital laboratory. The results become part of your hospital medical records, and you can get copies of lab work by going through the medical records department and signing a medical records release form. Make sure you give the hospital sufficient time to copy records, and be prepared to pay a small fee for records to be copied.

Q. What blood tests will need to be performed?
A. Here are some of the tests that may be recommended, their abbreviations, and their usefulness.

Test	Abbreviation	When	Purpose
Thyroid panel	TSH/T3/T4	Before diagnosis, baseline, and periodic check	Monitors thyroid function
Blood urea nitrogen/creatinine	BUN/CREAT	Baseline and periodic check	Monitors kidney function
Liver panel	ALT/ALP/AST/ ALB/bilirubin/ total protein	Baseline and periodic check	Monitors liver function
Lithium level	Li level	Periodic check while on lithium	Monitors for therapeutic range
Depakote level	Valproic acid level	Periodic check while on Depakote	Monitors for therapeutic range
Prolactin level	PRL	Periodic check while on antipsychotics	Monitors hormone balance

Fasting blood sugar	FBS	Periodic check while on antipsychotics	Monitors for diabetes
White blood cell count	WBC	Baseline and weekly while on Clozaril	Monitors for agranulocytosis, a severe reduction in white blood cells
Antinuclear antibody	ANA	As needed	Checks for autoimmune disorders
Vitamin B12 level	B12	As needed	Checks for deficiency
Folic acid test	Folate	As needed	Checks for deficiency
Lipid panel	HDL/LDL/trig	Periodically while on antipsychotics	Monitors for changes in cholesterol
Pregnancy test	hCG (blood test)	In teenage girls before beginning medications	Checks for pregnancy
Heavy metals profile	(No common abbreviation)	Before beginning medications or as needed	Checks for lead, mercury, and arsenic
Calcium	Ca	Periodically during treatment	Checks for appropriate levels
Magnesium	Mg	Periodically during treatment	Checks for appropriate levels
Genetic testing for HLA-B*1502	HLA-B*1502	For those of Asian descent before starting carbamazepine	Checks for a gene mutation that can cause a severe skin reaction
Human immunodeficiency virus	HIV	Before beginning medications or as needed	Checks for HIV

Q. Do medications have long-term effects?

A. Medications for bipolar disorder have both short-term and long-term effects. In the short term, these medications can calm a manic, depressive, or mixed episode. However, medication does not permanently erase symptoms—if medication is stopped, symptoms return. In the long term, these medications can make future episodes less frequent and less severe. In both the short and long term, treatment should increase your child's ability to function, learn, and grow appropriately. Additionally, some long-term treatment is showing promise in preventing degeneration in the brain that is thought to be caused by repeated bipolar disorder episodes.

Of course, not all short-term or long-term effects from medications will be positive. As a parent, it is important for you to monitor for negative effects and to report these to your child's physician. The physician will also monitor for negative effects through blood work. If a negative effect is serious, it is likely that a new medication choice will be made. If a negative effect is minor, it will likely not merit a change in treatment.

When determining whether to allow a side effect to persist long-term through continued use of a medication, be sure to consider how your child feels about it. For instance, if your child is very artistic but develops a tremor from his medication that inhibits this artistic expression, it could be very disturbing to him and may not be something that your child can live with as a long-term effect. If a medication provides an excellent mood-stabilizing effect but has one or two negative effects, sometimes an additional medication can be used to control the negative effects so that the medication may be continued for its long-term benefits on mood.

Q. Will medication cure my child?

A. While medications can help manage symptoms, these do not cure the illness. And while your child is young, you're probably managing his illness, but as he grows older, the responsibility will shift to him. Because this is not a curable disorder, it's important for you to prepare your child to manage this condition throughout his life. There are specific skills your child will need. A therapist can help him develop some of these skills, and you'll need to reinforce them at home. These skills will not be learned overnight and will be easier for your child to accomplish when he is stable. Here are the skills that are important for your child to develop:

- **Charting mood symptoms:** If your child is able to self-monitor for mood states and record them, he will have much more insight into his illness and managing symptoms.

- **Communicating with the doctor:** Help your child review mood charts and any concerns that he may have in advance of doctor's appointments. If necessary, practice what he will say to the doctor. The doctor should give your child time to express himself clearly.

- **Regularly taking medication:** Setting a daily timer or earning a reward for remembering can be ways to encourage young children to take their medications. Teach your older child how to fill medication containers and call for refills—however, make sure this is still done under close supervision. It is very easy for teenagers to make a mistake in medication dosage or to become noncompliant without direct supervision.

- **Self-advocating:** Teach your child to speak up for himself, particularly in school. These skills will help him self-advocate in his future workplace.

- **Building a support network:** Help your child build relationships and friendships that will support him in maintaining treatment.

Though medication will never cure your child's bipolar disorder, it can help keep it under control. Equally important is making sure that your child has the skills he needs to take care of himself as he transitions into adulthood.

Q. How does metabolism affect medications?

A. Your child's metabolism can have a great impact on the effectiveness of medications. Many medications are metabolized and eliminated through the liver by various enzymes. Some medications are ingested in an active form and can be immediately used by the body and eliminated, while other medications must be broken down by enzymes into a form the body can use. Your child can only receive a benefit from such medications if he has the right amount of these enzymes..

Different enzymes are responsible for breaking down different medications. CYP2D6 is an enzyme that breaks down about 25 percent of all medications. The production of this enzyme is genetically encoded, and people normally have two genes that are responsible for the production of CYP2D6. However, sometimes one or both of these genes are bad or don't exist, resulting in little or no production of this enzyme. When this is the case, medication that needs to be broken down before it can be used by the body will not have any beneficial effect. Medication that is active can't be eliminated from the body, which could result in toxic levels.

The opposite situation occurs when a person has three or more copies of the gene that controls this enzyme production. This person would be an extensive metabolizer, and his body would overproduce the CYP2D6 enzyme. When this happens, medication in the active form is eliminated from the body too quickly, preventing therapeutic action. Medication that needs to be broken down to be beneficial will be broken down very quickly, resulting in too much of the usable form in the body. Most people fall somewhere in between and respond to the normal dosages of medication, but if your child doesn't, then his doctor will want to choose medications that are metabolized by a different enzyme or to adjust the dosage of medication accordingly.

Q. Should my child have genetic testing to determine his metabolic rate?

A. There are genetic tests available that can give you information regarding the genes that produce the CYP2D6 enzyme and other enzymes that are responsible for metabolizing medications, and some doctors use these tests to help determine which medications and dosages would best suit your child. However, these tests are not yet routinely performed, and most insurance companies will not cover the expense incurred, which leaves parents to shoulder the burden of payment.

If your family has a history of medication sensitivity or if your child has had negative reactions to several medications, it may be worthwhile to have this testing done. The price for the test may actually save you money and heartache in the long run—you might avoid throwing money away on medications that prove ineffective for your child or lead to destabilization and costly hospital stays. Enzyme testing kits can be ordered online (http://www.dnadirect.com). Prices range from $200 to $800 depending on which drug metabolizing test is ordered. Some tests only check for the CYP2D6 enzyme, and others check for other enzymes that also metabolize medication. Testing usually involves swabbing the inside of your child's cheek to collect genetic information and mailing it to a lab.

If you are considering this testing, check with your child's doctor to determine the necessity of these results. Some doctors feel it is a useful tool, and others feel that this information can be gathered by close observation of symptoms. If you can afford the testing and decide to proceed, it will be important for you and your doctor to understand the meaning of the results and how it can translate into better treatment for your child.

Q. What if my child still has residual symptoms even after treatment?

A. It may be that once your child is treated, the more serious symptoms of the illness fade into the background. At this stage you may notice other residual symptoms that are not going away with the current treatment. First, you will want to make sure that what appears to be a residual symptom is not actually a medication side effect. For example, your child may be experiencing akathisia, which is a medication side effect that causes a feeling of inner restlessness. If the symptom is actually a medication side effect, then lowering the dose may give relief.

If the residual symptoms are coming from the illness, how you proceed will depend on the severity of these symptoms. If the symptoms are not too bothersome, it may not be worth it to alter treatment. You could end up chasing every symptom with a new medication and losing your child's overall progress and stability. It is also possible that therapy or changes in the environment can help address some of the symptoms, so those would be the first avenues to explore.

If, however, these symptoms are impairing your child's functioning, then he may need a new dosage prescribed. Checking to see if the current medications are at a therapeutic level is important if you are seeing residual symptoms. It may be, however, that the current medication treatment simply does not address these additional symptoms. Not every treatment works for every symptom. If that is the case, you should discuss other treatment options with your child's doctor. It may be determined that switching to a new medication is best or that adding a small dose of an additional medication is the answer.

Q. How does growth affect treatment?

A. As your child grows, his response to treatment or even the course of the illness may change. Being aware of how these factors interact is important to maintaining your child's stability. Some children continue with a chronic presentation of the illness. Other children, especially during adolescence, begin to have longer episodes of depression, mania, and wellness. Taking note of these changes may help you and your child's doctor find a new course of treatment.

Growth can also change how your child metabolizes medication. As he grows, he may require different dosages. Medication that used to be effective in smaller doses may not be enough for a growing child. On the other hand, some young children process medication out of the body very quickly, while older children may not go through their meds so fast. In this case, dosages may not change substantially as the child ages.

Also, older children have more treatment options than younger ones. Medications that are risky in young children may be safer for an older child to take. Parents also hope that growth will bring some maturity and more self-awareness, which can help your child cope with his symptoms in a healthier way. However, don't be surprised if this process takes longer than you would wish. As your child grows, so does his ability to express feelings. While it is good for your child to have an increased vocabulary for expressing emotions, you may go through many growing pains—this could be volatile or colorful. Bipolar disorder can complicate the normal trials of adolescence, making these years especially trying. Additionally, teens may start becoming more involved in treatment decisions, which can turn into another thing for you to fight over. Be sure to keep—or have your child keep—a record of his moods and reactions to treatment so you know what might be effective in treating his symptoms as he ages.

Q. Is my child ready to swallow pills?

A. Before trying to teach your child to swallow pills, make sure he is ready. A child who is very young, is unusually sensitive to textures and tastes, or has developmental delays may have trouble learning this skill. If your child falls into one of these categories, your doctor may want to start by prescribing some other form of medication besides pills, such as a liquid, chewable tablets, or sprinkle capsules, which can be opened and sprinkled over soft foods. If the doctor's medication choice does not come in one of these forms, check with a pharmacy that does compounding to see if the chosen medication can be made into liquid form. If not, your doctor may want to consider a different medication.

Even if your child is physically mature enough to learn to swallow pills, anxieties or phobias may be a problem. Your child may be worried that he will choke on the pills. In addition, your child may not understand the purpose of medication. When this is the case, he may worry excessively about swallowing medication. Having him talk to his therapist ahead of time may help alleviate these fears.

Additionally, children who are naturally contentious may refuse to learn this skill. Don't make learning to swallow medicine a power struggle between you and your child. If this happens, your child may become even more opposed to the task. Some children will respond to praise, incentives, and rewards for successfully swallowing pills. Address this issue with your child's doctor or therapist. It may be that for now an alternative medication choice will be better, and after your child's moods become more stable, he may be able to cooperate.

Q. How can I teach my child to swallow medication?

A. Wait until you believe that your child is physically and emotionally ready. Then, if you feel it is important or necessary for the medication, teach him how to swallow pills. Some kids catch on quickly, while other kids have a difficult time learning this skill. Here are some tactics to make it easier:

- **Set the stage:** Set aside plenty of "no pressure" time. Keep it fun and praise any progress. Take as many practice sessions as needed. End on a positive note.

- **Start small:** Use small candy—from sprinkles to mini M&M's—and start practicing with the smallest. Move to bigger sizes as your child masters each candy. Reinforce the skill daily.

- **Try several techniques:** There is no right or wrong way to swallow pills, only what works best for your child.
  - ❏ Try positioning the pill in different places in the mouth, such as under the tongue, in the middle of the tongue, or at the very back of the mouth. In each case, take one or more big gulps of liquid to wash it down.
  - ❏ Have your child chew a favorite food and then place the pill in the middle of the food before swallowing.
  - ❏ Put the pill in a spoonful of peanut butter, applesauce, or yogurt and swallow.
  - ❏ Try wetting the mouth before putting the pill in the mouth. Also, drinking liquid with a straw or a bottle may help medicine go down.
  - ❏ Have your child hold his head straight or slightly down when swallowing.

- **Use flavored drinks:** When medication has a bitter taste, it may help to use a flavored drink. Let your child choose a favorite or special drink to take with pills (but make sure the drink will not interact with the medication first).

- **Step back:** If you or your child start getting frustrated, step back from the situation. Give your child time to shake off the negative feelings before you keep trying or consider passing the job on to a trusted relative or therapist.

Q. What if my child refuses to take medicine?

A. Medication noncompliance is a huge issue in bipolar disorder. Periodic refusal to take medication can happen regardless of age, but it can be dangerous to abruptly stop medication and can cause a relapse of symptoms. So while you can and should try to make taking medication as comfortable as possible, medication compliance cannot be negotiable. If your young child starts refusing to take medication, swift consequences are needed to end the refusal. If your child learns that if he refuses his medication, he will not be able to play with friends—both because he refused and because he becomes unstable—then he may take his medication without complaint.

If your child is older, you want to get to the bottom of his refusal. It may simply be an effect of his mood, or it may be that he no longer feels that medication is needed. Or he could be experiencing a particularly unpleasant side effect. Having him talk with his doctor may help him realize the need for medication, or an adjustment in medication to avoid excessive side effects may be in order. If your older child continues to refuse medication, the alternative may be hospitalization and medications administered by injections. Generally, this is not appealing to any child and may get him to take his medication as prescribed. Additionally, it can be explained to older children that if they do not continue treatment, their moods will not be stable enough to do things that give them independence, such as driving or hanging out with friends. Children may test the limits in this area, but when it comes to their health, consistent treatment is vital—you have to find a way to get them treatment. How you approach the topic with your child could make a difference. Consider reading *How to Talk So Kids Will Listen and Listen So Kids Will Talk* by Adele Faber and Elaine Mazlish (for more information on this book and others, see Appendix A: Reading Lists, beginning on page 273).

Q. How do I explain the need for medicine to my child?

A. If a medication is prescribed, then it is likely that the doctor will discuss with your child why the medication is needed and what is hoped to be accomplished by taking it. Sometimes that explanation by itself is sufficient, but in other cases your child may still have questions about medication or feel uneasy. When addressing your child's concerns, a simple and direct tactic is usually best. Answer questions according to your child's age and ability to understand.

For a younger child, it may help to read books such as *Brandon and the Bipolar Bear* by Tracy Anglada. You may also want to casually talk about friends or family members who take medication for medical problems—for example, mention how grandpa's blood pressure medication keeps his heart healthy. If you use candy to help children learn how to swallow pills, emphasize that medication is not candy and that too much medication can make a person sick. Always keep medication out of the reach of children and preferably locked in a cabinet.

For older children, don't lecture them about taking their meds—look for natural ways to discuss their concerns about medication. Avoid comments that may make your child feel guilty about needing to take medication for a medical illness, such as telling him he has to take it because it's expensive or that he won't be like the other kids if he doesn't take it. Such comments could be unintentional, but they leave your child feeling like he is to blame for his illness. Encourage older children to learn about the illness and why medication is necessary. If your child is older, he should learn the names of the medications he takes, their dosage, and the purpose of each medication.

Older children may respond better to a third party than a parent. Encourage older children to direct questions or concerns about their medication directly to the doctor or therapist so they begin to establish a good patient/doctor relationship that will take them into adulthood.

Q. Will treating my child rob him of his gift?

A. You may be concerned that treating your child will affect his creativity or other gifts. Some may reason that if the great creative minds in history suspected of having bipolar disorder had been treated, perhaps they would not have given the same contributions to the world. This reasoning romanticizes suffering. While great works have come from suffering of all types, no one has ever chosen to be in pain—it was the unfortunate circumstance of his situation.

Good parents would never knowingly allow their child to suffer on the assumption that he will someday make a great contribution to society because of it. Parents should focus on raising happy, healthy children who grow to adulthood and have the ability to function within society and enjoy their lives.

As to the many gifted artists, writers, musicians, and so on who have suffered from untreated bipolar disorder, if their moods had been stabilized, perhaps many of them would not have been lost to a premature death, robbing society of any future contributions that could have been made. Additionally, many gifted individuals who did not take their own lives still lost years of time immobilized by depression. Some budding creative geniuses were not even able to bloom before being lost to suicide (check out http://www.notunnoticed.com). So, while the suffering of individuals with bipolar disorder may have resulted in some contributions to society, it has also taken them away—as well as made the sufferers live in misery.

While treatment will surely change your child's life course, it can also allow him the opportunity to stabilize and grow. You aren't robbing him of his gift, but you are helping him have enough control over his emotions to express his gift. To that end, carefully monitor medication side effects and levels so that your child is not unnecessarily experiencing negative side effects or overmedication that could negatively impact his ability to flourish.

Q. What will happen if the illness is left untreated?

A. If you choose to leave your child's illness untreated, either through denial or by a conscious decision, it is important to understand the ramifications of that decision on the life of your child. There are many risks associated with bipolar disorder, even in patients who are receiving treatment; these risks are substantially greater in those whose illness is untreated. The following are some of the behaviors shown to result from untreated bipolar disorder:

- **Drug and alcohol abuse:** Your child may attempt to self-medicate by abusing alcohol or drugs. In turn, alcohol and drug abuse may worsen the course and progression of bipolar disorder.

- **Self-harming behavior:** Your child may intentionally cause harm to himself with behaviors such as cutting. Additionally, reckless behavior while manic or careless behavior while depressed may lead to self-harm.

- **School failure:** Your child may drop out of school or fail classes or whole grade levels.

- **Running away:** Psychiatric disorders, including bipolar disorder, are risk factors for running away from home.

- **Failed relationships:** Your child may experience multiple failed relationships with family members, friends, and love interests due to untreated mood symptoms.

- **Increased mood episodes:** Your child may experience a greater number of mood episodes and a greater severity of mood symptoms without treatment.

- **Financial distress:** Your child may have difficulty holding a job and managing money.

- **Personality disorders:** Untreated childhood bipolar disorder is considered a risk factor for developing borderline personality disorder.

- **Arrests or imprisonment:** It is more likely that an untreated child with bipolar disorder will have difficulties that could lead to an arrest and imprisonment.

- **Suicide:** The risk of suicide is greater in children with bipolar disorder who are untreated.

- **Personal distress:** Your child may experience an increased amount of personal suffering and distress as a result of unchecked mood symptoms.

Chapter 7

COMPLEMENTARY AND ALTERNATIVE TREATMENT

- Are there treatment choices other than medication?
- What is complementary and alternative medicine (CAM) treatment?
- Why do people choose alternative approaches?
- Are alternative treatments natural?
- Are CAM treatments safe and effective?
- Do some parents have success using CAM?
- Can alternative treatments make my child worse?
- Can traditional treatment be enhanced?
- Can healthy diet make a difference?
- How can exercise be beneficial?
- Can I trust the claims of a CAM treatment?
- How do I research a CAM treatment?
- How can I approach my doctor with a treatment I'd like to try?
- What if I disagree with my doctor about CAM?

Q. Are there treatment choices other than medication?

A. As a parent, you have many important decisions to make about your child's care and well-being. This is a heavy responsibility, and a diagnosis of bipolar disorder can be a difficult time for parents. If you have doubts about your child's diagnosis, whether your child needs treatment, or if the recommended treatment is really appropriate for your child, discuss this frankly with your child's doctor. You will not be comfortable with treatment unless you understand why it is necessary and agree with the doctor's recommended approach. Become informed and educated about the topic of bipolar disorder in children. The more you know about your child's condition, the better equipped you will be to make decisions regarding treatment.

Not all parents want medical treatment for their child with bipolar disorder. This may result from family background, cultural pressures, strong biases, or a perceived stigma. Indeed, some parents choose to ignore warning signs and simply hope for the best outcome. This is a risky roll of the dice that can lead to tragic results.

There is another group of parents who want their child to be treated, but they want alternative treatment options. This is certainly different from rejecting all treatment, but it definitely involves some uncharted waters. As a parent, you have the right to investigate all treatment options, including alternatives. Talk to your doctor about all treatment decisions whether these are traditional or alternative. In the end, you will want to make treatment choices with your doctor that will be the best for your family and your child—the important thing is seeking the necessary treatment to make your child healthy and comfortable.

Q. What is complementary and alternative medicine (CAM) treatment?

A. Complementary and alternative medicine (CAM) treatments are those that fall out of the realm of traditional medical practice. Complementary treatments are those that are used in conjunction with traditional treatments. Alternative treatments are those that are used instead of traditional treatments. When a particular alternative or complementary treatment becomes accepted and proven in the medical community, it is no longer considered alternative. Some doctors use an integrative approach, meaning they use both traditional treatments and some selected complementary treatments based on the degree of scientific or clinical experience that has demonstrated a measure of benefit to the patient.

Because CAM encompasses anything out of the traditional realm, it includes a wide array of approaches and belief systems—and every approach has a base of supporters who believe it to be a worthwhile and effective means to health in general. Many of these approaches are accepted in certain cultural realms or have their basis in specific parts of the world. CAM treatments are generally not covered by medical insurance. The following are a few of the CAM approaches:

- **Homeopathy** uses highly diluted substances derived from plants, minerals, and animals. It aims to stimulate the body's own mechanisms to fight illness.

- **Dietary restriction** removes offending food items such as gluten or casein from the diet.

- **Dietary supplementation** adds vitamins, minerals, amino acids, and enzymes to the diet.

- **Mind/body methods** use meditation, biofeedback, yoga, and/or prayer. These aim to use the mind to promote healing in the body.

- **Chinese medicine** incorporates herbs, meditation, massage, and acupuncture.

- **Naturopathy** is a system of care based on the concept that nature heals and that the body has the power to maintain or return to a state of health. It encompasses a variety of approaches, including the ones above.

Q. Why do people choose alternative approaches?

A. Medical choices are very personal. In some ways, they are akin to religion and politics in that people feel very strongly about them. Some people are outspoken, and some are very private about their treatment decisions. Medical choices for children can be even harder as parents struggle with the idea that the choices they make now will have long-lasting consequences. The reasons that people may choose an alternative approach to treatment are many and varied.

Some choose CAM as a first approach to treating bipolar disorder with the belief that it is more natural and healthy. They may hope that using this intervention first may prevent or delay the need for traditional medical approaches. For some who are already involved in alternative treatment for other health issues, it may seem like a normal extension of their current choices. Others choose this approach after being sorely disappointed in traditional treatments and feeling that their needs have been failed by traditional medicine. This group arrives at their decision after having poor medical experiences and many failed treatments. They are hopeful that alternatives will provide something better. Still others are looking for the best possible outcome and wish to explore all potential possibilities, including treatment options that are unconventional. Many patients want to look at all options and mix and match treatment approaches.

Whether parents choose totally traditional approaches or a CAM approach for their child, they all want the same outcome. Each is looking for improved health, better functioning, and stability for their child.

Q. Are alternative treatments natural?

A. Many people feel more comfortable using natural products or treatments. While many treatments claim to be natural, this can be misleading. In general, a "natural" product is one that exists in or is formed by nature. For instance, vitamins and minerals are a natural part of our diets, and by that definition lithium is a natural product. However, synthetically reproducing these vitamins and minerals is not a natural process. Putting whole foods into pill form is also not a natural process, nor is it natural to take megadoses of vitamins and minerals. This does not necessarily mean that it is bad to use products or treatments labeled as natural or in quantities that would not normally be received in the diet—it may or may not be appropriate for any one individual depending on his specific health needs. That decision should be made by the physician and patient.

When naturally occurring products are used in megadoses or with the intent of controlling a disease, they become medicinal. One of the prominent discoveries of the action of vitamins was by Dr. James Lind, a naval surgeon who found that scurvy could be avoided by including citrus in the diets of sailors. Today, there are several vitamins, such as B12 and K, available by prescription for various conditions due to their recognized medicinal value. Currently, none of these are commonly prescribed for bipolar disorder.

When choosing any CAM product or therapy for a medicinal purpose, the important thing is to treat it as you would any other medical decision and to exercise just as much awareness, caution, and concern. Any treatment option must be weighed and considered carefully, just as you need to be aware of the pros and cons of treating with traditional means.

Q. Are CAM treatments safe and effective?

A. Using "natural" products or treatments may seem to be pure, normal to the human experience, and better, less invasive, and less dangerous than conventional treatments. However, this is not always the case— after all, both arsenic and cyanide are natural. Little is known about the safety and effectiveness of many CAM treatments, and even less is known about the safety and effectiveness of CAM in children. This is an area that is in dire need of further investigation.

The federal government has recognized this need and in 1992 established the National Center for Complementary and Alternative Medicine (NCCAM), which operates under the National Institutes of Health (NIH). Part of NCCAM's mission is "exploring complementary and alternative healing practices in the context of rigorous science" and providing this information to the public and professional sectors. For a list of completed research projects and future research into CAM, check their website at http://www.nccam.nih.gov.

In the past, it has also been impossible to know for sure that a supplement actually contains what the label says it does with no additional contaminates. Independent testing has revealed that some products are composed of less than half of the actual ingredient listed on the label. In June of 2007, the FDA announced a final rule that established good manufacturing practices for supplements, ensuring accurate labeling, quality products, and an absence of impurities. Additionally, the industry is required to report serious adverse events related to their product.

There is no guarantee that complementary or alternative treatments are safe and effective. Science is moving forward to answer these questions and to give us safer products, but in the meantime, if you are considering using an alternative treatment, don't assume it is safe just because you can buy it without a prescription. Do your research. If you decide to use a particular product, buy from a reputable company who does frequent quality testing and is committed to adhering to FDA standards for supplements. Also, check with your doctor to see if a specific supplement will require blood work to monitor its effects on the body.

Q. Do some parents have success using CAM?

A. There are growing numbers of parents who are making a conscious decision to actively pursue CAM treatments for their children with bipolar disorder. They may start by adding one or more complementary treatments to conventional medication or move completely to an alternative choice. The response to the treatment is as varied as the methods tried. Some people notice no difference in their symptoms, while others enjoy mild beneficial results. Still others have completely failed trials and return to traditional treatments. Finally, some report dramatic improvements. Success with CAM may depend on many factors:

- **Type of treatment:** Success may depend on the effect that a particular CAM treatment has on supporting healthy brain function in a particular individual. One person could have success with a specific approach due to his body chemistry and makeup, whereas another individual may have a different result. A treatment tailored to your specific child may be more effective than a one-size-fits-all approach.

- **Understanding of the treatment:** The patient's comprehension of the guidelines and principles behind the treatment could affect the outcome. Some CAM treatments call for strict dietary guidelines or other components that are necessary for it to be effective.

- **Adherence to the treatment:** As with any treatment method, the patient must comply with the rules of a CAM treatment, including allowing adequate time for the treatment to work.

- **Type of bipolar disorder:** It is not known if the various types of bipolar disorder respond differently to specific CAM treatments.

- **Experience of your physician:** The physician's specific skill and experience with using the CAM approach could affect the outcome.

If you have made the choice with your physician to try a CAM treatment, do all you can to ensure a successful trial. Learn about the treatment, the possible positive and negative consequences, and what to do if symptoms return. Network with other parents who are trying the same approach—just as when your child starts traditional treatments, it can be very reassuring and helpful to talk to others who have chosen the same path as you. Don't be afraid to abandon a failed trial and adjust as time goes on. Additionally, if you are going to immerse yourself in this approach, make sure that your doctor has extensive knowledge of both traditional and CAM approaches.

Q. Can alternative treatments make my child worse?

A. Certain CAM treatments carry the possibility of activating mania, just as certain conventional medications do. In particular, those CAM treatments that have an antidepressant or stimulant quality might induce mania in some children with bipolar disorder. The following are some examples:

- **St. John's Wort (hypericum):** This supplement is made from a plant and used for mild depressive symptoms. It has been reported to induce mania and even psychosis in patients with bipolar disorder. St. John's Wort can also negatively interact with some medications for bipolar disorder, including Tegretol.

- **SAMe (S-adenosyl-L-methionine):** This molecule comes from the essential amino acid L-methionine. SAMe has been shown to cause hypomania in some people with bipolar disorder. Additionally, one study (Antun, et al. 1971), which used high doses of L-methionine on patients who have schizophrenia-induced psychosis in over half of the participants.

- **5-HTP (5-hydroxytryptophan):** Because this amino acid boosts serotonin production, it has the potential to cause hypomania or mania.

- **Ginseng:** This popular herb is used as a supplement and can be found in some energy drinks. There are reports of ginseng-induced mania.

- **Ma-huang (ephedra):** This herbal supplement has been banned by the FDA. Ma-huang has been associated with inducing manic episodes and psychosis.

- **Vanadium:** An elevated level of this trace mineral has been found in the blood, hair, and tissue of patients with bipolar disorder. Reducing vanadium in the body has been shown to improve both manic and depressive symptoms, so supplementing with vanadium is not recommended. Foods containing vanadium include mushrooms, black pepper, parsley, dill seed, shellfish, and grain products.

- **Yohimbe:** This extract from tree bark has been known to induce mania and psychosis. It may interfere with lithium, Tegretol, and Depakote.

Q. Can traditional treatment be enhanced?

A. At some point in your child's treatment, you may wish to try something along with prescription medication to help reduce symptoms. The right complementary treatment has the potential to enhance traditional treatment—in fact, your doctor may even recommend one. Complementary treatments may help avoid a medication increase, improve cognition, or get your child through a seasonal mood change. Just like medication, the effects of complementary treatments should be closely monitored.

When deciding on a complementary treatment, you will want to research the treatment, weigh the pros and cons, discuss it with your child's psychiatrist, and monitor results. Your chosen complementary treatment will have the best chance of enhancing treatment if it fits the following criteria:

- **Does not interact with current treatment:** A complementary treatment should not negatively impact your child's current treatment.

- **Has a proven track record of improving symptoms:** Ideally, your child's physician would have other patients who showed improvement while on this complementary treatment or know of clinical trials that have shown improvement.

- **Does not induce symptoms:** A complementary treatment should not cause your child to become manic or depressed. If it does, adjusting the treatment or discontinuing will be necessary.

- **Fits into your family's budget:** Complementary treatments could be out of reach if they are very expensive.

- **Fits into your time schedule:** Some treatments may be so time-consuming that they create more stress than relief. A good fit for your family will also fit into your schedule.

Q. Can healthy diet make a difference?

A. Healthy eating is always a good thing. Your child's brain needs the proper nutrition to support healthy functioning. While eating healthy foods will not erase the illness, it can give your child's body more of an ability to deal with it and to function at the best possible level. Imbalances in blood sugar can contribute to increased irritability, depression, and mood swings in your child. Encourage your child to eat a balanced, healthy diet with frequent small meals and plenty of water. This is ideal to give support to the body and brain.

This can be easier said than done if you have a child with sensory sensitivities or a child who hyperfocuses on eating specific foods. Don't make food a source of arguments, but do make healthful foods available in abundance and set the example of healthful eating. Also, be aware of how your child reacts to sugar, high-carbohydrate foods, and caffeine. Every child is different. For some children, changing their food intake can substantially impact their symptoms. For others, it doesn't seem to make any difference. Either way, healthy eating is a good component to your child's overall wellness program.

There are some diets that claim broad-based improvements for children with behavioral and attentional difficulties. However, there is currently no evidence that any one particular diet is helpful for children with bipolar disorder. That is not to say that a particular diet won't help a specific child. Just as with medication, trial and error coupled with an accurate documentation of your child's reactions can help you know what kind of diet is best. Before starting any diet, check with your child's pediatrician and psychiatrist to see if it is appropriate for your child.

Q. How can exercise be beneficial?

A. In general, exercise is simply beneficial for good health. For children with bipolar disorder, getting proper exercise may have some added benefits. Here are some reasons to help your child develop a fun exercise program:

- **Energy outlet:** Exercise may help your child release pent up manic energy. Some teachers have actually found that when a child is manic in class, allowing him to run around outside is a helpful release.

- **Reduced symptoms:** Exercising has been shown to reduce stress, anxiety, and depressive symptoms. Considering that these can be some of the most challenging symptoms to address in bipolar disorder, implementing an exercise routine is a worthwhile venture.

- **Weight loss:** Many of the medications used to treat bipolar disorder can cause significant weight gain, which can have a negative impact on both self-esteem and health. Regular exercise can help counteract some of this effect.

- **Regulated sleep patterns:** Having a consistent exercise regime can help regulate your child's sleep patterns.

There are a few things to consider before initiating any exercise program. Consult with your child's doctor to make sure it is appropriate for your child's health. Also, one study noted that people with bipolar disorder have a reduced tolerance for exercise. While there may be many reasons for that, be sensitive to your child's abilities; finding fun ways to exercise may make it seem less like work and more like play. You may want to try such kid-friendly activities as swimming, biking, taking kickboxing classes, playing team sports, and rollerblading.

Q. Can I trust the claims of a CAM treatment?

A. There are various complementary and alternative treatments that claim to help everything from cancer to bipolar disorder. Simply making a claim does not automatically mean it is true or false. In this market, the saying is "buyers beware." Becoming an educated consumer is a must. While there may be some companies truly dedicated to their products and the health of their customers, there may be other companies interested in turning a quick profit without regard for long-term consequences. Even buying from a dedicated company that believes in its product and benefits doesn't automatically mean the product will be useful for your child. Before choosing a complementary or alternative treatment option for your child, it is vital to research the product or treatment and the claims it makes. Ask yourself the following questions:

- Is the product or treatment solely supported by testimonials, or have studies been done to back up the claims?
- If this is a product, are the ingredients listed or does it claim to have a "secret" ingredient?
- Have any of the ingredients or processes of this treatment been known to activate mania in bipolar disorder?
- Will this product or treatment interact negatively with current medications or treatments?
- Is my child's physician in agreement with trying this treatment?
- Is it financially within our reach to try this treatment, or will it involve a large investment that is not reimbursable by insurance?

- Have I fully researched this treatment option?
- Am I comfortable with this approach?
- Do I personally know others who have tried this treatment with positive or negative results?
- Do I have a support system in place if the trial proves ineffective or has a negative effect?

Q. How do I research a CAM treatment?

A. It would be impossible to cover every complementary and alternative treatment in existence, and new research that yields both positive and negative results will continue to be generated. Effort has been made in chapter 8 of this book to cover the CAM treatments that most parents would likely encounter if they were investigating this approach. If you are interested in trying a CAM treatment, be sure to check out research online. Don't be taken in by every claim, and make sure you make decisions based on more than the information given by those who stand to benefit from your use of their product.

The NIH and the National Library of Medicine have made abstracts of research studies available online at http://www.pubmed.gov. By searching relative keywords, you can locate both positive and negative study results on various traditional and CAM treatments. Additionally, you can see what clinical trials are being conducted by going to http://www.clinicaltrials.gov. NCCAM also has a wealth of information at http://www.nccam.nih.gov.

Try to find studies specific to children with bipolar disorder, and look for more than individual case studies and very small open-label trials. While these might form the basis for further investigation, they can't prove the effectiveness of any given treatment. The best studies are double-blind and placebo-controlled with a large number of participants. Even then, others should be able to duplicate the results, and in the best-case scenario, you'll be able to find another study that does just that.

While it may be tempting to just try any and every kind of treatment, the outcome could potentially be worse for your child. Another real danger is that it will delay treatment that has a track record of working. Research the treatment online and discuss your findings with your child's doctor before you decide on a course of treatment.

Q. How can I approach my doctor with a treatment I'd like to try?

A. It may be tempting for some parents of children with bipolar disorder to try complementary or alternative treatments without discussing them with the psychiatrist. Many parents dread such a conversation, anticipating a negative or even hostile response. However, initiating treatment without professional consultation is unwise. The doctor may know of an interaction or a negative response that could be harmful to your child.

Also, you are probably not the first parent to approach your doctor asking about alternatives to conventional medicine, and as complementary and alternative treatments continue to gain wider acceptance, you certainly won't be the last. You may also be surprised that even if your doctor doesn't feel there is a huge benefit to a CAM treatment, he may not think it would be harmful to try it. Medical professionals will generally respect your desire to try something else and be supportive. Here are some things to consider when preparing to speak with your child's psychiatrist about a CAM approach:

- **Do your homework:** Understand the treatment and why you would like to try it for your child.

- **Print out your research:** Before approaching your doctor, take the time to print out any important research information on the desired treatment.

- **Allow time for a discussion:** Make sure you have time to discuss the possibility of this treatment with the doctor. Don't casually bring it up when you have two minutes left in the appointment.

- **Be open to other options:** If your doctor realizes you wish to try a CAM treatment, he may already have a recommendation or an experience with an approach that differs from the one you're thinking of trying. Listen with an open mind, and see if it's something you're interested in.

Q. What if I disagree with my doctor about CAM?

A. Perhaps you have become convinced that a particular alternative or complementary treatment would be of value to your child. What if your child's psychiatrist is against this particular treatment approach—should you find another doctor? Before jumping to that conclusion, consider a few things:

- **Why does your child's doctor feel this way?** It may be that a lack of experience with this approach makes your child's doctor very cautious about using it.
- **Does he have a personal experience with failed trials of this approach?** Your doctor may have had other patients try this approach with poor results.
- **Is the research weak?** Your child's doctor may be aware that there is not enough research—or not enough quality research—on this approach.
- **Does this treatment have the possibility of ruining stability?** If your child has recently stabilized, your doctor may not want to risk a setback.
- **Is the doctor willing to allow a trial despite his disagreement?** Sometimes a doctor will allow a trial even if he is doubtful it will work.
- **Would he be open to a trial at a later date?** Maybe your doctor feels that now just isn't the right time.
- **Is this trial important enough to you to change physicians?** Only you can make this decision. How satisfied have you been with the care your child has received? How much do you really know about this new approach, and is it worth losing a comfortable doctor-patient relationship for possible greener grass on the other side of the fence?
- **Have you had clear and open dialogue about your feelings regarding this trial?** Are you making decisions based on your assumptions about how your doctor feels? Is your doctor aware of your feelings on CAM? Don't switch doctors without having a frank conversation with your child's physician.

Chapter 8

PROS AND CONS OF ALTERNATIVE TREATMENTS

Q. Should I try EMPowerplus supplements?

A. EMPowerplus is a vitamin/mineral/herbal supplement that claims to help those suffering from bipolar disorder. Some people view this product as miraculous, and others are opposed to the product and its marketing. The decision to try any specific treatment is a personal decision that must be made with your child's psychiatrist. Here are some pros and cons to weigh with your doctor regarding EMPowerplus:

Pros	Cons
Small open-label studies and case reports of children with behavior and mood problems have shown a decreased need for medication and an improvement in mood symptoms while on the original formulation of this product.	This product is known to cause adverse drug reactions when used with prescription medications.
There is reduced pricing available to low-income families who qualify.	This product is not usually covered by insurance.
The company implements a support system through personal phone calls, message boards, and mood charting.	Relatively few physicians are familiar with how to use the product, and the nonmedical support personnel may give medical advice.
There are few known side effects.	There are no studies on the long-term effects of the product.
More rigorous clinical trials have been approved.	The pills are large, and the recommended dose may range from eight to fifteen pills a day at approximately 33 cents a pill.
Available in a banana/orange-flavored powder form.	It may be difficult to discern between a relapse of the illness, an interaction with medication, a reaction to an ingredient in the product, or a medication withdrawal effect.
	Individual ingredients in this product when taken alone may not be appropriate for all patients with bipolar disorder. It is not known if the use of these ingredients in combination changes that effect.

Q. Should I try Equilib supplements?

A. The original formulation of EMPowerplus used in open-label studies later became known as Equilib when the companies involved in making and distributing the product parted ways. Equilib has since been reformulated and is distributed through Evince International and Earth's Pharmacy Nutritionals, neither of which is currently affiliated with the makers of the reformulated EMPowerplus. If you wish to try Equilib for your child, please discuss the advantages and disadvantages with your child's psychiatrist:

Pros	Cons
Small open-label studies and case reports of children with behavior and mood problems have shown a decreased need for medication and an improvement in mood symptoms while on the original formulation of this product.	This product may interact negatively in combination with prescription or nonprescription drugs.
The company offers discounts for bulk ordering.	This product is not usually covered by insurance.
The company implements the "safe call" support system, which involves an assigned support person, mood charting, and mood charts faxed to the participant's physician.	It may be difficult to discern between a relapse of the illness, an interaction with medication, a reaction to an ingredient in the product, or a medication withdrawal effect.
There are few known side effects.	Little is known about the long-term effects of the product.
Patients are encouraged to seek medical assistance, and support personnel do not recommend medication changes.	The pills are large, and the recommended dose may range from six to twenty-four pills a day at approximately 20 cents per pill.
Ongoing physician-assisted case studies are being conducted.	Relatively few physicians are familiar with how to use the product.
Available in orange-flavored powder form.	Individual ingredients in this product when taken alone may not be appropriate for all patients with bipolar disorder. It is not known if the use of these ingredients in combination changes that effect.

Q. Should I try "natural" lithium?

A. All of us get a certain amount of lithium naturally in the food we eat and the water we drink. Lithium is being studied to examine its effect on keeping the brain healthy and fighting the effects of Parkinson's and Alzheimer's disease. Lithium has long been used to treat bipolar disorder. In geographical areas where lithium in water sources is low, violent crime and suicide rates are higher. Hair samples from violent crime offenders show a reduced amount of lithium compared to healthy subjects. Lithium is obviously an important natural part of our diet.

As a mineral (as opposed to the manufactured synthetic form), it is available as a supplement in health food stores and on the internet. The dosing for lithium as a dietary supplement is very different from that of medicinal lithium. It may be tempting to simply order lithium in the dietary supplement form because it is available without a prescription, but before you do, talk to your child's psychiatrist and consider some pros and cons:

Pros	Cons
Some feel that natural lithium has fewer side effects.	Too much lithium can cause a toxic reaction, so medicinal use of lithium should be overseen by a physician.
In general, natural lithium does not require blood tests.	Buying natural lithium off the shelf gives you no assurance that the product actually contains the stated amount of lithium.
Natural lithium is an important part of a normal human diet.	Natural lithium is not covered by insurance and depending on the type purchased may be much more expensive than prescription lithium.
	Using lithium without a doctor's prescription has the potential to interact with other treatments.

Q. Should I use omega-3s?

A. Omega-3 fatty acids are considered by many to be "brain food." Omega-3 is made up of both eicosapentaenoic acid (EPA) and docosahexaenoic acid (DHA). Fish and seafood are good sources, and omega-3 can be purchased in supplement form. There are many varieties of omega-3 that have varying ratios of EPA to DHA. Some psychiatrists are recommending this essential fatty acid as a complementary treatment for children with bipolar disorder. As with any sort of treatment, you should carefully weigh the pros and cons before beginning:

Pros	Cons
A recent study of the OmegaBrite fish oil supplement in children with bipolar disorder showed a 50 percent reduction in symptoms for just over a third of the participants.	Most of the children did not achieve the 50 percent reduction in symptoms, which demonstrates that this may not be enough as a stand-alone treatment.
OmegaBrite is also available in flavored liquid for children.	It may be difficult to get your child to swallow fish oil products. They may have an oily consistency and a "fishy" aftertaste.
Omega-3 may be obtained by dietary intake of oily types of fish such as mackerel, salmon, and sardines.	Taking in a significant amount of omega-3 directly from fish could put you at risk for exposure to heavy metal toxins such as mercury.
Its very low side effect profile makes this an attractive add-on and first line intervention.	Omega-3 supplements are not covered by insurance.
Studies in adults have indicated that higher ratios of EPA to DHA may be the most beneficial for brain health.	The optimum dose and ratio of EPA to DHA is not clear and needs further investigation. Conflicting study outcomes have resulted from using various dosages.
No blood tests are required.	

Q. Should I use Free and Easy Wanderer Plus?

A. Free and Easy Wanderer Plus (FEWP), also known as *jia wei xiao yao*, is an herbal supplement used in Chinese medicine. Its name reflects the intended effect of the product—it is supposed to evoke a carefree and easygoing mood. FEWP is actually made up of a variety of herbs, and there are some variations on the product. It is most commonly taken to alleviate PMS symptoms and menstrual discomfort; however, it has recently been examined by the University of Hong Kong for possible benefits in bipolar depression and as a way to alleviate side effects from certain medications.

Pros	Cons
A double-blind, placebo-controlled , randomized study in adults with bipolar disorder demonstrated that FEWP as an add-on treatment to Tegretol decreased side effects, increased compliance, and improved symptoms related to depression in bipolar disorder.	No studies have been conducted with this product on children with bipolar disorder, either as an add-on or as a stand-alone treatment.
Bipolar depression is one of the most difficult phases to treat. If this product can demonstrate similar effectiveness as an add-on medication for children in the depressive phase, it could have promise.	No benefit was demonstrated in the adult group on manic symptoms.
	If there is an appropriate dosage for children, it has yet to be established.
	This product is not covered by insurance.
	Variations on this product may add additional unwanted ingredients that were not in the original testing.

Q. Should I use neurofeedback?
A. Neurofeedback, also called EEG biofeedback, is a process by which the brain is encouraged to change specific brain wave patterns. Electrodes are placed on the scalp, and the brain wave measurements are displayed on a computer screen through the use of a neurofeedback

machine and special software. The therapist programs the software to encourage or discourage specific brain waves based on your child's overall brain wave patterns and symptoms. When brain wave patterns are changed in a way that is desired, the brain is rewarded—usually by activating a video or a game on the computer screen. As long as the brain waves stay at the desired frequency, the video or game plays. As soon as the brain waves go out of this frequency, the video or game stops. As the brain learns how to make this desirable outcome happen again, it continues to be rewarded. Neurofeedback has been used for a variety of things, including ADHD, learning disabilities, and seizures. Here are some pros and cons to discuss with your doctor about neurofeedback as a complementary treatment:

Pros	Cons
May be covered by some insurance under psychotherapy.	This therapy is not usually covered by insurance and can be very expensive, ranging from $50 to $125 per session.
A two-year follow-up study of children with learning disabilities found that initial gains made with neurofeedback were sustained.	There are no studies on the effectiveness of neurofeedback in children or adults with bipolar disorder.
Some individual case reports have been positive.	Individual approaches and protocols vary considerably and could lead to mixed results.
Personal units can be purchased, and home training can be arranged through selected clinics, reducing some of the cost.	It is difficult to find providers who are experienced at using neurofeedback in children with bipolar disorder.
	As many as three sessions a week over an extended period may be required.

Q. Should I use acupuncture?

A. Acupuncture has become more widely accepted and used in the United States over the past few decades. According to NCCAM, more than eight million Americans have used acupuncture for a wide variety of health concerns. Acupuncture has been practiced for two thousand years and was introduced to the United States in the 1970s. It is the process of penetrating the skin with thin needles and manipulating the needles by hand or electrical impulse. The procedure is generally painless. If you are contemplating using acupuncture for your child, here are some things to consider with your child's physician:

Pros	Cons
The FDA has approved acupuncture by licensed practitioners. Needles must be sterile, nontoxic, and for single use only.	There have been no clinical trials in children with bipolar disorder to evaluate the effectiveness of acupuncture as a complementary or alternative treatment.
Several studies have demonstrated that acupuncture may be an effective complementary treatment in adults with depression and bipolar disorder. Acupuncture was found to be as effective as tricyclic antidepressants.	Validity of studies in adults has been called into question by some physicians, and no studies have compared acupuncture to mood stabilizers or lithium.
Patients in a mental health setting who used acupuncture as a complement to regular treatment reported "marked improvement" in overall health.	Different types of acupuncture procedures and the skill of the clinician may affect the outcome.
One study, which monitored blood and urine before and after acupuncture, noted an influence on the level of neurotransmitters, especially those related to depression.	If sterile needles are not used, infection may result.
Acupuncture is more widely covered by insurance than other CAM treatments.	It is not known if acupuncture can activate mania.

Q. Should I use massage therapy?

A. There are over eighty types of massage therapy, all of which involve techniques that manipulate the muscles and soft tissue and that increase blood flow and oxygen. It may be used in conjunction with aromatherapy and sound therapy to encourage a relaxed state. Massage therapy is regulated on a state-by-state basis. Some states require massage therapists to be licensed and hold a national certification, while others have very minimal requirements to hold a state certification. Massage is considered in some instances to be part of conventional medicine, especially in the case of treatment for injury. When massage is used for therapeutic benefits outside this range, it may be considered a CAM technique.

Pros	Cons
Parents who were taught massage techniques for their child with a disability reported less anxiety in themselves as well as improvement in their children. Massage may be a unique, soothing technique and a bonding experience between parent and child.	The effects of various massage therapies have not been specifically studied in children or adults with bipolar disorder.
One study compared massage therapy to relaxation therapy in a group of aggressive adolescents. The massage therapy group showed reduced anxiety and aggressiveness compared to the relaxation group.	Massage therapy is not generally covered by insurance except in the cases of injury or accident.
A study published in the *Journal of the American Academy of Child and Adolescent Psychiatry* (1992 Jan 31(1):125–31) reported the effects of massage in a group of children and adolescents hospitalized for depression. The study noted a decrease in depression/anxiety and stress hormones and an increase in cooperation and sleep.	There are many different types of massage and skill levels of massage therapists, which may ultimately influence outcome.

Q. Should my child see a chiropractor?

A. Chiropractic care involves using the hands to manipulate the spine. Some theories promote the idea that misalignment in the spine interferes with nerve flow and has an effect on various bodily functions. Use of chiropractic manipulation has been documented as far back as the fifth century B.C. and has been practiced in the United States for more than a hundred years.

Chiropractors must complete three years of college plus an additional four years of education at a chiropractic college. Each state regulates chiropractic licensing and continuing education requirements. Chiropractic care is most widely accepted for its use in low back pain. Additionally, some chiropractic techniques claim to have broad benefits for many health care issues, though this view is generally less accepted and not well established.

Pros	Cons
Chiropractic care is sometimes covered by insurance.	There are no studies on the use of chiropractic care for bipolar disorder in adults or children.
One published case study suggested that a man whose bipolar disorder symptom onset occurred after head injury benefited from upper cervical chiropractic care.	The safety of upper cervical manipulations has not been well established. Upper cervical manipulation is considered more risky than standard chiropractic care and may carry a risk of stroke.
Various relaxation techniques may be implemented in general chiropractic care that could lead to a reduction in stress-induced anxiety.	Chiropractors who claim to use specialized treatment may require an expensive out-of-area trip and are generally considered "out of network" for insurance. Initial visits may be hundreds of dollars out of pocket.
	General chiropractic care may require visits several times a week, making it an investment in time and money.
	There are different types of chiropractic care, and skill levels vary from office to office.

Q. What is light/dark therapy?

A. Light/dark therapy uses sunlight and darkness in an attempt to regulate the body's internal clock, which appears to be maladjusted in patients with bipolar disorder. Exposure to full-spectrum light has been shown to help reduce seasonal depression, known to be a common component in bipolar disorder. The therapy basically entails patients sitting in front of a light box. However, parents must watch for emerging signs of mania or hypomania. As with medication, starting low and going slow may give the best chance of avoiding an induced hypomanic state. Slowly raising the amount of time in front of the light box can help your child discover the right amount of time for him. Be aware that this time may need to be adjusted as the season and your child's mood changes.

Dark therapy is an investigational approach to inducing sleep and improving manic symptoms. It's basically the opposite of light therapy: exposing patients to periods of darkness. One study used dark therapy as an add-on treatment to medications. Those who added imposed darkness from 6:00 p.m. to 8:00 a.m. to their treatment experienced significantly faster improvement in symptoms and earlier hospital discharge and required less medication. Because complete darkness is difficult to impose for that time period, investigation is now turning to "virtual darkness" through amber lenses that block blue light. When blue light is blocked, the body naturally recognizes night and produces melatonin, which helps regulate the sleep/wake cycle. It is not known whether this therapy can induce depression.

Q. What is electroconvulsive therapy?

A. Electroconvulsive therapy (ECT) is a process in which electrical currents are briefly sent into portions of the brain, causing a controlled seizure. ECT is not really a CAM treatment. In fact, it has been accepted and used in psychiatry for years in the adult population. However, it has a controversial history and is not used very frequently in young people. Because it is a nondrug therapy and not typically a mainstream choice for young people, we are discussing it in this chapter.

It is somewhat ironic that the main mood stabilizers are anticonvulsant medications, but inducing a controlled seizure may yield positive effects on mood disorders, especially on the depressive and psychotic symptoms. It is unknown exactly how ECT produces positive results. It is speculated that it has a broad range of effects on several neurotransmitter systems in the brain. Other speculations include the idea that while the brain fights the effects of the convulsive activity, permanent, positive changes are made in the brain. According to current treatment guidelines, ECT would only be considered as a last resort for adolescents.

Immediate side effects of ECT include headache, nausea, memory loss, and aching muscles. Long-term negative effects may include memory loss and altered personality, but it is not conclusively known what long-term effects may be present when ECT is used to treat young people. It is a procedure that should not be undertaken lightly and or without full disclosure about possible effects.

Q. Can personal awareness be beneficial?

A. There are a large variety of therapeutic techniques—progressive muscle relaxation, yoga, autogenics, guided imagery, and so on—that include components of personal awareness, mindfulness, meditation, and so forth. The techniques differ by country, personal belief, and type of therapy. Some focus on relaxation, while others promote an awareness of self, mood states, and thoughts. Both relaxation and awareness are vital components to living a healthy life with bipolar disorder. In fact, meditation has been shown to alter the physical structure of the brain; one study indicated that meditation increased cortical thickness in the brain regions that control sensory processing and attention.

Meditation practices vary considerably, so you should find one that coincides with the needs and beliefs of your family. Children with bipolar disorder don't come ready-made with the skills necessary to meditate. While some children are generally more insightful than others about their mood states, all children can benefit by learning relaxation techniques and by becoming aware of shifts in their moods. Many therapists incorporate this into their sessions, and parents can assist in this process by supporting awareness and calming techniques.

Pilot studies have shown that mindfulness-based cognitive therapy (MBCT), a therapy that combines meditation practices and cognitive therapy, may prevent the brain from falling back into certain patterns of activation that correspond to depression. This is showing promise in preventing recurring suicidal thoughts during depression. Benefits of MBCT can include the following:

- Acceptance of the illness
- Increased awareness of the need for treatment
- Awareness of thoughts and mood shifts
- Recognition of negative thoughts as mental events that should be allowed to pass rather than as certitudes that define the person
- Help with implementing self-awareness skills in everyday life

Q. Can animal therapy help?

A. When you mention animals as they relate to people with disabilities, most people think of guide dogs for the blind. Formal training for guide dogs began over seventy-five years ago, but for centuries before that, various animals have been used for therapeutic purposes. There are several ways in which animals may prove beneficial to children with bipolar disorder. Here are a few:

- **Emotional support:** A variety of animals from rabbits to ferrets to dogs can comfort, soothe, and provide emotional support to children with bipolar disorder. Additionally, the responsibility of caring for another living creature and having that creature return affection has social, emotional, and possible cognitive benefits. If you are considering purchasing a pet for emotional support, make sure it is a pet that fits the needs of your family and that can be cared for appropriately. It is important to ensure the safety of both your family members and the animal.

- **Therapeutic interaction:** There are various types of specific interaction with animals that have therapeutic benefits. One such interaction is equine-facilitated learning (EFL), which involves interacting with horses. This specific interaction helps the child learn about himself through leading and guiding the actions of a horse. Through this horse/child interaction, the child is actually working on such skills as multitasking, sequencing, and attention. Along with calming, it also has proven useful in improving self-esteem, communication, confidence, and self-awareness. For more information, visit http://www.wayofthehorse.org.

- **Psychiatric service animals:** Service animals are specifically trained to do tasks for those who are substantially impaired. They do more than provide emotional comfort—they may be able to assist during a panic attack, interrupt repetitive behaviors, remind the owner to take medication, and mitigate paranoia among other things. For more information, visit http://www.psychdog.org.

Q. What is the placebo effect?

A. In studies that try to validate the effectiveness of any one treatment, the treatment may be compared to a "placebo," or inactive agent. Placebos for alternative treatments may be difficult to construct—they need to mimic the alternative enough to convince the test subjects that it is the treatment, while not delivering the active ingredient. The active treating agent needs to perform better than the placebo to prove its effectiveness.

Ironically, even people given a placebo versus the active treating agent show improvement. Those given placebos also have negative reactions, implying that a real effect is taking place. There is debate among the medical community as to why this happens. Some feel that simply anticipating a negative or positive response colors the patient's objective measurement of results. Also, unrelated events in a person's life may have an effect that the research doesn't account for, such as an end to seasonal depression. Others feel that the therapeutic environment in which the placebo is received brings about real measurable benefits for the patient or that, for some reason, real neurochemical changes take place in the brain when a placebo is used. Research is trying to track down the placebo effect. Recent studies by Dr. Zubieta, associate research scientist at the University of Michigan Molecular and Behavioral Neurosciences Institute, and his team demonstrate that patients who felt pain relief with a placebo actually experienced the release of pain-numbing brain chemicals. The future possibilities of this powerful mind/body connection have yet to be explored.

Some may argue that it doesn't matter why something works, only that it does. Parents also sometimes feel that studies don't matter if a particular treatment works for their child. Become educated, explore all your options, consult with your doctor, and use trial and error to find the treatment that works best for your child and for you.

Chapter 9

LEARNING AND DEVELOPMENT

- Does bipolar disorder affect learning?
- What areas of the brain may show abnormalities in children with bipolar disorder?
- How can I understand brain abnormalities in childhood bipolar disorder?
- What can I do to minimize impairment?
- How can I strengthen my child's cognitive abilities?
- What is executive functioning?
- How does treatment impact learning?
- Will my child have a learning disability?
- Why is writing so difficult for my child?
- How does bipolar disorder impact development?
- Can my child regain lost functioning?
- How can I help prevent lost functioning?
- How is social learning impaired?
- What challenges will my child face socially?
- How can I use social stories and role playing?
- How can I help my child interpret emotion?

Q. Does bipolar disorder affect learning?

A. Your child may spend a large part of the day involved with school and school-related activities such as homework and extracurricular activities. How well he is able to function in this environment can set your child up for success or failure more so than even his intelligence or determination. Children with bipolar disorder may be very intelligent; in fact, some of them are gifted. Even so, the disorder has been shown to affect learning. In one sampling of children with bipolar disorder between the ages of eight and eleven, 80 percent required special education services to make adequate progress in school.

The brain pathways involved in learning are complex. They involve gathering information through the senses, decoding and processing that information, comparing the information to previously held knowledge, consolidating it into a newly acquired memory, and reforming it to apply in new circumstances. Therefore, it is understandable that an illness that has an effect on the brain could cause difficulties in this process.

Childhood bipolar disorder may interrupt the pathways to learning in several prominent ways, such as through mood states, abnormalities in both the structure and function of the brain, and deficits in cognition and executive functioning. Additionally, co-occurring conditions including learning disabilities can interfere with the child's ability to make adequate progress in the school setting. Even treatment can, at times, make learning a challenge due to medication side effects. Even though bipolar disorder can affect the *way* your child learns, it does not mean that he *cannot* learn. Adequate support in the school setting will make learning easier. Additionally, you may be amazed at the strides in learning that can be accomplished during times of stability.

Q. What areas of the brain may show abnormalities in children with bipolar disorder?

Brain region	Abnormality	Areas that may be impacted
Anterior cingulate cortex	Changes in gray matter with development, lower glutamine levels, decreased response to emotional faces, increased DNA fragmentation in some neurons	Cognitive function, decision making, and emotion
Cingulate gyrus	Smaller volume of gray matter in the left anterior portion of the cingulate gyrus	Emotional response to stimuli and aggression
Frontal lobe	White matter lesions that worsen over time	Impulse control, planning, judgment, reasoning, attention, language, problem solving, and socializing
Fusiform gyrus	Increased gray matter	Processing of stimuli related to social interaction, face recognition, and emotional context
Hippocampus	Reduced volume, especially in girls	Formation of memories and associations
Motor cortex	Increased gray matter	Motor movement
Orbitofrontal cortex	Abnormal gray matter volumes	Mood, motivation, responsibility, and addiction
Prefrontal cortex	Lower ratios of N-acetylaspartate/creatine, decreased gray matter in the left, increased gray matter ventrally, abnormal activation	Planning, sequencing, working memory, judgment, and social control

Brain region	Abnormality	Areas that may be impacted
Putamen	Enlarged and increased activation	Motor control and sensory motor integration
Right and left amygdala	Reduced gray matter, abnormal development of the left amygdala, increased activation to emotional faces	Processing of emotional significance and perception
Right nucleus accumbens	Larger volume pronounced in prepuberty	Modulation of desire, satisfaction, and inhibition
Septum pellucidum	Cavity separating two membranes that would normally fuse during infancy found to be present and enlarged in adults with childhood-onset bipolar disorder	Modulation of emotional expression
Striatum	Abnormal volume changes that progress with age	Motor activity, learning by habit, and cognitive function
Superior parietal lobule	Decreased gray matter	Spatial orientation
Superior temporal gyrus	Smaller total volume in the left, decreased white matter	Insight, speech, information processing, and music
Temporal lobe	Reduced average volume, increased gray matter (left side)	Integration of sensory information and memory
Thalamus	Increased activation	Processing of sensory information
Whole brain	Smaller total volume	Multiple areas

Q. How can I understand brain abnormalities in childhood bipolar disorder?

A. Even scientists and researchers are still struggling to understand what these abnormalities mean. As a parent, the most important thing is to realize that these physical abnormalities do exist and that your child is going to need your understanding and support to deal with the effects of this illness on his day-to-day life and learning. Here is a list of definitions that may help you to understand some of the listed abnormalities a little better:

- **Activation:** When brain cells become active and give off an increased electrical discharge. Areas may be overactive if they give off more electrical discharge than they should or give off the discharge at the wrong time. Areas may be underactive if they do not give off the amount of electrical discharge that they should.

- **Creatine:** An amino acid that is involved in energy production.

- **DNA fragmentation:** When cells die, their DNA becomes fragmented or broken. Having increased DNA fragmentation is a sign of increased cell death.

- **Gray matter:** Part of the brain made up of cell bodies and responsible for processing information.

- **Glutamine:** An amino acid that is made by the body. Stress may be a factor if the body has a reduced amount of glutamine.

- **N-acetylaspartate:** A chemical that is only found in neurons and is considered a marker for the health of neurons. Reduced amounts indicate poor functioning of the neuron possibly due to damage or cell death. Reduced N-acetylaspartate is also seen in neurological conditions such as Alzheimer's disease and epilepsy.

- **Volume:** The amount of space that an object occupies.

- **White matter:** Part of the brain made up of nerve fibers that have a protective coating that is white in appearance. The white matter helps different parts of the brain communicate with each other and the rest of the body.

- **White matter lesions:** Areas where the protective coating on the neurons is no longer there, causing the neurons to function improperly.

Q. What can I do to minimize impairment?

A. Having one or more abnormalities in the brain does not automatically mean that a child's functioning will be impaired, nor does having structurally sound regions of the brain guarantee that these structures will function properly. In bipolar disorder, it appears to be the combination, severity, timing, and progression of both abnormal structure and brain function that lead to impairment—meaning that the amount of impairment will differ depending on the severity and timing of the bipolar disorder onset and where the child is in his cognitive development.

One of the major systems affected by pediatric bipolar disorder is the limbic system and the closely surrounding areas. The limbic system is involved in the interpretation of sensory information, the regulation of emotional responses, and the creation of memory. Other brain regions affected by the disorder are important for mood, concentration, working memory, motor movement, planning, judgment, organization, information processing, communication, and attention.

Is it any wonder then that your child may struggle to interact at home, may feel overwhelmed with the tasks assigned at school, and may have difficulty maintaining friendships? As a parent, you likely wish to diminish the effects that brain abnormalities have on your child's course of illness. What can be done? Studies of the progression of the illness give a clue. These studies have implicated an increase in some brain abnormalities related to repeated mood episodes. Thus one study showed that repeated periods of depressive episodes correlated with a decrease in patient IQ scores. This decline in cognition and functioning may *not* be regained once the mood is restabilized.

Research is exploring the possibility that medications such as lithium may have neuroprotective and restorative properties, perhaps even the ability to reverse some abnormalities. As a parent, your choice to treat your child with medication now may indeed make a big difference in how extensively brain abnormalities will progress and hinder your child's future functioning. Preventing mood episodes, establishing appropriate treatment, and arranging support for your child at school should be a high priority.

Q. How can I strengthen my child's cognitive abilities?

A. Cognition can be thought of as the basic set of learning skills. Having the ability to maintain attention, focus on a topic, remember the topic, process and respond to information, and organize thoughts are all involved in cognition. A child's ability to read, write, perform mathematic computations, participate in class, and demonstrate acquired knowledge is all affected by cognition. While we have seen that your child's ability to do those things can be impaired by active mood states such as mania or depression, cognitive dysfunction can also be present even when your child is in a stable mood. Cognition can also be affected by your child's quality of sleep and nutrition.

You can help your child strengthen weak areas of cognition. First, determine the extent and areas of your child's cognitive dysfunction. Educational testing may be necessary to uncover areas of weakness. Understanding which areas of cognition your child struggles with and to what degree will give you a place to start. A special teacher or therapist may need to work with your child on severely impaired cognitive skills.

Strengthen cognitive skills at home by playing memory or computer-based brain games with your child. Also, give your child tools to work around faulty cognition. If memory is a problem, teach your child memory tricks such as rhyming or picture association. Your child may benefit from using tools such as organizers and daily planners. Try different things until you find something that seems to be working, and be sure your child maintains a healthy diet, exercise, and sleep schedule. Remember, nobody has perfect cognition, and it can change over the course of time. Helping your child make the most of his cognition will make learning and daily tasks easier for him.

Q. What is executive functioning?

A. Executive functioning is a specific set of cognitive skills needed to perform complex tasks, including the planning, sequencing, and organizing skills your child needs to break down large projects into manageable pieces. Executive functioning also involves the ability to reevaluate, shift gears, and inhibit actions. Generally, executive functions are thought to originate from the frontal and prefrontal lobes of the brain but also involve interaction and communication with other areas of the brain.

Deficits in executive functioning can make advancing to the higher grades of school difficult for your child because he is expected to have the ability to tackle more detailed and larger projects. He may be poorly organized and have difficulty breaking large tasks down into incremental steps. Your child may also find it incredibly difficult to let go of an old plan that does not work in favor of a new plan. Needing to accomplish the task a specific way can also make working as part of an interactive, cooperative team difficult for your child. Finally, difficulty inhibiting actions may cause your child to be easily sidetracked, perhaps latching onto very small details that have little to do with the final project at hand.

Poor executive functioning is very often present in children with bipolar disorder. This deficit can contribute to frustration, irritability, poor self-esteem, and mood swings, and you need to find ways to help your child with this type of functioning. You can minimize their frustrations by helping with both homework and household tasks that require executive functioning skills. In a cooperative effort, you, your child, and your child's teacher can break down larger tasks, set time lines for the completion of these tasks, evaluate progress, and make necessary adjustments.

Q. How does treatment impact learning?

A. Comprehensively treating bipolar disorder with a combination of medication and psychotherapy can have a positive impact on your child's learning. Minimizing the symptoms of bipolar disorder can increase your child's ability to attend school and to take in information while in the classroom. Success in the classroom builds your child's confidence, and he will attempt greater and more positive steps forward. Without the distracting, racing thoughts or the sudden changes in energy that can plague your child, school may become much easier. Additionally, treatment can prevent future mood episodes that contribute to a decline in cognition. Treatment can improve your child's prognosis.

However, individual responses to treatment can vary. One side effect of concern with some medications is cognitive dulling. You should be aware that if your child has a sudden difficulty with schoolwork that coincides with the beginning of a new medication, this could be a sign of cognitive dulling. Some medications are more known for causing this type of side effect than others, and some children seem more susceptible to it. If cognition becomes a concern, an adjustment in dosage or type of medication may be necessary. Being alert to this possibility can prevent prolonged, medication-induced cognitive difficulties.

It should also be recognized that negative reactions to medication trials or changing medication regimes can at times interfere with school. When this occurs, it's important to have a safety net in place for your child. See Chapter 10 to learn what protections and accommodations your child can receive in the school setting.

Q. Will my child have a learning disability?

A. Bipolar disorder is an illness that can cause difficulties with learning, but it is not a learning disability. Many children with bipolar disorder do have a learning disability in addition to their illness, and it may or may not be caused by the same underlying neurological deficits. If your child with bipolar disorder has excessive difficulty with tasks related to learning, he should be tested for a possible learning disability. However, he may not have a learning disability at all and may have little difficulty in school once his symptoms are being treated and are no longer interfering in the classroom.

Learning disabilities tend to run in families and can take on many forms. They can interfere with your child's ability to read, speak, write, process information, or perform mathematics. Generally speaking, a learning disability is present when a child's intelligence sharply contrasts with his ability to learn or demonstrate knowledge. So, a child whose academic performance in one or more areas is several grade levels below what is expected for his IQ may have a learning disability. When considering this topic, keep in mind that even gifted students can have learning disabilities. Learning disabilities may be very specific, only hampering the student in one area such as math, or they may have more global effects. For instance, a learning disability in reading may have consequences in all subjects because reading plays a role in acquiring knowledge in areas like science and history. Reading disabilities can even hinder math skills due to difficulty with directions or with word problems. Without appropriate intervention, a learning disability can make life very difficult for a child. If your child is already struggling with bipolar disorder, recognizing additional learning disabilities and compensating for them can be an aid to managing the illness. If you have concerns in this area, write to your child's school to request a complete educational evaluation to determine if there is an underlying learning disability. Also, familiarize yourself with education law by visiting http://www.wrightslaw.com.

Q. Why is writing so difficult for my child?

A. Does your child end up in tears at homework time? Are broken pencils and crumpled sheets of paper the end result of hours of work? Difficulties with writing may be the cause. If so, your child is not alone. A good proportion of children with the disorder struggle to write. While studies need to explore this area more fully, reports of parents and some experts in the field show that approximately half of all children with bipolar disorder also have a learning disability in the area of writing.

Many of the functions that are impaired in children with bipolar disorder are heavily involved in the writing process. Writing requires sustaining attention and holding an idea in working memory while integrating that idea with the motor skills necessary to produce written language. Your child may get lost in this process due to a misstep in one or more of these functions. By the time pencil gets put to paper, the idea may no longer be available to record. Additionally, the psychosis experienced by some young people with bipolar disorder may be implicated in their writing struggles. One study indicated that young people who are experiencing psychosis have a diminished ability to write.

Reflection on the writings of famous authors with the illness, such as Virginia Woolf, reveals differences in writing that are dependent on mood cycles. Your child's writing difficulties may be steady across mood states or may vary to some degree according to the mood state and depending on the underlying neurological cause of the problem.

Q. How does bipolar disorder impact development?

A. When a child is developing normally, parents barely give the process a second thought. It's only when development does not meet up with normal expectations that an alarm is raised. When a chronic illness presents itself in youth, there are bound to be repercussions in the child's development—and this is true of childhood bipolar disorder. There are several factors that play into the degree of impact that the illness will have on your child's development: the age of onset, the severity of symptoms, the length of time your child stays unstable, and the response your child has to medical treatment.

Many children with bipolar disorder are actually developmentally advanced before the illness manifests, but an earlier age of onset means that fewer milestones have been met while your child is healthy. Having more milestones to reach after the onset of chronic illness increases the likelihood that one or more of them could be delayed or not attained. Also, a more severe form of the illness may mean a greater degree of impaired brain functioning. These deficits can affect how a child develops. In addition, lengthy periods of instability can cause hospitalizations and lost time at school, with friends, and in extracurricular activities. This has an unavoidable impact on your child's development. While other kids may be naturally learning social interaction on a football field, your child may be unavailable. Early intervention and response to treatment, however, may be a better predictor of how your child develops than anything else, as reduced time spent in active mood cycles has been linked to better functioning.

Q. Can my child regain lost functioning?

A. Children are amazingly flexible creatures with a wonderful capacity to grow, and learning and development is a process that never really ceases. Though the major developmental goals are expected to be achieved by adulthood, this does not mean that a child who has not fully developed won't continue to make some degree of progress. Even in healthy children, the frontal lobes of the brain don't fully mature until early adulthood. For children with an illness, a delay in development may just mean that the child takes longer than healthy peers to reach similar development.

What may be more difficult for a parent than delayed development is when they see that their child has actually gone backward and lost functioning. This can happen during periods of instability. The burning question then is, will my child regain his former functioning? If this is his first instance of instability, he has a very good chance of fully recovering the functioning that may be lost during this period. However, your child may be less likely to fully recover lost functioning after repeated episodes of instability. Additionally, recovery may take longer.

In the case of lost development, it is best to focus on helping your child work on skills to improve functioning in the present state. Keeping expectations at the previous level will frustrate both you and your child and will not give your child the tools necessary to advance. You may want to think of advancement as a staircase. When a child takes a few steps backward, he is not starting all over at the bottom again, but you also may have to take a few steps backward to reach out and help him move forward.

Q. How can I help prevent lost functioning?

A. Some of the impact of bipolar disorder on your child's functioning and development can't be changed, but there are things you can do to help. One of the main enemies of your child's functionality is stress. Stress is a toxin to children with bipolar disorder. It can induce instability, which is a major culprit in reduced functioning and developmental gaps. Stress should be dealt with on two fronts: reduction and coping skills.

It is not possible to remove all stress from your child's life, but stress reduction techniques should be a major part of your family's routine. Recognize that even good things can cause stress. Make sure your child is engaged but not overscheduled. A routine that is too busy creates much stress. In addition to eliminating unnecessary stress, teach your child how to cope with the necessary stress that comes with life.

There are many techniques that can help your child deal with stress. A skilled therapist can help you and your child learn these techniques. Additionally, you may want to help your child find an outlet for stress, such as playing a musical instrument, exercising, praying, or meditating. Being able to self-soothe from the stresses of life is a skill that will not happen overnight and will not be learned by an unstable child, but don't give up teaching this important skill both directly and by example. Once mastered, this can be an incredible lifelong asset that will help optimize your child's future functioning.

Q. How is social learning impaired?

A. Academic learning is obviously vital to a child's progression, but social learning can be just as important to a child's development and functionality. While social learning isn't tested and graded in the same way, it is an important topic in school. Some teachers work on a child's social skills by assigning a team project, and nonacademic school time is the groundwork for social learning. Discussions at the lunch table may give a wealth of social lessons. Additionally, family interaction is another time for children to acquire the social skills they will need to be successful in life. Your child with bipolar disorder may not always act in a socially appropriate manner. There are a couple reasons why this may be true.

Some children with bipolar disorder understand social appropriateness but are unable to maintain appropriate interaction when in an active mood state. Your child's mood cycles may temporarily overtake everything else and prevent him from applying the social skills he already has acquired. When this is the case, stabilizing your child will enable him to use his social skills. Other children with the disorder are impaired in their social development and understanding. These social deficits are recognizably lacking even when the child is in a stable condition—the necessity of polite interaction, the ability to make friends, or the understanding of inappropriate interaction may be beyond the child's grasp.

Altered perception of other people's emotions also negatively affects the social interactions of children with bipolar disorder. Successful social interaction partially relies on being able to interpret body language, voice intonation, and facial expressions correctly. Processing facial emotions is impaired in children with bipolar disorder. Neutral faces are perceived as hostile. If your child with bipolar disorder incorrectly perceives another child as being hostile, it is unlikely that he will interact with that child appropriately. Interpretation of the emotional meaning of speech is also impaired.

Q. What challenges will my child face socially?

A. The very nature of bipolar disorder may, in some cases, attract friends. Your child may display a contagious exuberance. Especially in the teen years, silly, goofy, and extreme daredevil displays may actually contribute to social popularity. Your child's passionate personality can help him in the social arena.

However, while the fun-loving nature of hypomania may attract friendships initially, this attraction often dries up when the illness progresses to full-blown mania. During these times, your child's behavior may become increasingly inappropriate and offensive. Mania may cause impaired judgment and lead your child into impulsive decisions. Embarrassing situations at school can result from your child's uninhibited actions. Friendships can be damaged, and your child may get a reputation that makes future social interaction difficult.

Depression too can leave a negative mark on your child's social life. Withdrawing into isolation and refusing to associate with others can leave friends feeling left out and unwanted. Certainly depression can get in the way of establishing new friendships as well. Rapid cycling between the two states can cause friends to become confused and lead to ruined relationships.

Some children and families choose to talk openly about bipolar disorder to close friends. While it is true that this can cause some people to back away due to fear and stigma, others become steadfast friends who are better able to understand the confusing aspects of your child's personality. Seeking out positive social interactions for your child can help create an environment of success. Just as failure in the social arena tends to be contagious, so does success. As your child stabilizes with treatment, you may also find that previously damaged friendships slowly repair, and your child may enjoy an unexpected second chance.

Q. How can I use social stories and role playing?

A. Social stories and role playing are tools that can help strengthen the areas in which your child's social skills are weak. Social stories are brief stories that describe a social situation, how other people in the situation may act or feel, and how your child could successfully handle the situation. Role playing is acting out these scenarios. Social stories and role playing can be practiced with a therapist or mental health professional and also reinforced at home.

The first step to utilizing these tools effectively is to understand your child's areas of weakness. If your child has specific gaps in understanding social interactions, identify these gaps and address them one at a time. Write a very brief, direct, and descriptive account of the social situation with which your child has trouble. Be sure to include how other people feel and how your child should react. Including your child in writing the story may help him remember what to do. A social scenario could be as simple as standing in line for lunch or as complex as how to approach a classmate at recess. Once you have written the social story, have fun with it by role playing. As always, keep in mind that this intervention will be more successful if your child is stable.

If your child already understands appropriate interaction but has trouble implementing it due to mood states, practice the same scenarios with your child, but modify them by adding information about how to handle strong emotions. These stories may include instruction on how to successfully get out of situations without losing emotional control. Have the child practice asking for help, asking to be excused to go to the counselor's office, or simply expressing himself in a way that doesn't have negative social consequences, such as saying, "I don't feel good today."

Q. How can I help my child interpret emotion?

A. Correctly recognizing and interpreting the emotions of others is a key factor in successful social interaction. Your child with bipolar disorder may be overly sensitive to the feelings of others or may misconstrue their emotions as negative or harsh. The way the brain interprets emotions, especially as they relate to facial expressions, is an underlying deficit in childhood bipolar disorder. Helping your child recognize and correctly interpret emotion in others may be an ongoing challenge.

It's important to create dialogue with your child about feelings and emotions. Talk about how emotions look on faces. Ask questions that draw out the child's opinion, and try to correct faulty assumptions. For example, you can ask, "How do you think Mrs. Neighbor was feeling today?" If the response is, "I think she was angry," you might say, "Sometimes that's how people look when they are in a hurry even if they aren't angry. Do you think maybe she was just in a hurry?" Be patient if your child persists in faulty assumptions. Your child is basing his conclusion on reality as his brain has interpreted it.

Also, recognize that sometimes you may need to correct faulty thinking about your own emotions. You may have to say to your child, "I'm not mad. I'm just trying to concentrate hard, which makes my face look serious." In addition, when choosing therapists, doctors, or teachers, be aware that your child may respond better to people whose faces reflect less neutral or serious expressions and more obviously friendly expressions.

You may also wish to use flash cards and games that highlight emotions as expressed on faces. Two particularly useful games are the Feelings game and the Emotions game, which are free online at http://www.do2learn.com.

Chapter 10

YOUR CHILD AT SCHOOL

- How will mania affect my child at school?
- How will depression affect my child at school?
- How will sensory processing affect my child's performance at school?
- What laws protect students with disabilities?
- How do I get my child evaluated under the Individuals with Disabilities Education Act (IDEA)?
- What is an appropriate classification under IDEA?
- What if my child is denied services?
- What if I don't agree with the school?
- What is an individual education plan (IEP)?
- How should I prepare for the first IEP meeting?
- What is a functional behavioral assessment (FBA)?
- How can I develop a positive relationship with the school?
- What can I do if the relationship is adversarial?
- What information should I provide for the teacher?
- What if my child is too unstable to attend school?
- What accommodations can help my child?
- What kind of classroom environment is appropriate?
- Can the school discipline my child?
- What is a manifestation determination hearing?
- What if the IEP is not implemented?

Q. How will mania affect my child at school?

A. The school environment generally requires a student to be seated, quiet, attentive, and ready to learn. Mania can put your child's brain and body into overdrive, making concentration and even holding still a near impossibility. When your child's brain is flooded with racing thoughts, the teacher's lecture may barely be heard, let alone retained. Ability to follow directions is overwhelmed by all your child's extra energy, and his focus and ability to hold information is hampered. Paying attention long enough to write down homework assignments, let alone do classroom work, would be a tremendous feat.

Additionally, your child may be filled with an inner restlessness that, even when contained, is a constant pressure in need of release. When this release does happen, it could come in the form of loud, distracting noises, goofing off, clowning around, singing, dancing, and generally causing what could be quite a large disturbance in a quiet classroom. The next stop for your child may be a trip to the counselor, dean, or principal's office.

When mania is expressed in an agitated, irritable state, this can be bad for the child, his peers, and the teacher in the classroom. Progression to thoughts of paranoia could cause your child to be unusually fearful of normal, routine activities at school. Grandiosity may cause your child to feel superior to all school authorities and to reject the very idea that he even needs to attend class.

The only benefit to mania in the school setting may come in the form of hypomania, which could increase a child's focus and productivity. Unfortunately, the time your child spends in hypomania compared to the other mood states may be small. Mania needs to be controlled to allow the best possible classroom experience for your child.

Q. How will depression affect my child at school?

A. The effects of depression on the school day will start before your child even makes it to school in the morning. The decreased energy your child feels during depression will make getting out of bed, combing his hair, and putting on clothing an exhausting thing to even contemplate. In addition, even the thought of interacting with others at school while depressed is enough to make his stomach churn. Absences during depression may be one of the biggest hindrances to learning.

Even if your child is able to force himself to go to school, he may not be "available" for education. Your child may lay his head on the desk and even sleep in class. Depression messes with your child's motivation. If he is able to keep his eyes open in class, he may simply stare at his work. Mental fog and a lack of concentration make thinking and schoolwork a chore. Slowed reaction time and a feeling of heaviness can make getting out school supplies and sharpening a pencil tasks that consume half of a school period. As your child tries to focus on the teacher's lecture, what he hears may sound much like the teacher in Charlie Brown cartoons: a bunch of sounds, but no coherent words. During depression, the brain just isn't able to sort out the information in a way that is understandable and beneficial to the student.

As your child switches between states of low and high energy, school officials are sometimes confused. They may feel that your child is choosing to be lazy in one class period and disruptive in another when in fact these periods may coincide with switches between the mood states. Talk to each teacher and give them information to help them understand bipolar disorder.

Q. How will sensory processing affect my child's performance at school?

A. Some of the brain pathways affected by childhood bipolar disorder are also involved with sensory and information processing, and many children with bipolar disorder have issues with sensory processing. To perceive the world around them, children take in information through all the senses. Once this information is gathered, the brain has to decide what information is important, what information is threatening, and what information should be ignored.

When the brain does not filter out unimportant information, the child becomes highly aware of noise. This poses a special problem in the school environment. Your child may not be able to shut out noises like a foot tapping behind him, a pencil scraping the paper next to him, or the air conditioning humming in the background. This flood of sensory information may crowd out your child's ability to focus on instructions from the teacher.

When sensory information is incorrectly processed as a threat, then your child may have an unusually strong, inappropriate reaction that may lead to trouble in school. In bipolar disorder, amygdala dysfunction is thought to be responsible for the inappropriate tagging of harmless information as threatening. In the school environment, this may mean that a friendly pat on the shoulder by a teacher or fellow student may be perceived as an intrusion or a threatening gesture that can provoke anything from responding with a snippy, irritated remark to hitting or running away. Additionally, when your child is reprimanded by the teacher or other adults, the amygdala may again take over and cause a survival reaction out of proportion to the event.

Q. What laws protect students with disabilities?

A. People with disabilities are protected against discrimination by federal law in the United States. There are two primary laws that provide this protection: section 504 of the Rehabilitation Act of 1973 and the Americans with Disabilities Act. Both laws make it illegal to discriminate against people with disabilities. Section 504 includes federal and state entities who receive federal funding, and the Disability Act widened the scope of protection to include entities that don't receive federal funds. If your child is considered to have an impairment that substantially limits one or more major life activities, then he may qualify for protection under these laws. Major life activities specifically include learning. However, your child will not automatically qualify for protection under section 504 at school. He must be evaluated and be determined to qualify, at which time a document will be drawn up in accord with the law. This legal document, called a 504 plan, will list the accommodations that are necessary for the child's specific disability. For more information, visit the website of the U.S. Department of Education's Office for Civil Rights at http://www.ed.gov/ocr.

Additionally, children with disabilities may qualify for protection under the Individuals with Disabilities Education Act of 2004 (IDEA). This law provides that children who qualify due to a disability receive special assistance in school. This is not an antidiscrimination law and provides more than equal access to education—it provides specialized instruction and related services to individuals who have a qualifying disability that interferes with their educational progress. Special education services do not have to be given in a special classroom and may include interventions in the traditional classroom.

Q. How do I get my child evaluated under the Individuals with Disabilities Education Act (IDEA)?

A. Your child does not automatically qualify for protection and services under IDEA; he must be evaluated and found to be eligible under the requirements of the law. While school districts are required to actively find students who have disabilities and need special education services, your child may or may not be evaluated unless you specifically request such an evaluation. Bipolar disorder is not a learning disability, but it is a disability, and your child may have enough symptoms that interrupt his learning that he will qualify for help.

You may want to send a written request for an evaluation to the school's special education administrator and give copies of this request to your child's principal and teacher. While a phone call may seem easier, it does not document your request, your concerns, or the date. A letter also gives you the opportunity to outline your specific concerns in a professional manner and ask for a complete, multifactored evaluation to determine if your child is eligible for services under IDEA.

Under current federal law, this evaluation is to be completed within sixty days of your consent. Some school districts may prolong this process by failing to give you the forms needed to sign consent. Delay tactics are common due to the costly nature of giving services to children with disabilities. You may want to specifically state in your request letter that the letter should also be viewed as consent for testing to proceed. It is likely that you will still need to sign a form from the school, but this may expedite the process. State and local authorities are allowed to establish their own procedures for the evaluation, but these should be in accord with the federal law. Check with your state Department of Education for your state's regulations.

Q. What is an appropriate classification under IDEA?

A. To qualify under IDEA, your child must fall within one of thirteen categories of disability. The following are the thirteen classifications as they are listed in the regulations of the law:

- Autism
- Deaf-blindness
- Deafness
- Emotional disturbance
- Hearing impairment
- Mental retardation
- Multiple disabilities
- Orthopedic impairment
- Other health impairment
- Specific learning disability
- Speech or language impairment
- Traumatic brain injury
- Visual impairment

Children with bipolar disorder are frequently put into the categories of emotional disturbance (ED) or other health impairment (OHI). It is important to understand the difference between these categories. ED includes children with schizophrenia, while OHI includes children with ADHD; bipolar disorder is not specifically categorized. This could lead to some confusion about classification, since symptoms of bipolar disorder can be similar and overlap with symptoms of both ADHD and schizophrenia in some cases.

The overall description of each category could fit a child with bipolar disorder with one significant exception. The ED classification states that the child's inability to learn cannot be explained by health factors. Classifying the child under ED may lead to school personnel treating the symptoms as if they are willful behaviors instead of part of a serious health condition. OHI, on the other hand, is a more appropriate classification for bipolar disorder because it specifically relates the learning issue to a chronic or acute health problem.

In most states, a child's needs, not his classification, determine what services can be provided, so it's more important to properly identify and address his needs than it is to get the perfect classification. A classification is also not set in stone, so a parent could request a change if it has shown an ill effect.

Q. What if my child is denied services?

A. Not every child who is evaluated will qualify for special education services under IDEA. Having a medical diagnosis does not automatically qualify your child for services. Eligibility will not be determined solely on private evaluations or doctor's reports, though these are considered. For a child with any disability to qualify under IDEA, that disability must clearly impact his education, and there must be a demonstrated need for special education and related services. It will help if you clearly understand your child's disability and how that disability impacts his education.

Providing information on your child's disability may help the school understand the specific issues related to his needs. If the school refuses to evaluate your child or denies services to your child under IDEA, then they must provide the following statements to you in writing:

- Statement of the specific action refused
- Reason the action was refused and a description of what was used as a basis for the refusal
- Statement of procedural safeguards or how to obtain these safeguards
- Sources for parents to contact to obtain assistance
- Other options considered and why these were rejected
- Description of factors relevant to the refusal

This notification under the law is called a "Prior Written Notice." If your school does not provide you with this notification, you may wish to request it to understand what basis the school is using to deny services and if other services such as those under section 504 were considered. If you believe that your child is being wrongly denied, you may be able to request an independent educational evaluation (IEE), which is an evaluation completed by a neutral party. In some cases, a good advocate can assist you in getting your child the services he needs.

Q. What if I don't agree with the school?

A. It would be unusual if everyone agreed with each other all the time, particularly about the proper care of children. When dealing with your child's school, you should expect and prepare for a certain amount of disagreement to take place. These disagreements may arise regarding your child's needs, services, evaluation, qualification, classification, or educational program, and they can be charged with strong feelings on both sides. The best approach is to settle the dispute in a professional manner with the team of people who have been assigned to your child's case. They will be delivering services to your child, so it is in your best interest to establish and maintain a good working relationship.

Of course, not all disputes will be resolved in this manner. If this approach fails, consult the procedural safeguards for your state. The school is required to give you this document when you request an evaluation. If you did not receive a copy, ask for one. This document will help you find out what your rights are when you disagree with a school's treatment of your child and will give you the basics regarding your options in settling disputes with the school. IEEs, mediation, filing of complaints, and due process hearings can all be used to challenge a school, but keep in mind that some of these options are legal proceedings and should not be undertaken unless you are fully aware of what is required under the law.

Become educated about your rights. While you don't have to be a lawyer, the more you understand about education law, the better prepared you will be to advocate for your child. There are a few resources that can help; both http://www.wrightslaw.com and http://www.starfishadvocacy.org are websites that help parents become educated advocates. Additionally, in very difficult cases you may want to engage a professional educational advocate or a lawyer.

Q. What is an individual education plan (IEP)?

A. If your child is found to be eligible for assistance under IDEA, an individual education plan (IEP) will be developed to meet his specific needs. This is the plan that will guide your child's services and educational program. According to the law, it should include the following:

- Present level of performance
- Measurable annual goals
- How often and by what means progress will be measured
- Statement of services, modifications, and supports to be provided
- Explanation of how much your child will participate with nondisabled peers
- Statement of accommodations on district and state assessments
- Date for beginning services and frequency, location, and duration of those services
- Statement of transition services when the child turns sixteen

This plan is made by the IEP team. The team consists of you as the parent, one or more of your child's regular education teachers, one or more of your child's special education teachers, a representative of the local educational agency, an individual who can interpret the results of educational evaluations, other people who have knowledge or expertise regarding your child as desired by you or the school, and the child himself when appropriate. The IEP team should consider the strengths of your child, your concerns as the parent, the most recent evaluation results, and the needs of your child in the areas of academics, functioning, and development. The team must also consider behavior and positive behavior supports, which should include proactive measures like having a safe person and place your child can go to when he feels overwhelmed. The team should also consider any need for assistive technology, such as a word processor for typing. The IEP team should review the IEP no less than annually. A pilot program allows for a multiyear IEP, but this would likely not fit the needs of a child with bipolar disorder. Revisions to the IEP may be made by reconvening an IEP meeting or by adding an amendment when there is agreement on a change.

Q. How should I prepare for the first IEP meeting?

A. The first IEP meeting can be nerve-wracking—it is at this first meeting that important decisions will be made that start your child on the road to receiving services. Even if it is just for moral support, you may want to bring someone with you. In addition, being prepared can increase your confidence and ultimately benefit your child by resulting in a well-developed plan that can help him succeed in school. Here are some tips to help you prepare:

- **Request results of assessments in advance:** This will give you time to fully review the information and understand the results.

- **Dress for success:** Treat this as a business meeting, and dress appropriately. It will help you have confidence and gain the respect of other team members.

- **Understand your role:** The law recognizes you as a team member who has valuable knowledge about your child. You are at this meeting because you play an active role on the IEP team.

- **Be willing to negotiate:** Recognize that there is a certain amount of negotiation in drawing up an IEP. Know what issues are vital and what other issues are less important so that you can carefully choose your battles. Be aware that you will be revisiting your child's needs over time, so not everything needs to be accomplished right away.

- **Don't come empty-handed:** If you can bring a treat for the meeting (doughnuts, for example), it will automatically break the ice and promote a pleasant atmosphere. In addition, bring a list of your child's strengths, your concerns, and any and all information to give to the team regarding his disability.

Q. What is a functional behavioral assessment (FBA)?

A. If your child is found to qualify under IDEA, an IEP will be drawn up. According to the IDEA statute 1414(d)(3)(B), special factors, including behavior, must be considered when developing the IEP. In cases where a child's behavior impedes his learning or that of others, the IEP team is required by law to consider the use of positive behavioral interventions, supports, and other strategies to address the behavior.

To address behavior, schools may use a functional behavioral assessment (FBA). In fact, they are required to do so if the child has been removed from a school or program due to a behavior violation. An FBA collects important information regarding when and why aberrant behavior occurs and evaluates those things that may precede a specific behavior. The assessment is designed to make positive changes to help avoid the negative behavior. The quality of an FBA may vary depending on the person evaluating the child's behavior and his expertise.

Once this information has been gathered, a behavior intervention plan (BIP) is written to address what positive interventions should be implemented to help the child modify the negative behavior. This is not a discipline plan but an intervention plan that should be written by the IEP team which includes you as the parent. You have valuable information to help the team understand your child's behaviors and triggers.

Q. How can I develop a positive relationship with the school?

A. A positive relationship with school personnel can mean the difference between a successful school year for your child and one full of heartache. Developing a positive relationship with the school personnel does not happen without effort on your part. Here are some simple ways to start:

- **Always express appreciation.** In every communication with the school, whether written or in person, start with the positives. Thanking teachers or administrators for the effort they put forth can set the tone of a meeting or conversation.

- **Recognize the other person's opinion.** Even if you do not agree with a teacher, recognize his position and opinion. Acknowledging the other individual and listening shows mutual respect and allows communication to remain open.

- **Avoid polarizing situations.** If the school or teacher has made a mistake, avoid polarizing the parties involved. Rather than focusing on maliciously proving the school wrong, help the school rectify the situation and provide your child with the support he needs to be successful.

- **Be willing to consider options.** You may not always agree with the recommendations made for your child, but be willing to consider options. Keeping an open mind may help your child experience success in ways that you did not imagine. If you remain open-minded, the school may also be more willing to try new things.

- **Be ready to help.** Educating a child with bipolar disorder is a very difficult task. If the teacher perceives that you are a parent who is ready and willing to help, this will foster a positive relationship.

Q. What can I do if the relationship is adversarial?

A. It could be that you haven't gotten off to a good start with the school system; perhaps your child has had many poor experiences or the school has made it difficult to go through the IDEA evaluation process. It is important to keep your perspective and to keep your eye on the goal of obtaining an appropriate education for your child with a disability. Focus on that goal and what will get you there, not on all the little things that get in the way.

Become educated about your rights and be proactive. Your child's school may be more careful to comply with the law if they realize that you know exactly what you're entitled to receive from them. Document every communication with the school. If possible, communicate by letters or emails to establish a paper trail documenting your concerns. When a conversation on the phone does take place, document it and follow up with a letter restating the concern. Try to remain businesslike and professional. You may need to draft several copies of your emails or letters to the school, removing any harsh language or accusatory tone. State the facts along with your concerns, and invite the school into a working relationship.

If your child's rights have been severely trampled on and the school refuses to work with you, you may need to consider hiring an advocate or a lawyer. Switching schools may also be necessary. Happily, in many situations, persistence and hard work may turn an adversarial relationship into one in which the educators are anxious to help your child. Consider reading *Getting to Yes: Negotiating Agreement Without Giving In* by Roger Fisher and William L. Ury and *Getting Past No* by William Ury.

Q. What information should I provide for the teacher?

A. Teaching is a challenging occupation that requires patience and hard work, but it is ultimately very rewarding. Teaching a child with bipolar disorder multiplies those challenges, but in many ways it also increases the benefits. However, sending your child to a teacher who is not informed about how to recognize the symptoms of bipolar disorder and deal with them in the classroom can be disastrous.

Open a dialogue with your child's teacher immediately—don't wait for your child to experience a meltdown or depression before discussing your child's disorder. While the IEP will document many of the concerns of bipolar disorder, don't leave it to chance that your child's teacher will understand completely. Also, be prepared to have several conferences and visits with your child's teacher throughout the school year. Teachers will need reminders and perhaps will need to be made aware of new symptoms.

Be sure to give the teacher printed information written specifically for teachers dealing with children who have bipolar disorder. Too much information could be overwhelming, but concise information in doses throughout the year can be extremely helpful. You can find printable handouts, newsletters, fact sheets, and brochures and DVDs and interactive CDs for teachers on the internet. Check out these resources for teacher information:

- http://www.bipolarchild.com
- http://www.bpchildren.com
- http://www.bpchildresearch.org
- http://www.bpkids.org
- http://www.nami.org
- http://www.schoolbehavior.com
- http://www.starfishadvocacy.org

Q. What if my child is too unstable to attend school?

A. There may be times when your child is simply too unstable to attend school. When this is the case, sending him to school could have very negative consequences both for him personally and for the school in general. It may be that calling in sick for a few days while the psychiatrist adjusts medications will be enough to get him through this rough spot. Because bipolar disorder is a medical condition, it is accurate to explain that the child is sick and to keep him home.

In other cases, it may be necessary for your child to take a longer break from school. When this is the case, you can request that your child be put on a homebound teaching program through the IEP. You should get a written request from your child's psychiatrist that explains why homebound instruction is needed and for what period it's deemed necessary. Homebound instruction is not meant to be a permanent solution but is a temporary intervention for a child whose medical condition is fragile. The level of instruction for homebound teaching varies by state but is very limited compared to traditional attendance in school. If it becomes clear that a child is in need of more comprehensive care, it may be necessary for the school to rethink the child's classroom accommodations and educational program so that he can successfully attend school and get the level of help he needs.

When your child returns to school from homebound instruction, it may be necessary to slowly reintegrate him into the classroom so he has time to get used to it again. You could start by sending him to just one class at school, then working up to a half or whole day of attendance as the child readjusts.

Q. What accommodations can help my child?

A. To understand what accommodations are appropriate for your child, first write a list of your child's difficulties in school and then consider what intervention would be appropriate.

Child's difficulty	Possible accommodations
Trouble paying attention in class due to external stimulation/noise	• Reduce class size • Provide seating near the front • Use headphones to block out noise
Easily overwhelmed and frustrated; shuts down when presented with large amounts of work	• Present worksheets one at a time vs. large packets of work • Reduce the amount of work

Frequent mood swings that alternately cause both slow and lethargic or loud and energetic behaviors	• Ignore minor behaviors during mood swings • Allow him to run outside to expend energy • Give extended time on assignments
Many physical complaints, such as headaches, stomachaches, and backaches	• Allow the child to go to the nurse when he feels ill • Give nurse instructions from child's doctor regarding what interventions are necessary (ibuprofen, acetaminophen, crackers, ginger ale, a five-minute rest, and so on)
Dry mouth and increased thirst due to medication	• Allow the child to have a water bottle in class
Frequent urination caused by medication	• Allow the child to use the bathroom as needed
Significant writing disability and hand tremors from medication	• Allow the child to dictate answers to the teacher • Reduce writing assignments • Give the child a copy of all classroom notes • Use occupational therapy for handwriting issues • Use word processor to type
Obsession over the safety of family members	• Allow the child to call home
Difficulty with social interaction	• Involve the child in a social skills group with the behavioral specialist
Behaviors such as crying in class or angry outbursts	• Have an emergency card or private signal to teacher for escape from the classroom before a meltdown and have a safe contact person to go to

Q. What kind of classroom environment is appropriate?

A. Some classrooms seem to breed success for children with bipolar disorder, while others seem to set them up for failure. Although each child is different, there are some common themes in classroom environments that foster success:

- **Routine:** Your child's ever-changing moods and inability to regulate himself can become a huge problem if he doesn't know what to expect within his environment. Your child may be unable to shift gears easily without provoking a mood episode, making structure and routine vital.

- **Flexibility:** Flexibility should complement routine. What is true for your child one hour or day may not be true the next. A flexible teaching approach to accommodate for changing moods is crucial.

- **Collaboration:** Environments that invite your child to be an active participant can help engage your child and keep him focused. Solving challenging situations together will help your child feel like part of the solution instead of part of the problem, which will help him maintain a positive mood.

- **Warm expression:** If an instructor looks serious or stern, your child may misperceive this as hostility and anger. A warm expression will be easier for your child to read.

- **Willingness to accommodate:** Teachers who are willing and cooperative in implementing your child's IEP will foster an environment of success.

- **Willingness to learn:** A teacher who is willing to learn about bipolar disorder and its effects on a student will be more likely to create a positive learning environment for your child.

- **Small class size:** In general, small classroom sizes are more appropriate for children with bipolar disorder. Smaller class sizes equal less stimuli and noise.

- **Fresh start:** A teaching environment that judges the child on past successes or failures can be very difficult. Starting fresh each day will help prevent your child from giving up.

Q. Can the school discipline my child?

A. The appropriate school setting, medical treatment, accommodations, and interventions can help keep your child from facing serious disciplinary issues at school. Unfortunately, even with the best interventions, your child may have an episode at school that leads to disciplinary action. Here is a brief overview of what IDEA says about disciplining a child with a disability who has violated a student code of conduct rule:

- School personnel may consider unique circumstances when determining whether to order a change in placement, such as removing your child from his school to place him in an alternative school.
- The child may be suspended or moved to an appropriate alternative placement for not more than ten consecutive school days. More than ten days would constitute a change in the child's educational placement. Before such a change could take place the IEP team would need to meet and decide on an appropriate placement.
- If the code of conduct violation includes possession of a weapon or illegal drugs or inflicts serious bodily injury to another person, then the child may be removed to an alternate setting for no more than forty-five days.
- The school must notify parents of disciplinary actions on the same day the decision is made.
- A child with a disability who has a change of placement must continue to receive education services that will enable him to participate in the general education curriculum and to progress toward the IEP goals. A functional behavioral assessment, behavior intervention services, and modifications should be reviewed to avoid a recurrence of the violation.
- IDEA does not prohibit the school authorities from reporting criminal actions to law enforcement.

- Within ten school days of a decision to change the placement of the child due to a code violation, a manifestation determination hearing must be held.

Q. What is a manifestation determination hearing?

A. A manifestation determination hearing is a meeting that seeks to determine if the child's behavior was a manifestation of his illness. The meeting includes the parents, local educational agency, and relevant members of the IEP team. Information in the students file should be reviewed, including the IEP, teacher reports, and information from the parents. Parents may want to bring any assessments or reports from the physician for consideration. The behavior will be deemed a manifestation of the illness if it fulfills one of these two determining factors:

1. Was it caused by or did it have a direct and substantial relationship to the child's disability?
2. Was it the direct result of the school agency's failure to implement the IEP?

If the behavior was due to the illness, the school must conduct a functional behavioral assessment and implement a behavior intervention plan (or modify an existing one) to address the behavior. The child can be suspended for up to ten days but will be returned to the previous placement unless both the parents and the school agency agree to a change. Exceptions to returning to the previous placement are made when the violation involves a weapon or illegal drugs or causes serious bodily injury. In this case, the child can stay in an alternate setting away from school for up to forty-five days.

If the behavior is not shown to be a manifestation of the illness, the child may receive the same manner and length of discipline as a child who does not have a disability. An appeal can be made by a parent who disagrees with the results of the manifestation hearing, or the school agency may appeal if they feel that maintaining the current placement is likely to result in injury to the child or others. No matter what the hearing determines, a child with a disability is still entitled to receive a free and appropriate public education. The local school agency must ensure this.

Q. What if the IEP is not implemented?

A. You might have the best IEP in the world, but if it is not implemented, then it can't help your child. If one or more teachers do not seem to be following the IEP, first seek clarification. Read the IEP to confirm that the particular service or accommodation was included in the document and that you understand how it is to be implemented. If there are unclear phrases in the IEP that could be leading to confusion, request an IEP meeting to clarify.

If the service or accommodation is clearly stated in the IEP, then contact the teacher or school to review your concerns. Always be pleasant and businesslike in your communications. An emailed reminder may remedy the situation, and no further action may be needed. Let teachers know that you are ready to support their efforts in the classroom to help your child be successful. Become active and involved.

If personal communication with your child's teacher does not remedy the situation, convene an IEP meeting. If the situation persists, consider taking the teacher out of the equation. It may be easier and more productive to switch an uncooperative team player than to try to force compliance. While a forced compliance is possible through complaints to the state or litigation, compliance may be begrudging and not really give your child the environment he needs. Finding a positive resolution that maintains a good working relationship with the school is always preferable. If you do decide to pursue legal means, consult with an advocate or lawyer and fully know your rights.

Chapter 11

HOSPITALIZATION

- When does a child need hospitalization?
- What types of hospitals treat bipolar disorder?
- How can I find out about services in advance?
- How can a hospital stay be beneficial?
- What should I expect?
- How can I make the stay more comfortable?
- How can I make the stay more positive for my child?
- How can I assure continuity of care?
- What should I tell family and friends?
- How can I help the transition back home go more smoothly?
- What if the hospital stay did not help?
- What are my rights?
- What if I have a complaint about the hospital?
- What is a partial hospitalization program?
- When is long-term care needed?
- Should I feel guilty about extended care?
- How do I choose an appropriate residential treatment facility?
- What about a boot camp or military-type program?
- What questions should I ask?
- What are the possible drawbacks of a residential placement?

Q. When does a child need hospitalization?

A. Bipolar disorder is an illness that sometimes requires the extra care and medical supervision that comes with hospital stays. While difficult, hospital stays may be necessary if your child is in crisis. Very serious symptoms require a very serious reaction. The goal of any hospital stay is to stabilize a medical situation and to move the patient toward wellness that can be maintained in an outpatient environment. Talk to your child's doctor about what symptoms would require hospitalization. Here are some situations that could lead to hospitalization:

- **Suicidal ideas or attempts:** If your child is a danger to himself, a hospital stay could save his life. Immediate stabilization of the crisis and round-the-clock medical supervision can be provided to ensure that the child does not take his own life.

- **Violence toward others:** If your child is expressing violent behaviors, a hospital stay may be necessary to bring the illness under control so your child does not threaten the safety of others.

- **Complete medication changes:** If your child's treatment is not effectively controlling his illness and it is determined that a complete and drastic change in treatment is necessary, this may need to be done in a hospital setting for supervision.

- **Episode of psychosis:** Symptoms of psychosis such as hallucinations, delusions, false beliefs, and paranoia may require a hospital stay depending on the severity of the symptoms.

- **Drug addiction:** If your child also has an addiction to illegal drugs, he may require a program that specializes in mood disorders and drug addiction.

Q. What types of hospitals treat bipolar disorder?

A. Not all hospitals are prepared to treat a child or teen with bipolar disorder. The most appropriate hospital is a psychiatric hospital with separate specialized programs for children and teens. Your child's psychiatrist can both help you determine the need for hospitalization and refer you to an appropriate facility. It would be inappropriate for children to be in the same unit as adults with bipolar disorder because their needs are far different. Programs for children may be part of a hospital system but in a separate location from the main hospital. Many times these programs are termed "behavioral health" programs.

Hospital services for children with bipolar disorder may include the following:

- **Crisis services:** Crisis services generally focus on the short-term goal of stabilizing the child and providing a safe environment.

- **Acute inpatient services:** Inpatient hospitalizations may focus on both the short-term goal of stabilization and the long-term goal of maintaining wellness. Inpatient programs may include medication changes, school programs, group and individual therapy, family therapy, social skills education, and training on awareness of moods and behaviors.

- **Day treatment:** Day treatments are for children who need intensive services but may be well enough to stay at home during the evening and nighttime.

- **Outpatient services:** Hospitals may have an outpatient program that includes counseling, support services, and referrals for other community-based services.

Q. How can I find out about services in advance?

A. The first source of information about where to take your child in an emergency is your child's psychiatrist. He likely has experience with the local hospitals and knows their track record of caring for children. He should also know which hospitals work cooperatively with him as a physician and may be aware of the emergency services and age-appropriate programs available. Even if hospitalization is not a current issue, check with your doctor now to know what hospital he recommends.

Another good source of information is local support groups. This consumer base may have firsthand knowledge of both good and bad experiences with the local hospitals. They may be able to recommend a good hospital or emergency service. They may also be able to give you information and tips that only a fellow parent who has been to that hospital could provide. This is only one of the many reasons to be active in local support groups. Do keep in mind, however, that individual experiences will vary greatly. If your doctor recommends a hospital where someone else had a poor experience, that doesn't necessarily mean that your experience there will be poor.

Another way to check out a hospital is online. Many hospitals have websites and information regarding their programs available on the internet. Having this information in print can help ease your mind and familiarize you with the facility. Some websites even have virtual tours. While this doesn't replace an on-site visit, it can help give you a feel for the hospital.

Q. How can a hospital stay be beneficial?

A. As scary as it can be to contemplate a hospital stay, it is sometimes necessary and can be extremely beneficial, even lifesaving. If a child in your family is in the middle of a crisis, you may not even realize how much that crisis is affecting and draining each and every family member. It also may be difficult to realize how prolonged periods of instability are impacting your child and his siblings. While hospital stays are not for every child, there are situations in which it can be just what is needed to start recovery. It can also prove to be a time of healing for the family, especially if they are involved in family-based interventions and therapy.

Some children end up in the hospital as their first introduction to psychiatric treatment due to a severe crisis. When this happens, a hospital stay may have immediate lifesaving benefits. Additionally, a hospital stay may help stabilize the child, first by using fast-acting medication, and second by initiating longer-term medication and treatment. While the hospital stay brings its own stresses, it also removes the child from the regular environment and outside stresses such as public school. This change to a more sheltered environment may help the child stabilize. Additionally, the child may learn coping skills and learn how to recognize the illness and identify triggers. There may also be transitional services put into place to help the child ease back into family life and school life once he is released.

Q. What should I expect?

A. You should expect to be kept informed about what is going on with your child's treatment. You can also expect that your privacy will be protected and that your child will be kept safe not only from self-harm but also from being harmed by any other patient. Ask about the hospital's safety plan for the patients. Find out the name of the head nurse assigned to your child's case and how you can contact this person with any questions.

Most likely a treatment plan will be drawn up. Many hospitals include the parents as an integral part of this treatment plan. You have valuable information about your child's medical history, symptom history, and reaction to medications. Your input is vital.

Find out how often the psychiatrist visits and when you can talk to him. Ideally, your child's current psychiatrist would also be the treating physician, but this may not be the case if your child's psychiatrist is not associated with a hospital. If it is a new doctor for your child, find out if he will be consulting with your child's psychiatrist. Having a new doctor can bring both advantages and disadvantages. Sometimes a fresh perspective can send you in a new treatment direction that can be beneficial. At the same time, a new doctor does not have personal knowledge of your child's treatment history. It's very important for him to consult you and your child's current doctor before making a treatment plan.

Q. How can I make the stay more comfortable?

A. Your child may experience a certain amount of discomfort when he is away from familiar surroundings; a hospital stay may produce much anxiety. As a parent, you likely wish to make this experience as good as it can possibly be, and you may be able to help make the transition into the hospital easier. Staying calm can help—if your child senses that you are overly disturbed about a hospital stay, it may feed into his own anxiety about it. Open communication about why the hospital stay is needed may be helpful; however, if your child is having delusional thoughts, you may not be able to have a rational conversation.

Ask the hospital about what you should and should not bring. There will likely be restrictions on anything that would be considered dangerous to your child or to another patient. Things that may seem harmless to you at first glance could be prohibited. Glass objects will not be allowed. This means that flowers cannot be in a glass vase, and pictures should not be in a frame with glass. Consider sending a picture or two without a frame. It could be of you, a sibling, or even a cherished pet. These may be a comfort if your child gets homesick. Check to see if stuffed animals are allowed. Even older kids may find childhood objects from home comforting during this time.

Also check policies for visitation and phone calls. This will help you keep in touch with your child while he is in the hospital. Generally, psychiatric hospitals do not allow parents to stay overnight, so take full advantage of other means of staying in contact.

Q. How can I make the stay more positive for my child?

A. As much as we would like to say that every hospital stay is a good one, this is not always the case. The level of care and the skill of the treatment team may vary dramatically from place to place. This makes many parents wary of hospitalizations even if their child is in need of admission. What can you do to help make your child's hospital stay a good one?

- **Prepare:** Always prepare for the possibility that your child may need to be hospitalized to get a greater level of care. Hopefully this won't be necessary, but know in advance what hospitals are in your area and which of these hospitals is appropriate for your child in a psychiatric emergency. If you have to make this decision in the middle of a crisis, you will be under added stress.

- **Take a tour:** If possible, tour the facility in advance to see if it is appropriate for your child. Take note of the cleanliness and the friendliness of the hospital. Check to see if it is well staffed. Make sure the staff appreciates parent involvement. Ask about hospital policies.

- **Be involved:** Be an active part of your child's hospital stay and recovery. Make yourself available for family therapy and consults with the doctor.

- **Communicate:** If you have concerns, don't hesitate to speak up. Know in advance whom you can talk to about your child's case.

- **Check insurance:** Check in advance to see what hospital coverage your insurance provides. Knowing what your financial obligations will be can help you feel more relaxed about a hospital stay.

Filling out the crisis plan template in Appendix D can help you be prepared in case of a hospitalization. For further instructions on filling out the crisis plan, refer to Chapter 4.

Q. How can I assure continuity of care?

A. If your child's regular psychiatrist can't visit him in the hospital, this may make you worry about the continuity of your child's care. Ask to sign release of information forms immediately upon admission so that the psychiatrist in charge of treatment at the hospital will be able to access your child's records and to communicate with your child's regular psychiatrist. Make sure that the treating physician and staff are aware of current medications, and find out if these will be provided by the hospital pharmacy or if you should bring in a supply. Find out when you can meet with the treatment team. Checking with the head nurse to verify medications is also a good idea—you don't want to discover three days into the hospital stay that one of your child's regular medications has been overlooked.

If your child needs hospitalization, it is quite likely that medication will be changed. In fact, you may find yourself getting frustrated if the doctor in charge doesn't change your child's treatment. Make sure that the hospital understands that you wish to be consulted regarding all changes in medication. Insist on being included in the development of a treatment plan.

This is a frustrating and emotionally charged time period at best. If you have concerns about the level and continuity of care that your child is receiving, you may find it beneficial to write a list of your concerns so that these are on paper. Having this list in front of you can be a lifesaver, especially if you only have a few minutes to share your thoughts with the doctor or nurse. You don't want to realize after you hang up or leave a meeting that you have forgotten something important.

Q. What should I tell family and friends?

A. If your child goes into the hospital to have surgery or to recuperate from an illness such as pneumonia, you're likely to tell family, friends, and neighbors to build a support system. When a child is admitted to a psychiatric hospital after a severe episode, things are different. Why does this happen, and what can you do to change or deal with this situation?

- **Shame and embarrassment:** Sometimes we as parents build a wall of shame and don't open up to anyone about what's going on. Have you given people the opportunity to reach out and support you? You may be pleasantly surprised by the results. *Give people the opportunity to support you.*

- **Awkwardness:** Another reason for lack of support may come from people's own awkwardness in these situations. Sometimes the right words are just not there and everything seems inadequate, so people do nothing. *Don't be afraid to express your needs.* Many people are willing to help but don't know how. Let them know if you need a meal, childcare for a sibling, or anything else.

- **Privacy:** Your child, especially if he is a teen, may want you to keep things private. While you should respect this wish, *you still need support as a parent.* This illness doesn't just affect the person who is suffering with it, it affects the entire family. In this case you may want to seek the more anonymous support that online forums can bring. But in addition, make sure that your child works with his therapist and treatment team on issues related to embarrassment about the illness.

The best way to approach this conversation is to be open and truthful. You don't have to share all the details of what led up to the hospitalization, but do emphasize that your child is ill, that it is a difficult time, and that your family would appreciate any support. Let your child's teacher know if he would like to receive cards from school friends and classmates.

Q. How can I make the transition back home go more smoothly?

A. Once your child is ready for release from the hospital, there should be a transition plan drawn up by the team caring for him. Ask to be part of this transition planning so you can be fully aware of the steps that will get your child through this time. Change in general is difficult for children with bipolar disorder. Even though your child may want to return home, this change can still pose challenges. You will want to make this transitional time as smooth as possible. The first thing to do is to get rid of a few misconceptions about what this time will be like:

- **Myth #1: My child will be completely stable.** A hospital stay is generally not long enough to totally stabilize a child; but steps should have been taken on the path to stability, and beneficial treatment changes should have been made.

- **Myth #2: My child can resume all previous activities.** Even though your child may be past a particular crisis that made hospitalization necessary, remember that your child is still in a fragile state. It is very important to make sure that stress is reduced in your child's environment and that he is able to get sufficient rest and to follow up with his psychiatrist.

- **Myth #3: My child can return to school immediately with no transition.** Make sure the transition plan from the hospital addresses school concerns. Meet with your child's IEP team or school before his return to review and modify his plan to address the current circumstances. If he has no supports already in place, make sure that an emergency plan is drawn up. Your child may need such things as homebound instruction, half-day slow transitions, no homework, and reduced assignments.

Plan with your school, your doctor, and your family to prepare for your child's release; that should go a long way toward helping you keep the stress level down and your child stable.

Q. What if the hospital stay did not help?

A. One of the most difficult scenarios is if your child is at the end of his planned hospital stay and is no better or maybe even worse than he was at admission. Unfortunately, bipolar disorder doesn't always cooperate with our imposed time lines or those of our insurance companies. It's likely that you wanted your child stabilized yesterday, not a month from now. But if your child is not well, it's time to step back and reevaluate the plan. Discharge may no longer be appropriate, or your child may need to enter another facility or program. If your child has improved but still needs a high level of care, it may be appropriate for your child to attend a partial hospitalization program or a day program.

Additionally, as a parent and the manager of your child's treatment team, you will also want to consider whether or not the medical facility is at fault. It may simply be the severity of your child's current episode that is the problem, but it could also be the skill of the personnel or the environment of this facility. Though you likely worked very hard to pick the most appropriate treatment center, it may not turn out as well as it could. If the medical professionals working with your child have not been responsive in treating your child, working with you, and consulting with your child's psychiatrist or if they are using totally behavioral approaches and no medication, then it may be time to terminate the relationship with this facility and to seek medical care elsewhere.

Q. What are my rights?

A. When your child is hospitalized, you have both rights and responsibilities. Some of your rights are established by the Health Insurance Portability and Accountability Act of 1996 (HIPAA). This law sets requirements for the privacy of medical records and requires medical centers such as hospitals to disclose their privacy policies to you.

Additionally, as a parent you also have the right to be informed regarding your child's treatment and to give or withhold consent. Sometimes you'll give consent verbally, such as when a new medication is started and you are in agreement with the physician. Other times you will need to sign an order giving or refusing consent to a procedure. You have the right to have the risks and benefits of any procedure fully explained to you before making a decision regarding consent. If you do not agree to a particular treatment, it is likely that you and your child's doctor can find an alternate treatment on which you both agree. In some unusual cases, a doctor can seek a court order to force treatment when parents disagree.

During a hospital admission, you will likely be asked to sign a whole slew of paperwork regarding your child's treatment and care. Read this paperwork carefully before you sign. Some of it will be about filing insurance and so forth, but other paperwork will be about treatment. If you don't understand something, do not feel foolish. Ask for clarification—you have the right to understand what it means. If you are uncomfortable with the language or broad permissions being requested, you can strike these out or modify them before signing.

Q. What if I have a complaint about the hospital?

A. If you feel that your rights as a parent or your child's rights are being violated by a hospital or if you have any other complaint, first try to solve the problem by speaking to those involved. Talk through your concerns with your child's nurse, a head nurse, or the doctor—it may be enough to correct the situation. If you can't fix the problem this way, address it at the next level. Most hospitals have a complaint procedure that ends at the top, which is usually the organization that manages the hospital. If you still cannot get resolution, you may wish to file a health care complaint with your state. Each state has an agency for handling health care issues. Links to your state's health administration agency can be found at http://www.statelocalgov.net/50states-health.cfm.

If the complaint involves a violation of privacy laws, then you can file a complaint with the U.S. Department of Health and Human Services' Office for Civil Rights (OCR). You have 180 days from the time of the suspected violation to submit a written complaint. To find out more about filing a complaint, go to the OCR/HIPAA website at http://www.hhs.gov/ocr/hipaa/.

If you have exhausted your complaint procedures and you feel that there was a severe denial of rights that harmed your child, then you may wish to seek the advice of a competent attorney. Your decision to pursue litigation should factor in the extra time and expense such litigation will incur and the extra toll it could take on your family. It's really a matter of picking your battles carefully. Your main focus should remain on the care and well-being of your child.

Q. What is a partial hospitalization program?

A. A partial hospitalization program is less intensive than the twenty-four-hour setting of a hospital but more intensive than an outpatient program. In these programs, the patient will spend his day in a therapeutic environment, which may also include school. A partial program is not for emergency treatment. This intervention may be used as a step down from an inpatient stay before returning to home full time or may be used when full hospitalization is not required. The program may work for the following issues:

- **Medication stabilization:** A partial program can monitor and try to improve your child's stabilization on medications.

- **Social skills:** The program may target improvement in social skills.

- **Occupational therapy:** Some programs incorporate an occupational therapy component, which is specialized therapy aimed at increasing a patient's ability to function independently.

- **Anger management:** Your child may learn anger management skills.

- **Therapy:** Both group and individual therapy can help your child begin to recognize various mood states.

- **Coping skills:** The program may help your child replace unhealthy behaviors with improved coping skills.

- **Family education:** Most programs try to educate the family regarding the child's illness and to teach them techniques to manage it.

There are many partial hospitalization programs that address various psychiatric issues. Not every program will be appropriate for your child. Some hospitals have programs specific to autism or developmental disabilities, while others are geared toward children with obsessive-compulsive disorder. Doing your homework ahead of time will help assure that the program chosen is appropriate for children with bipolar disorder. Check with your doctor to find a local program that is right for your child.

Q. When is long-term care needed?

A. Both partial programs and inpatient hospital stays, while intensive, are still relatively short-term interventions. If your child is unstable, you may worry that he will require longer, more intensive care. Many parents worry about the possibility that their child will ultimately need a residential program. Most children with bipolar disorder can be successfully treated at home with outside interventions and support, but some critically ill children require a more intensive level of treatment.

Children requiring this level of intervention may be aggressive to the point of being a danger to themselves or others. They are not able to function and interact within the household framework and may be at high risk for ending up in the juvenile justice system. This behavior could be caused by a lack of response to medication, the severity of their illness, a drug addiction, or multiple co-occurring illnesses with bipolar disorder. Residential treatment may last from weeks to months or even years depending on the child's response to the intervention. The goal of treatment is to stabilize the child and help him return home.

It is nothing short of agonizing when parents are faced with these difficult treatment decisions. If your child does need this level of intervention, you should not feel that somehow it is your fault. The degree to which your child needs a specific intervention speaks more to the severity of his illness than to the care and concern of his parents.

Q. Should I feel guilty about extended care?

A. If you are considering the possibility that your child may need hospitalization, then it is a scary time filled with uncertainties. It can also be filled with guilt. You may feel that a hospital stay is somehow due to a failure on your part. You are not alone; many other parents have felt this way too. It was no truer for them than it is for you. *Seeking treatment for your child is never a failure; it is a step on the road to success.* Your child's increased symptoms are not a failure on your part. They are an indicator of your child's medical condition.

Guilt can be intensified if the treatment or hospital stay was not a positive experience. But were you the one who caused the hospital stay to be negative? It is doubtful that this could be your fault, and it's more likely due to the skill of a particular facility, the effectiveness of the chosen intervention, and the level of your child's instability. What if it is your own child who makes you feel guilty for a needed hospital stay? Remember that unstable children with bipolar disorder tend to place a lot of blame. Also, when scared, your child may lash out at those he loves the most. While this may be painful, try not to internalize it. Seek emotional support of your own with a skilled therapist who understands your situation. You need to be able to process these events and to come out strong enough to continue advocating for your child.

Q. How do I choose an appropriate residential treatment facility?

A. If your child does need to attend a residential treatment facility, you are now in the unenviable position of needing to find a good placement. In some cases, your doctor may be aware of a good, appropriate facility close to home. It's preferable that the facility be associated with a hospital system where your child has received treatment in the past. When the placement is covered by insurance, this also can affect where your child is sent. At times, the expense of the educational part of a residential treatment facility is covered by the public school system under IDEA. When a school system cannot provide an appropriate educational setting, they may give specific recommendations to alternative programs. A parent will want to evaluate any recommended placement for appropriateness.

Many times, however, it is up to the parents to find and finance an appropriate placement. Residential facilities vary widely in their programs, educational components, quality of staff, philosophy, and quality of medical care. A facility that looks good on paper may not be the right place for your child. If you are searching for an appropriate placement, you may wish to enlist outside professional help; an excellent resource can be an educational consultant, an independent counselor who helps parents plan a child's education. Many consultants specialize in students with special needs. This specialization may increase the chances that you are aware of your choices and avoid placements that could have a poor outcome for your child. Considering the relatively large financial burden of a placement of this sort, the cost of the consultant may be well worth the investment.

A listing of educational consultants can be found at the Independent Educational Consultants Association (IECA) website: http://www. educationalconsulting.org. Additional resources may be found at http:// www.strugglingteens.com. Also, checking with families who have children in a particular placement may give you clues as to whether the facility is appropriate for your child.

Q. What about a boot camp or military-type program?

A. No doubt everyone would like to have a well-behaved and respectful child. There are various military-style camps that may appeal to parents who feel that discipline is the answer to their child's difficult behavior. However, many boot camps now recognize that their programs are not appropriate for young people with a psychiatric illness, whether it is bipolar disorder, depression, or another illness. Many times they will refuse to even allow enrollment, recognizing that such a child needs medical intervention with behavior modifications implemented in a therapeutic environment.

Military-style programs and boot camps are based on the idea that the child or teen is simply choosing to behave badly. The goal of these programs is to assert strong physical punishment and authority over the child to modify such behavior. Sometimes tactics include attempts to psychologically "break" the child. This type of program does not take into account difficulties as a result of an illness. No amount of punishment will stop a child from hallucinating. No amount of tough approaches will change the abnormalities in the brain that prevent the child from functioning in the current environment. Sending a fragile, emotionally distressed child to one of these programs is a recipe for disaster.

These types of programs, however, may not always be easy to identify. There are some that maintain the same coercion techniques and near-abusive methods under a glossy and sometimes even religious exterior. Terms such as "teen revitalizing" are sometimes used to mask the same harsh philosophies of boot camps. Be wary of any program that attempts to address depression by teaching teens "accountability." Find out the philosophy behind the program before making any choice.

Q. What questions should I ask?

A. There are many questions that should be asked of a program before you decide if it's the right placement for your child. This is a very individual process and will center on your child's specific needs. As you narrow down your choices and consider a placement, make sure you tour the facility and ask the necessary questions. Here is a general list of questions, but you will also want to include questions that address the unique needs of your child:

- What type of therapy is used?
- How often is therapy administered?
- What is the level of medical care?
- How many people are on staff?
- How many are medical personnel?
- Is there one psychiatrist who will regularly see my child?
- Are there trained psychiatric nurses on staff?
- How often will I be able to communicate with my child?
- Will my child be allowed to come home for visits?
- How will medication changes be handled?
- How often will I receive a report on my child?
- How is discipline handled?
- What are your policies regarding the use of physical restraints?
- Are there any complaints or legal actions pending against your facility?

- Have there been any abuse allegations?
- What is your educational program?
- Are you licensed?
- May I tour your facility?
- How often will I be allowed to visit through the year?

Also check to see if this facility or program is accredited by the Joint Commission on Accreditation of Healthcare Organizations (JCAHO). JCAHO is a nonprofit organization that accredits health care institutions after they pass an unannounced evaluation. It is concerned with issues surrounding patient rights, cleanliness, medication safety, and health care excellence. To check if a facility is accredited, go to http://www.qualitycheck.org.

Q. What are the possible drawbacks of a residential placement?

A. Before making placement decisions, you must weigh the good and the bad and be fully aware of potential drawbacks to the placement. Here are some of the difficult realities that may face parents who are considering more intensive treatments:

- **Financial burden:** The sad reality is that many people do not have sufficient finances or insurance coverage to pay for long stays in hospitals, outpatient programs, and residential facilities. Parents sometimes find themselves in the horrible predicament of being asked to relinquish custody to the state to obtain treatment.

- **Lack of appropriate facilities:** Even when insurance or finances are adequate, it is difficult to find a facility nearby to care for your child. Sometimes children end up being placed hours or even states away.

- **Minimal therapeutic interventions:** Residential facilities may not always provide the intensive intervention that your child needs. Facilities may lack funding to provide adequate treatment or staff.

- **Release before stabilization:** Parents sometimes report receiving their child back from a residential placement in a completely unstable condition, no better than when he was admitted. This sometimes occurs when the treatment team is forced to discharge a child due to insurance constraints.

- **Exposure to the behavior of others:** A child may be negatively influenced by the other children hospitalized for psychiatric care—he could pick up behaviors such as cutting, bulimia, and drug use.

This is a sad and scary commentary on the state of mental health affairs for our children. To receive the sometimes lifesaving treatment offered, parents must make hard and occasionally terrible decisions. It may be that your child has a totally positive experience with a good outcome, but the negative side of these placements should make parents aware of the vital importance of using a facility with a very good reputation.

Chapter 12

INTENSE PARENTING

- What are the special parenting challenges of having a child with bipolar disorder?
- How does my child's stability affect parenting?
- What levels of illness require different parenting?
- What is the same in every parenting mode?
- What are the variables in each mode?
- How do family attitudes affect recovery?
- How do I parent in emergency mode?
- How do I parent in critical mode?
- How do I parent in transitional mode?
- How do I parent in modified mode?
- How do I parent in wellness mode?
- What are the warning signs of backsliding?
- What should I do when my child backslides?
- What are the special needs of siblings?
- What if siblings show the same behaviors?
- What if parents disagree on how to raise the children?
- Should my child be disciplined while unstable?
- What if my child becomes violent?
- What should I do if Child Protective Services gets involved?
- How can a single parent manage?
- Where can I find support?

Q. What are the special parenting challenges of having a child with bipolar disorder?

A. It is challenging to raise any child with a chronic illness; there are physical, economic, and emotional drains on the parents. In addition, childhood bipolar disorder comes with its own unique set of difficulties.

One of the biggest challenges you may face as a parent is the uncertainty of your child's ever-changing moods. For example, you may still be trying to recover from angry words your child hurled at you, but your child may have moved on, singing silly songs and skipping around the house with no idea why you would still be upset. Or you may know the feeling in the pit of your stomach when your child comes through the door at the end of a school day and you brace for the unknown mood that will follow. Another challenge is the constant need to educate others about your child's disability. Repeatedly educating extended family, teachers, and others who come in contact with your child can become tiresome. A third challenge is recognizing the more subtle ways that the illness impacts your child and finding the appropriate interventions to help him navigate around these difficulties.

Likely you have learned firsthand that traditional parenting techniques sadly fall short of meeting your child's needs. You may also feel that if you get one more well-meaning piece of parenting advice, you will get sick on the spot or at least loan your child out so that neighbors and some professionals can see how their approach works in real time. You know your child best. You know what you have tried in the past and how your child reacts to specific tactics. However, you may long for some real guidance that will work for your family.

Q. How does my child's stability affect parenting?

A. You always need to be aware of your child's mood and level of stability and to slip into the appropriate parenting mode while simultaneously trying to guide your child to a higher level of stability. In most adult wellness models, the patient must stay in tune with his own changing moods and adjust accordingly; but with childhood bipolar disorder, you become the monitor of your child's wellness and resulting needs. Your child with bipolar disorder will have varying abilities according to his stability. This may change frequently, especially as treatment is just being established or during times of transition. As abilities change, your expectations of your child should be modified.

This flexible parenting style responds to the changing needs of your child. The illness modifies your child's ability, so you need to modify your parental reactions. It may be easier to understand this flexible approach by comparing it to parenting another child with a chronic illness. For instance, would you expect a child whose asthma has flared up to complete his usual task of mowing the lawn, or would you modify that expectation until he is well? How would your expectations for that child change when his asthma is well controlled? Would you permanently alter an expectation if it triggered a worsening of his condition? The answers are obvious. Illness does change the needs of your child.

So, why do parents feel guilty for parenting a child with bipolar disorder differently from a healthy child? Your child's illness may not be obvious to the outside world, and that can make it feel awkward to parent in this way. Furthermore, the signs of the illness aren't as clear-cut as wheezing but may be such things as anger and irritability—the very things that would likely result in disciplinary actions for a healthy child. But no matter how it might look to the outside world (with the obvious exception of abuse), you should never feel guilty for parenting in a way that works for your specific child.

Q. What levels of illness require different parenting?

A. Your child has varying degrees of stability, each of which may require different parenting approaches. Each child will begin on a different place on this scale and will go up and down depending on the course of his illness. As a parent, you will want to evaluate where your child falls on this scale with each mood shift and to parent accordingly. The goal is to help your child function safely where he is while moving him forward to a healthier level of stability.

It's important to realize that your child will not go from being severely ill to being well—there will be a progression toward wellness. Likewise, parenting should not skip from emergency mode to wellness mode. Your parenting will adjust gradually as your child's state changes.

Level of stability	Parental concern	Parenting mode
Severely ill	Your child is completely unstable; you are concerned for the safety and well-being of your child or others	Emergency mode
Critically ill	Your child is just recuperating from severe illness or is very fragile with frequent and severe mood swings; he does not function well in the outside world or at home	Critical mode
Moderately ill	Your child is experiencing frequent mood swings but is functioning to some degree in the outside world or at home; your child may do well in one environment and not another	Transitional mode
Mildly ill/partially stable	Your child is experiencing some minor mood instability but is functioning fairly well both in the outside world and at home; stress may still induce an exaggerated response, but he recuperates quickly and is able to resume activities	Modified mode
Well/stable	Your child's mood is stable, and he is currently functioning normally in the outside world and at home	Wellness mode

Q. What is the same in every parenting mode?

A. There are a few things that should stay the same no matter what parenting mode you are in or what state of stability your child is in. These are the rules and approaches that can't be modified regardless of the current severity of symptoms:

- **Your child's illness cannot compromise the safety of someone else in the household.** If safety becomes an issue, a higher level of care is necessary. Animals should also be included in household safety.
- **Treatment is nonnegotiable.** There are no circumstances in which treatment becomes a negotiation tool. Compliance with medication, doctor's visits, and therapy is part of each of the parenting modes.
- **Parents work as a team.** No matter which mode parents are in, they should work together to accomplish the goal. Both parents need to understand how the child's level of stability changes parenting objectives. For this to be accomplished, both parents need to understand the illness.
- **Structure and routine are critical to each parenting mode.** No matter which mode you are in, try to maintain key routines in the household to the degree possible for the circumstance. Things as basic as mealtimes and bedtimes can bring comfort when they are predictable and routine.
- **As the parent, you are the authority in the household.** When you make decisions as to how to parent in different circumstances, you are doing so by reason of your authority—and not by giving up your authority. However, whether your child is able to acknowledge that authority in extreme mood states may be a different matter altogether. Power struggles that ultimately push your buttons and are not beneficial to moving your child to the next level of stability should be avoided. So choose your battles carefully, but remember who's in charge.

Q. What are the variables in each mode?

A. There are many variables that will affect your parenting in each parenting mode. The differences in each mode can benefit your child and help move him to the next level of stability. Variables that change

Level of stability	Parental responsibility	Parenting mode
Severely ill	• *Expectations:* On hold • *Medical care:* Intensive emergency services • *Stress:* Remove stress • *Goal:* Ensure your child's survival	Emergency mode
Critically ill	• *Expectations:* Still on hold • *Medical care:* Intensive, frequent follow-up • *Stress:* Remove stress • *Goal:* Help your child recover	Critical mode
Moderately ill	• *Expectations:* Reduced • *Medical care:* Consistent, frequent follow-up • *Stress:* Reduce stress • *Goal:* Build on current functioning	Transitional mode
Mildly ill/partially stable	• *Expectations:* Gradually increase • *Medical care:* Regular follow-up • *Stress:* Reduce stress • *Goal:* Help your child build skills	Modified mode
Well/stable	• *Expectations:* Increase according to ability • *Medical care:* Maintenance • *Stress:* Help child regulate stress as needed • *Goal:* Maintain wellness, help child learn self-monitoring, and recover lost functioning	Wellness mode

with each level of stability include your child's moods, medical needs, ability to function, and ability to handle stress. As a parent, you will need to be flexible in meeting the needs of your child depending on the state of his illness. Please refer to the brief comparison chart on page 190 to learn how your parental behavior will change in each parenting mode.

Q. How do family attitudes affect recovery?

A. Your attitude toward your child and his illness can make a big difference in the speed and thoroughness of his recovery. Studies on how families express their emotions have given us some helpful guidance on things to avoid no matter what parenting mode is necessary. Please note that these attitudes and beliefs can also have a negative impact when coming from other primary people in the child's life, such as teachers. The following approaches could make your child's condition worse:

- Believing that the illness and symptoms are the child's fault
- Having screaming fights, yelling, and engaging in demeaning name-calling
- Making negative or critical comments about your child's illness ("Oh, I guess you are going to blame your bipolar disorder again.")
- Making negative or critical comments about your child's personality ("You are so lazy!")
- Blaming yourself and feeling overly guilty about your child's illness
- Using angry, harsh, and loud speech during a crisis
- Using facial expressions that tell your child you are disgusted or don't care
- Blaming your child

The following approaches can help your child no matter what state he is in or what parenting mode you are in:

- Learning about the illness and understanding it
- Using a low, calm, steady voice, even when your child is out of control
- Understanding that your child's illness is to blame, not your child
- Knowing that your child's illness is not your fault

- Using positive remarks about your child and his illness when possible ("What a great artist you are! You know, a lot of artists have bipolar disorder.")
- Refusing to engage in a shouting or fighting match when your child is unstable
- Supporting your child but allowing him to have outside success independent of you
- Having compassion and empathy for your child without pitying him or viewing him as a victim

Q. How do I parent in emergency mode?

A. We all hope that we will never have to parent in this way—it's necessitated by only the most difficult circumstances that can surround a child with bipolar disorder. This is when the illness is at its very worst and treatment is nonexistent, ineffective, or part of the problem. It is at this moment that your child will need you more than ever, though he may not treat you well or want your help. Parenting in emergency mode is quite likely the scariest moment parents can have with their child. Even

Child's state	Your child is severely ill. His primary need is to be kept safe so that he will not be a casualty of his illness. Suicide or violence toward others is a great risk.
Parent's goal	Your goal as a parent during this time is to maintain safety for your child and family. All other concerns are inconsequential. No other parenting goals can be achieved without basic safety.
Exercising parental authority	• Access immediate medical attention for your child; quite possibly, this may occur through emergency services and may lead to hospitalization. • Place siblings in a safe environment, possibly with another family member, until the crisis is stabilized.
Achieving the next level of stability	Your child must have medical intervention before he can move toward the next level of stability, which will include recuperation from the current episode.

so, it can sometimes be difficult to recognize when we as parents need to go into emergency mode. We could be lulled into thinking that suicidal gestures or comments are not a real threat or that the child simply needs to pull himself together. Additionally, the child may slip so quickly into this severe phase that it may not be recognized soon enough to help.

Q. How do I parent in critical mode?

A. Critical mode is also a phase of high alert—your child is only one step away from an emergency. This phase requires vigilance. It may be that a new treatment has been implemented and you are waiting for

Child's state	Your child is critically ill. His health is fragile and erratic. He may be recuperating from a crisis or on the verge of one. He does not function well at home or away. Safety is still a paramount concern.
Parent's goal	Your goal as a parent during this time is to prevent the further deterioration of health, to promote recuperation, and to maintain a safe environment.
Exercising parental authority	• Arrange necessary medical care. Your child may need an outpatient program or at least very frequent medical attention. • Maintain close supervision. Your child may be too fragile to be left alone. • Reduce as much stress as possible. • Keep a calm environment. • Allow other matters to drop unless they are extremely important. • Work with the school. Your child may need homebound services or a high level of educational intervention.
Achieving the next level of stability	Recuperation from a crisis takes time. Weeks may pass before your child begins to function to a higher degree. Continuing to give your child an appropriate recuperation environment or crisis prevention environment will be important to get him to the next level of stability.

results or that your child has just passed through an emergency. Parenting in this phase is still primarily concerned with helping the child survive and keeping everyone safe. Skill-building and learning cannot take place until your child is at a higher level of stability.

Q. How do I parent in transitional mode?

A. In transitional mode, your child is not on the verge of a crisis, and you are well past an emergency. Safety, while always a concern, has become much less of an issue. After being on high alert for so long, parents may try to switch to parenting in wellness mode without gradually increasing responsibilities and expectations, which is an important way to slowly ease your child back to a healthy state. A premature switch to parenting

Child's state	Your child is moderately ill. He has frequent mood swings, but he is functioning partially.
Parent's goal	Your goal as a parent during this time is to gradually help your child to build on his functioning and to learn to identify mood states and triggers.
Exercising parental authority	• Regularly follow up with medical care and reevaluate treatment with your child's physician. Your child may benefit from psychotherapy to help him identify triggers. • Continue stress reductions and maintain a calm environment. • Allow small matters to drop, but gradually start addressing issues that you may have had to let go of earlier. Consider doing this with the help of a therapist. • Work with the school. Accommodations and stress reduction at school are vital to prevent relapse.
Achieving the next level of stability	This level puts you squarely in the middle. It is just as possible to go backward to critically or severely ill as it is to go forward to mildly ill or well. Address additional issues that could be a roadblock to moving forward (learning disabilities, hidden medical problems like thyroid issues or sleep apnea, and so on).

in wellness mode can sabotage your child's progression toward wellness and may be enough to put your child back into a crisis state. Children in this time period are still moderately ill and need more intervention to move them toward wellness.

Q. How do I parent in modified mode?

A. Parenting in modified mode is focused on taking the opportunity to improve your child's functioning while still giving him enough support to succeed in new areas. Skills and development may have been lost

Child's state	Your child is mildly ill and can be categorized as partially stable. His moods are fairly consistent, and he functions fairly well. Unexpected situations, changes, or undue stress can still cause exaggerated responses and recurrence of minor instability.
Parent's goal	Your goal as a parent during this time is to identify areas that could solidify your child's stability and to help your child learn new skills that could not be mastered during instability.
Exercising parental authority	• Follow up with maintenance medical care. • Focus on helping your child learn self-calming techniques, mood and trigger identification, and socializing skills. • Gradually increase your child's responsibilities and expectations. • Arrange for your child to have successful outside interactions. • Work with the school to continue accommodations as appropriate and to make up for academic concepts that may have been lost.
Achieving the next level of stability	Be consistent with medication. Missing doses of medication makes it easier to go backward instead of forward. Avoid things like excessive caffeine and late-night bedtimes, which can throw off stability. Improve healthy living habits in the areas of nutrition, sleep, and personal interactions.

while your child was less stable, so in this mode you want to concentrate on restoring any lost skills while encouraging new ones.

Gradually increasing responsibilities while in this mode may be met with some resistance but is a necessary part of moving your child forward. Start slowly and use consistent rewards to encourage your child to be receptive to these added challenges. Giving your child the opportunity to have more responsibility also gives your child the chance to feel success and pride.

Q. How do I parent in wellness mode?

A. Wellness mode should not be mistaken for an easy task or for "normal" parenting. Even in wellness mode, you must parent according to the special needs of your individual child. As a parent, you must recognize the limitations that may come with executive functioning deficits, sensory integration difficulties, attentional or anxiety problems, and the constant risk of relapse.

Child's state	Your child is stable. He has the normal variations of moods that would be appropriate for his age. However, bipolar disorder still leaves its mark in areas that may or may not be visible to the outside world.
Parent's goal	Your goal is to optimize the length of this period of stability, to monitor for early warning signs of setbacks, to optimize your child's functioning by strengthening areas of weakness, and to understand any limitations that result from the illness.
Exercising parental authority	• Follow up with maintenance medical care. • Focus on helping your child learn life skills and possibly preparing for a vocation or further education if age appropriate. • Learn what your child's limitations are and work within this framework to help your child use his strengths to navigate around the weaknesses. • Maintain your child's responsibilities and expectations.

	• Arrange for your child to have regular, independent outside interactions. • Work with the school to continue accommodations as appropriate and encourage academic strides while your child is well.
Increasing time in this level of stability and preventing setbacks	Maintain wellness as long as possible by keeping your child medication-compliant, being in tune with your child's moods, and making adjustments as necessary. Fully understand the needs of your child. Teach your child self-monitoring techniques and healthy living techniques to minimize relapse now and later in life.

Q. What are the warning signs of backsliding?

A. Even when you try to minimize the time your child spends in states of instability, there will be times when he backslides into a lesser degree of stability. This is the nature of the illness. Being aware of early signs that your child is slipping in stability can help you address this more quickly. Be especially aware of possible warning signs if your child is experiencing a period of transition such as changing schools or moving, as this could precipitate instability. Also be aware that changing seasons, changing hormones, and growth spurts can also bring changes in stability. If all the warning signs are missed, you may find yourself back in emergency mode. Of course, every child can have an "off" day, but seeing warning signs over several days should be cause for concern. Here are some early warning signs that your child's stability is slipping:

- Your child regresses or begins to go backward in emotional behavior, throwing tantrums or otherwise behaving in a difficult way.
- Your child's functioning in school or at home begins to deteriorate.
- Your child is "on edge" and easily set off.
- You begin seeing increased symptoms of mania, depression, or both.
- Your child's tolerance for frustration decreases.

- Your child's ability to handle stimulation (noises, bright lights, and so on) decreases.
- Your child's sleeping pattern is thrown off.
- Your child's eating habits are different.
- Your child's interaction with family members deteriorates.
- Your child's interest in previous activities decreases or intensifies.
- Your child may have a specific sign or indication unique to himself.

Q. What should I do when my child backslides?

A. Children with bipolar disorder have frequent relapses. This is very difficult for parents. Once your child is well, you want him to stay well. Somehow, it feels like a failure to move back to a previous parenting mode when your child begins losing stability. But accepting and realizing that this *will* happen can help you to be ready for this reality and to minimize its effect. The sooner you can intervene, the more likely that the setback will be less severe and shorter.

Take some time to reevaluate your child's needs and to adjust your parenting mode accordingly when your child starts to backslide. If you switch gears early on, you will have a better chance of helping your child regain stability quickly. If you attempt to keep parenting in the same way while your child's stability has slipped back, you may find yourself in a more severe crisis requiring more drastic measures. Here are some things to do as soon as you notice a problem:

- Reduce stress! Reduce stress! Reduce stress!
- Attempt to regulate sleeping patterns.
- Address your concerns with your child to see if there is a stressor or trigger causing the setback.
- Communicate with the school to arrange for extra supports and monitoring. Make sure that established interventions are being followed.
- Follow up with your child's therapist and psychiatrist.
- If your child has a medication that requires a blood test to check therapeutic levels, ask for a test to make sure the levels have not dropped.

- If you have seasonal interventions approved by your child's psychiatrist, you may need to modify their use. For example, if your child uses a light box for added seasonal depression, it may be time to increase or decrease its use.

Q. What are the special needs of siblings?

A. Siblings of children with bipolar disorder also have special needs that must be addressed. They are living in households where their parents' time, resources, and energies are taxed to the maximum with an ill child. They are not simply bystanders but are often directly affected by their sibling's illness. An older sibling may feel that the parent is simply spoiling the younger sibling and letting him "get away" with things. A younger sibling may begin to accept an older sibling's mood instability as the norm and emulate it.

As a parent, it is not your job to parent each child exactly the same. It is your job to meet the needs of each child. This may confuse siblings when they see you adjust your parenting style for an ill child while the rules remain constant for them. Children in general love to point out when an injustice has been done by saying (or screaming), "It's not FAIR!" They are right. Bipolar disorder is not fair, but it is a reality that parents must address with all the siblings in the household.

Educate the siblings about the illness as appropriate for their age. Hiding the diagnosis from siblings is a huge disservice to them and will only lead to further confusion. Children do have the capacity to understand that there are special needs. Adequately meeting the well sibling's needs will increase his ability to deal with his ill sibling. In fact, sometimes it is a sibling who becomes one of the greatest advocates for his brother or sister.

Here are some ways to meet the needs of siblings:

- Arrange special one-on-one time with one parent and siblings.
- Educate the siblings about the illness. (Sibling books can be found at http://www.bpchildren.com.)
- Include siblings in family therapy, or arrange their own sessions.
- Consider letting siblings join a sibling group or attend a sibshop, which is a workshop for siblings of children with special needs (http://www.siblingsupport.org).

- Validate and respect the feelings of siblings.
- Make sure siblings have time with friends and extended family.
- Give siblings a space of their own.
- Make sure that siblings are safe and feel safe.

Q. What if siblings show the same behaviors?

A. You may notice that a sibling is starting to manifest the same behaviors as your child with bipolar disorder. This can happen for two reasons. First, it could be a manifestation of the illness. Bipolar disorder runs in families, and a sibling of a child with bipolar disorder will have a greater chance of having the illness than the average person. Second, the sibling may have started to mimic the behaviors of your child with bipolar disorder.

If the symptoms that you are seeing are severe, let a psychiatrist decide if it is mimicking or a presentation of the illness. If they are milder behaviors, talk to your child and reinforce behavior that is acceptable. Also make clear what the consequences of difficult behaviors will be. If your child is able to modify behavior with typical parenting intervention, then it is not likely a manifestation of the illness. However, if these problems persist, then you will want to take the sibling for an evaluation. Even if the sibling doesn't have bipolar disorder, he may need therapy to work through sibling issues.

Some parents find it exceedingly difficult to get help when a second child has an onset of the illness. Many parents hold onto the idea that having at least one "well" child proves that their parenting is not at fault. But seeking help for a second child is not a failure any more than it was for the first child. This is not about how you as a parent can feel justified. It's about making sure that all children in your family are appropriately cared for.

Q. What if parents disagree on how to raise the children?

A. On a perfect planet, all parental teams would agree on how to raise their children. Unfortunately, that planet is not ours! Parents with "typical" children frequently disagree on how to approach parenting, and having a child with special needs makes it much more challenging. There are several scenarios that can occur.

The first is that one parent understands the illness and is trying to parent accordingly, while the other parent refuses to accept that there is any problem. A second scenario is that both parents accept that there is an illness, but one "checks out" mentally and gives little support, while the other parent becomes overwhelmed. A third scenario is that one of the parents may simply be too overwhelmed with his own strong emotions to adequately address the needs of the child. Or maybe both parents recognize and understand the illness but still disagree on how to handle the child.

It is very important to try to come together when parenting a child with bipolar disorder. Your child needs both of you to understand his needs and address them together. Agreeing on the same parenting goals may take some time but will be worth the effort. Here are some ways to begin working together:

- Go to doctor appointments together so that both parents have an opportunity to ask questions and gain information.
- Join a local support group together where both parents can talk to other parents of children with bipolar disorder about what techniques have been successful.
- If a parent has an untreated or undiagnosed condition, make treatment for the parent a priority.
- Handle disagreements in private, not in front of the children.
- Recognize the areas you do agree on, and start from there.
- Consider family therapy.

Q. Should my child be disciplined while unstable?

A. Discipline is the art of teaching your child through training; it is not about punishment for undesirable actions. Good, effective discipline recognizes a child's ability, age, and development and adjusts accordingly. You never want your child to be without guidance, training, and discipline. While training should be continuous, the goal and method of this training changes according to stability.

During times of instability, training will let go of unimportant things and focus on things such as health, safety, and regaining emotional control. Work with your child's therapist to teach your child appropriate strategies that will help him handle strong emotions. Reward him for recognizing his emotions and for implementing any self-calming technique. If you engage your child in shouting matches when emotions are running high, you are not training him to quiet strong emotions—you're teaching him how to escalate a situation.

What if your child damages property when unstable? Your child won't benefit from a long lecture in the heat of the moment, but when the situation has passed, it may be appropriate to impose restitution for the damage. Don't use harsh discipline or guilt to try to prevent a future episode. This will be ineffective and may have negative consequences on self-esteem. However, children with bipolar disorder can learn that their actions, even when unstable, affect other people—require an apology and replacement of items damaged. Teaching your child to repair both relationships and material things is a good life lesson.

As your child comes nearer to stability, discipline will adjust again. You can start to pick a skill or two to begin working on with clear expectations and positive reinforcement. Help your child find success and build on it. Periods of stability can inspire tremendous leaps of growth in maturity.

Q. What if my child becomes violent?

A. When very unstable, some children with bipolar disorder become physically aggressive or violent. This behavior may include hitting, kicking, punching, and spitting at other people. Especially during periods of psychosis, a child may feel threatened and lash out. Though this behavior is more than likely not under the child's control during a mood episode, you can't let it continue. It's not good or healthy for you, your family, or the child.

If your child becomes violent, make sure that siblings go to a safe place in the house. If you can maintain household safety until the episode passes, then do so, but follow up with a call to the psychiatrist. Some children will calm down if they are held firmly, but others may get more agitated. Trying to restrain your child when he is agitated could cause injury to you or to your child. Check with your child's psychiatrist in advance to see if he feels this is appropriate for your child. If he feels that using restraint on your child is sometimes necessary for safety, then make sure you are taught how to do this in a safe manner that will not harm your child. If you cannot maintain the safety of all in the household, you may have no choice but to call 911. Immediate medical attention must be sought to intervene. If violence is an unusual occurrence that marks a regression or is the result of a recent change in treatment, it should be addressed immediately by informing your child's psychiatrist so he can adjust the treatment.

However, if violence is taking place regularly despite aggressive medical treatment, then it is time to reevaluate that treatment. First, make sure that none of the medications are having an adverse reaction that is actually worsening your child's condition. Is your child taking any "high-risk" medications that could be making things worse? Are medications at their optimal dosing? A consult with an expert in the field may give you a new direction to go in or provide more answers. Your child could have additional co-occurring conditions that are complicating treatment.

If you have done what you can to ensure that current treatment is appropriate and the violent behavior continues, it may be time to implement a higher level of therapeutic intervention. This could include hospitalization or day treatment. More intensive care may be necessary at least for a time to move your child into a safer level of functioning.

Q. What should I do if Child Protective Services gets involved?

A. Children with bipolar disorder sometimes exhibit behaviors that are confusing to other people. If someone has no understanding of the illness or its symptoms, they may make an allegation of abuse based on false assumptions about the cause of the behaviors. For instance, about a quarter of children with bipolar disorder show hypersexuality as a symptom of their illness before they reach puberty. Up to 70 percent show this symptom after reaching puberty. Especially when a manic child is hypersexual, an outsider might conclude that the only basis for such behavior is sexual abuse in the household. Additionally, self-inflicted wounds could be blamed on parents, or the sound of a raging child through apartment walls may lead the neighbors to incorrect conclusions about what is taking place. Even statements made by the child when in a state of psychosis could mislead other adults.

In light of the risks of a possible false allegation of abuse, it is important for parents to be educated. One hopes this never happens; however, there are a few things you can do in advance to help your situation. First of all, learn your rights as a parent—you will be less likely to sign them away or verbally renounce them if Child Protective Services (CPS) comes to check in on your family. To learn more about your rights, visit http://www.accused.com and http://www.fightcps.com.

Keep documentation of your child's medical history and medications. If your child has had overtly hypersexual symptoms, put your concerns regarding these symptoms in writing to your child's doctor and keep a copy. If CPS does become involved, ask for your lawyer to be present during questioning, and tape-record or document all conversations. If your child is already in foster care, then comply with reunification requirements. For a referral to a lawyer, visit http://www.falseallegation.org.

Q. How can a single parent manage?

A. If you are a single parent raising a child with bipolar disorder, your job is undeniably difficult. What are some realistic things you can do to be successful?

- **Prioritize:** You may have to let lesser items go while making sure that vital tasks are still accomplished.

- **Simplify:** The less you have to bog you down, the easier it will be to handle the responsibilities of raising a child with bipolar disorder. While this is easier said than done, you may have to say no to unnecessary demands on your time and your finances.

- **Rest:** When you go full speed twenty-four hours a day, you will burn out. Take care of yourself, and make sure you get needed rest.

- **Rely on others:** Single parents may try to avoid relying on other people, but you should always accept help when you need it. Try to build a support system of families, friends, or people in your religious organization. These are the people you can call to pick your child up from school or help you not just in an emergency but also with the difficult day-to-day affairs of raising your child.

- **Get support:** In addition to the support you receive from family and friends, try to connect with other single parents in a similar circumstance. It helps to be able to talk to someone who really knows what it's like to be in your shoes.

- **Collaborate:** If your child's other parent is in the picture, try to work collaboratively on parenting issues. While it can be exceedingly difficult to deal with an ex, you may need to find a way to work together to parent this child. This may be easier after years have passed and emotions are not raw from a breakup.

Q. Where can I find support?

A. Families who have a child with bipolar disorder need support from those who understand the illness. Sometimes extended families, church members, and friends are great supports, and if so, lean on them. If they aren't supportive, you may find that with time they will grow in their understanding. Even so, you likely need support now, not when others are ready to help. You may also find yourself longing for the support that comes from talking to other parents in the same situation. There are many support groups both online and in person that can help fulfill this need. Some of these groups are specifically for parents who have children with bipolar disorder, and others are a little broader and may include parents who have children with a variety of challenges.

Your child's psychiatrist may be aware of local support groups. Both the National Alliance on Mental Illness (http://www.nami.org) and the Depression and Bipolar Support Alliance (http://www.dbsalliance.org) have chapters all over the country where you can find support. A search on their website will give you links and contacts for groups near you. Also, many community treatment centers and hospitals have support groups associated with them, so check these local resources. Sometimes the newspaper will carry a listing of times of group meetings.

At http://www.bpkids.org, you will find a listing for local support groups, or you can join one of their email support groups. These support groups do more than simply encourage; they educate their members about brain illness and advocacy. You will find this a valuable way to continue expanding your knowledge about the illness.

Chapter 13

HELPING YOUR CHILD FIND HIS WAY

- How can I help my child self-calm?
- How can I teach my child to identify moods?
- How can I help my children get along with each other?
- How do I help my child see the positives?
- How can I identify and nurture my child's gifts?
- How can I foster strength and resilience?
- How can I create positive experiences?
- How can I nurture self-esteem?
- How can I encourage his dreams?
- Why do I need an action plan?
- What is the first step in my plan?
- What is the destination?
- How do I map the course?
- How do I develop goals?
- How do I reach the goals?
- How do I identify roadblocks?
- What is an example of an "action plan"?
- What are more "area of need" examples?
- Do I need to make these plans with my child?
- How can I teach my child to make a plan?
- What if I'm too overwhelmed to make a plan?

Q. How can I help my child self-calm?

A. One of the most important skills for your child to learn is how to self-calm. While this won't be something he can accomplish when he is very unstable, it is something to start working on as your child begins to stabilize. Some children will instinctively do things to calm themselves down, but a parent could work against this without even realizing it. For instance, one thing that might help your child self-calm is removing himself from a situation. This sounds great, but if your child is in the middle of a disagreement with you or a teacher and he walks away, the adult may not recognize that this is indeed what the child needs to do to calm down. Forcing the child to stay may actually work against him as he learns and practices self-calming techniques. Eventually, you will want his emotions to be in check enough that he can stay and work through the issue, but until then, walking away may be a way for him to prevent a total loss of control over his emotions.

Additional tools for self-calming can be music, art, and poetry or almost anything that is soothing to your child. You may wish to establish a "calm corner" with your child in advance of an episode. You and your child can create a special place where he can go when feeling upset, overwhelmed, or out of control or when he just needs a break from stress. This is not a punishment spot but a safe spot where relaxation is practiced. Encourage your child to visit this spot and to practice calming techniques regularly.

Q. How can I teach my child to identify moods?

A. Identifying and naming moods is an important step in helping your child have a sense of control over his emotions. It can be quite difficult for children to know what they are feeling and to put a name to it, and even more so if that child has bipolar disorder. Especially as your child grows older, it is very important for him to be able to recognize, identify, and verbalize his moods. Begin this process at a young age. First, help your child learn about each emotion, what it feels like, and what it looks like. *My Roller Coaster Feelings Workbook* by Bryna Hebert is a great resource to help a young child begin recognizing emotions. Other books on feelings may also be appropriate to help your child.

You should also make statements to your child that identify moods. Simple statements like "I feel frustrated" or "Johnny seems happy" can help your child see the correlation between body language and emotion. Additionally, you can help your child start tracking his own moods by using a simple mood chart. A free, printable mood chart for children can be found in the "Fun for Kids" section at http://www.bpchildren.com. Set aside a few minutes each day to help your child record his moods for the day. Keep this time positive—it's not an opportunity to scold or to make your child feel bad. It is simply a time to recognize feelings. As your child improves his ability to recognize his own moods, he is taking the first steps toward self-management of his illness.

Q. How can I help my children get along with each other?

A. Fighting can be a big issue in households with more than one child, and your child with bipolar disorder may be particularly difficult for siblings to get along with. His low tolerance for frustration can make playtime more like a war zone. Additionally, stressful interaction with the other siblings may trigger a mood episode in your child with bipolar disorder, or alternately, he might incite or aggravate the other children to fulfill his need for stimulation. Boredom can indeed be the enemy! Then, of course, some households have more than one child with bipolar disorder. This double blessing is a double challenge. Here are some ideas to help things run more smoothly:

- **Have separate rooms:** It is important for each of your children to have his own space. Your children with and without bipolar disorder both need to have a spot to go to when things are too tense. Being in the same room makes it difficult to separate them when necessary.

- **Have an "open door" policy:** When one child is unstable, it is important to closely supervise sibling interaction; make sure that the door to whichever room they're in remains open at all times You need to be able to check often and both see and hear what is going on in the room.

- **Schedule activity:** Your child with bipolar disorder is less likely to cause contention if he is engaged in an activity. He may qualify to be enrolled in a mentoring program, or you may be able to find a friend within your religious organization who will buddy up with him. Taking him out for an occasional separate activity can give the other kids in the family a needed break as well as help keep your child with bipolar disorder focused.

Q. How do I help my child see the positives?

A. Just as some parents may find it difficult to focus on the positives of raising a child with bipolar disorder, some children may find no positives in having the illness. As you strive to achieve and maintain a positive attitude about your parenting, seek to help your child find the good in it as well.

The changes in your child's brain that may cause instability in emotions may also cause creativity or giftedness in another area. Your child may be a talented artist, poet, inventor, or philosopher. Perhaps he has unique negotiation skills. His obsessive nature may make him proficient in a specific area of knowledge. Additionally, battling against an illness at such a young age may have given him an insight into the emotions of others who suffer. It may have given him a unique and compassionate perspective on life.

Help your child find his silver lining and identify positives in the midst of negatives. This can be exceedingly difficult, especially if he is unstable. But as time goes by, you may be surprised to see his confidence in the skill area you've emphasized as a positive. Also, when the whole family comes to view the child in a positive manner, then the family is in a better position to support and encourage him—even siblings should be encouraged to find the positives of having a sibling with bipolar disorder. By helping your entire family realize the unique gifts of your child with bipolar disorder, you will help him feel less like "damaged goods" and more like an amazingly special individual who has both challenges and gifts to offer. He may feel less like a burden to the family and more like a contributing member.

Q. How can I identify and nurture my child's gifts?

A. First, realize that your child does have gifts—watch for them and look for opportunities to draw them out. To identify your child's gifts, try exposing him to various creative outlets such as art and music. Notice what your child is attracted to, but don't immediately discount areas that he may fear; overcoming a fear could lead to recognition of a gift that neither you nor your child would expect. For instance, one young man with bipolar disorder was terrified of getting up in front of his class to speak. This same young man now is a proficient public speaker who motivates others.

Also, think about those qualities that may cause your child to struggle now. Once he has gained some maturity and more control over them, they may be the very things that are a gift. Many of the negative symptoms in bipolar disorder can turn into positives when the symptom is modified through medical treatment and channeled appropriately, such as the following:

- **Anger:** When your child has the ability to control this emotion, it can turn into a passion against injustice.

- **Excessive energy:** When controlled and toned down, manic energy can help your child get things done later in life. Many people with bipolar disorder credit their college degrees to hypomanic energy.

- **Depression:** When treated, depressive traits can give a person the ability to be reflective and philosophical.

- **Hyperfocus:** Modifying hyperfocus to be simply "focus" can be a very positive thing—in the working world, they may call this person a goal-oriented achiever.

- **Anxiety:** Too much anxiety is bad, but being mildly anxious may provide a sharpened awareness of surroundings and other people.

- **Obsessions:** While obsessions are intrusions, their milder counterpart is organizational skills. Many successful people are a tad obsessive.

- **Hallucinations:** Children who are prone to hallucinations also may be very visual and imaginative. Once hallucinations are controlled, your child may be able to retain his visualization abilities.

Q. How can I foster strength and resilience?

A. Strength is a person's capacity to endure, and resilience is the ability to spring back after being stretched to the limit. Clearly, these traits are important for both children with bipolar disorder and their parents. We all possess a measure of strength and resilience, sometimes much more than we realize. Fostering these qualities in ourselves and our children can be extremely beneficial.

While one person may be strong on his own, an interconnected group is even stronger. If a rope is made up of a single cord, it will snap more easily than if it is made of several cords intertwined. Both you and your child need to be interconnected with others in ways that make you stronger. Build strong relationships and help your child do the same with people who will be there to believe in him and to give him strength even when he might not have enough on his own. Resiliency is built by learning from mistakes and building on successes. See your missteps not as failures, but as opportunities to learn and grow. Foster this same attitude in your child; don't overprotect him from making mistakes, but help him learn from them. Important life lessons can be learned this way, but at the same time, be sure to give your child plenty of opportunities for success.

No matter what the current level of strength and resiliency in your family, you can increase it. In this way, you will be helping yourself and your child prepare for a successful future while dealing with this illness.

Q. How can I create positive experiences?

A. You may be concerned that repeated negative experiences will have a lasting effect on both yourself and your child. Indeed, negative interaction with each other and outsiders can tear down the strength and resiliency of your family. It is important to foster positive experiences whenever possible. This is generally easier when you are associating with people who are understanding and receptive. If you are always around people who are negative to your family and your child, then your experiences are likely to be negative. This can even be true between yourself and your child. If you are always dwelling on the negatives surrounding your child's actions or illness, you will have a lot of negative experiences.

Consciously set up positive experiences. To do this, you need to understand your child's current abilities and what environment could foster a successful experience. Taking an unstable child into a shopping mall with tons of stimulation and things on which to hyperfocus will pretty much guarantee a negative experience. Watching a favorite movie at home with that child may end up being a much better experience. While stability will naturally increase the possible positive experiences, try to create as many as possible for the current mood state. Also, don't negate a positive experience with a later negative one. For instance, if you and your child shared a positive experience together at the park but a meltdown ensued on the way home, you still shared something good together. You still gained from the positive experience. It does mean, however, that your child still has difficulty transitioning from one event to another. Separate out the events. Use missteps as an opportunity to learn where your child is still having difficulty.

Q. How can I nurture self-esteem?

A. Nurturing self-esteem in a child whose illness tells him to hate himself is a real challenge. Nurturing your own self-esteem when typical parenting has failed is also a challenge. Think of encouraging self-esteem as laying the foundation of a strong home: even when times are tough and your self-esteem or that of your child is waning, the underlying foundation of self-esteem is still there.

Beware of things that will undermine your foundation of self-esteem. Negative talk is one of the fastest ways to undermine self-esteem. While sometimes this talk comes from others, it may also come from you. Do you repeatedly tell yourself that you are a bad parent? If you make one mistake, do you tell yourself you are a failure? Your thoughts matter. Focus on turning negative self-talk into positive statements. Recognize when you are doing a really good job of parenting in very difficult circumstances. When you make a mistake, remember it is just that—a mistake—and we all make them. Pick a few good qualities to recognize in yourself. When you start to engage in negative self-talk, stop and repeat your good qualities.

Practice doing the same with your child. Don't speak negatively to him—he likely has his own negative inner voice that needs countering. If you speak negatively to him as well, it will simply reinforce the negativity of his inner voice. Avoid sweeping statements that blame and accuse, like

"You always do..." or "You never do...." Replace these with statements such as "I know this can be a challenge for you, but I also know you have a great mind that can find a way around this problem." Look for every opportunity to praise yourself, your child, and everyone in your family—that way, you'll build a self-esteem foundation you can rely on when times get tough.

Q. How can I encourage his dreams?

A. Many parents feel conflicted about encouraging their child with bipolar disorder to pursue his dreams. As parents, it can be difficult to know when to encourage a dream and when to give your child a reality check. Even if it's clear that they're following something that won't happen, if you tell them so, you could risk a breakdown.

Certainly some actors, politicians, musicians, and businesspeople have bipolar disorder. Don't be quick to crush your child's dreams or to tell him that something is unrealistic. If he is manic or grandiose, you likely can't reason with him anyway, and the fantasy may pass as he stabilizes. Also recognize that all children have dreams both realistic and unrealistic as they grow.

If this dream is a lasting and reasonable goal, even if it is ambitious, encourage your child to reach his dream by setting up smaller goals that could lead there. For instance, if acting is an interest, you may consider enrolling him in a local theatre group. This could help him see if the interest is something he wants to continue to pursue or if it's not really for him after all. If you are constantly pointing out the negatives of a particular dream, then you become the enemy. Your child may decide that you just don't want him to succeed and hyperfocus on the goal even more. Help your child be the one to discover what's right for him—let him explore lots of options and find what he likes.

Q. Why do I need an action plan?

A. Raising a child with bipolar disorder can be rewarding and challenging. In the most difficult times, you may be overwhelmed and emotionally drained. This can make it difficult to decide what you should do; in fact, it can freeze you in your tracks. On the flip side, when things are going well, it may be tempting to just "go with the flow." After all, it is a nice break from the difficult times. But neither of these approaches will help move your child toward better functioning. As the old saying goes, "If you have no plan, then you plan to fail." You would not be reading this book if you wanted to fail. You want clear direction. Making a plan for your child is a way to take what you have learned from this book and to apply it directly for the benefit of your family and your child.

Some people feel a bit silly writing down an action plan. But why should you? Do you budget your money? That is a monthly spending action plan. Do you have a mortgage? That is your bank's action plan for repayment. Do you have a will? That is your action plan for what should be done with your finances when you die. Do you write a grocery list? That is your shopping action plan. Is your child's health any less important? If making an action plan feels silly to you, put that feeling aside for now and do it anyway. You will be amazed at how this simple act will give you direction and focus and help you along your path.

Q. What is the first step in my plan?

A. An action plan doesn't have to be complicated—straightforward and concise plans are the easiest to follow. A good action plan outlines the following:

- Where you are now
- Where you are going
- What you need to do to get there
- How to overcome obstacles on the way
- How to take care of yourself

The first step in making your action plan is to reflect on where you are now. Title a sheet of paper "current status." Reflect on how your family is functioning, where your child is at medically, and your own emotional state. Go back to the parenting modes in Chapter 12 and determine which one best fits your current situation. Keep this current status statement to one paragraph; if you get too complicated, it will be more difficult to draw up your action plans. Don't be surprised if you feel emotional during this exercise. It can be difficult to actually put your current status in writing—somehow it makes the situation feel more real. But don't give up. This is just the first step to getting where you want to go. Here is an example of a possible current status:

Current status: Our family is currently in critical mode. Johnny was just diagnosed and is having frequent mood swings and is agitated easily. I am very frustrated with the school because they don't seem to be helping. My husband doesn't know how to approach our son in a way that keeps things calm. I'm concerned that Mary is not getting enough attention since our energies are focused on her brother.

Q. What is the destination?

A. After recording the status of your family right now, you need to figure out where you want to be. In the next step, you will record where you want your family and your child with bipolar disorder to end up. The final destination is really not an end point for your child, but it is where you want your child to be by the time he reaches adulthood. After that, he will be charting his own course. Take some time to think about the future. Be specific about what you want for your children, but be general enough to be flexible for their goals. Write a destination for both parents and children. A paragraph for each should suffice:

Destination (parents): Our family will be a supportive unit working together to help our children find success while we also pursue our own interests. I would like to become a counselor or an advocate helping other families. Hubby would like to advance in his field of work.

Destination (Johnny and Mary): Our children will be able to live as independently as possible. They will be prepared to either hold a job or pursue additional education of their choosing (online classes, vocational school, or college). Johnny will be able to interact with other people and manage his illness. Mary will understand her brother's illness and be well adjusted. They will both hold a strong moral and ethical code to guide them in whatever goals they choose. They will understand their strengths and use these to get around areas of weakness.

Q. How do I map the course?

A. Now that you know both where you are and where you need to go, the next logical question is, how do I get there? You need to identify the path to take. Using your destination statement, break down each goal into several categories. For example, the most common would be "education," "work skills," "social skills," and "medical management." There may be other areas according to your child's specific needs. Once you have identified the major areas of concern, ask what is lacking in each area. These will be the basis for determining the steps you need to take to reach your ultimate destination. Here are some example questions to help you:

If *education* is a concern:

Has my child been tested for learning disabilities?	yes	no
Are there additional learning struggles that have not been addressed?	yes	no
Does he have an IEP?	yes	no
Are accommodations being implemented?	yes	no
Does the current setting address his needs?	yes	no

If *work skills* are a concern:

Has my child talked about future employment?	yes	no
Is my child engaged in any volunteer work?	yes	no
Does my child have a part-time job?	yes	no
If my child is in high school, has the IEP addressed transition?	yes	no
Does my child have responsibilities at home?	yes	no

If *social skills* are a concern:

Is the IEP addressing social skills?	yes	no
Is my child in therapy to learn to interact appropriately?	yes	no
Does my child have opportunities to strengthen these skills?	yes	no

If *medical management* is a concern:

Has my child been evaluated by a psychiatrist?	yes	no

Does my child need a higher level of medical care?   yes   no
Does he need a second opinion?   yes   no
Are there other medical concerns to address?   yes   no

The answers to these questions will show you the actions you need to take.

Q. How do I develop goals?

A. There are several types of goals that you want to develop. You already have the end goal in mind, and now you want to develop short-term goals and midrange goals. The short-term goals will be the ones you focus on immediately—longer-range goals can't be accomplished without the help of these short-term goals. When making goals, it is helpful to work backward. When you see clearly where you want to go, it is easier to know what steps to take. Here are some examples:

Area of need: *Education*	*Johnny does not have an IEP or any accommodations in school.*
Destination goal	Johnny will be prepared to pursue additional education of his choosing.
Midrange goal	Johnny will find success in school through appropriate supports for his disability.
Midrange goal	Johnny will have an IEP or 504 plan by the end of this school year.
Short-term goal	I will write a letter to the school requesting a complete multifactored evaluation to determine if Johnny qualifies for services.
Short-term goal	I will learn more about my child's educational rights.
Area of need: *Medical management*	*Johnny began taking medication two weeks ago, but he has only slightly improved. Our next doctor appointment is still two weeks away.*
Destination goal	Johnny will be able to interact with other people and to manage his illness.
Midrange goal	Johnny will stabilize medically so he can grow in maturity and learn to manage his illness.

Short-term goal	I will monitor Johnny closely in case his symptoms escalate and he needs to be hospitalized.
Short-term goal	I will start charting Johnny's moods.
Short-term goal	I will call the doctor tomorrow and give an update to see if he should be seen sooner.

Q. How do I reach the goals?

A. Once you have developed goals in all your child's areas of concerns, you may feel empowered because you now have a clear path to take toward your child's wellness. At the same time, it could also be overwhelming if you try to focus on everything at once; if you become overwhelmed, this makes it difficult to take the first steps toward your goals. Once the action plan is written, pick the area that's more critical right now and one short-term goal to accomplish. That's it: one area and one goal. Then take that action. Guess what? Now you are one step closer to your destination. Once your short-term goal has been accomplished, you can either cross it off or write the completion date next to the goal.

Pace yourself. This is a marathon, not a sprint. Slow and steady will get you through your goals. As short-term goals get crossed off, it will be necessary to pencil in more short-term goals to get you to your midrange goals. If you find that a short-term goal just isn't working out like you had hoped, there is a nifty little device at the end of your pencil that can change that. Erase and replace. Realize that there may be several ways to reach the same destination—be flexible. Choosing better, alternate paths is always good.

To be successful in this process, it's helpful to surround yourself with supportive people who encourage reaching these goals. It is especially helpful if both parents become engaged in the process of setting and reaching goals; that way, you can help each other and might find new and important short-term goals when you work together.

Q. How do I identify roadblocks?

A. Roadblocks may come in many forms: some that are easily recognized and some that are in disguise. A roadblock is anything that keeps you from reaching one of your goals, whether it is a short-term goal or the final destination. Here are some common roadblocks:

- **Discouragement:** Discouragement can be one of the biggest obstacles to reaching your goals. When you feel discouraged, focus on how much progress has been made instead of how much further there is to go. Take some time to recharge. Changing your focus may help you see that this roadblock is much smaller than it seemed at first. Once you have it in perspective, you may be able to jump right over it.

- **Lack of education:** Not knowing how to go about accomplishing a goal can be very intimidating, especially when you are dealing with legal rights. If you are hit by this roadblock, then change your short-term goal in that area to getting the education you need to move forward. Like most roadblocks, this will evaporate when it is addressed.

- **Finances:** This roadblock is perhaps the most frustrating. If you know what services your child needs but can't access these due to financial constraints, it can feel like a dead end. If this roadblock is in your way, change your short-term goal to investigating other financial options. There are generally alternate routes around this block.

- **Bureaucracy:** Dealing with systems of care, education, government, and insurance can be another big roadblock. Sometimes it feels like the red tape alone will bury your action plan. When this roadblock is in your path, it's not a matter of removing it but a matter of navigating through it. Look for someone who has experience and tap into it. We all need a guide at certain points in the journey.

Q. What is an example of an "action plan"?

A. This example action plan deals with one major issue for a child named Brianna who has bipolar disorder. An action plan template can be found in Appendix C.

Action Plan for Brianna
dd/mm/yyyy

Current status	Our family is in transitional mode. Brianna functions in school, but she loses it at home. She is experiencing extreme frustration over homework, especially writing assignments. She is having difficulty with her sleep/wake cycle. We are following the therapist's advice to let go of minor issues for now. We are focusing on having a successful morning routine.
Destination	Brianna wants to become a veterinary assistant. She will have the skills needed to live independently and work in her chosen field. Brianna will be able to manage her illness and self-report to her doctor. Brianna will understand personal interaction and be able to have meaningful relationships.
Area of need: *Education*	*Brianna's IEP is not addressing homework issues and her extreme difficulty with handwriting.*
Destination goal	Brianna needs the skills to work in her chosen field. She will need handwriting or keyboarding skills.
Midrange goal	She will receive occupational therapy or assistive technology to address handwriting concerns.
Midrange goal	I will give her the tools and accommodations she needs to make it through her afternoon homework without melting down.
Short-term goal	I will write to the school requesting an IEP meeting to discuss handwriting and homework concerns. I will prepare a letter to bring to this meeting requesting an evaluation for occupational therapy services and assistive technology services due to issues with handwriting.
Short-term goal	Hubby will call the insurance company to see if it pays for a private occupational therapy evaluation.

Q. What are more "area of need" examples?

A. After Brianna's mother wrote the letter to the school and her father called the insurance company, Brianna's mother felt so encouraged that she was able to then address several more areas of need by writing out more goals based on the current status and desired destination.

Area of need: *Work skills*	*Brianna will need controlled exposure to her desired field of work.*
Destination goal	Brianna would like to be a veterinary assistant.
Midrange goal	Brianna will take an online course to prepare her for this position.
Midrange goal	Brianna will work part-time at a local vet office for training and experience.
Short-term goal	Brianna and I will surf the internet together to find information for online schools in this field.
Short-term goal	I will call the local animal shelter to see if Brianna and I can volunteer on Wednesdays after school.

Area of need: *Medical management*	*Brianna's sleep issues are significantly interfering with her functioning.*
Destination goal	Brianna's sleep/wake cycle will be evened out enough to allow for her to function well during the day.
Midrange goal	Brianna will be able to wake up to an alarm clock and to get ready for school with minimal prompting (two wake-up prompts from us).
Midrange goal	Use a dawn simulator as recommended by the psychiatrist to help Brianna with morning wakefulness.
Short-term goal	Hubby will look for budgeting options to save money for a dawn simulator. (Possibly ask grandma to consider contributing to this instead of her usual school clothes purchase for Brianna.)
Short-term goal	I will schedule an appointment with the sleep specialist who was recommended by Brianna's psychiatrist to rule out an additional sleep disorder.
Short-term goal	Start melatonin as recommended by the psychiatrist to promote a better sleep/wake cycle.

Q. Do I need to make these plans with my child?

A. The action plan centers on your child's needs and future, but it is *your* action plan for your child's benefit. Certainly it should be made only after considering your child's particular and unique needs and desires, but it does not necessitate the direct involvement of your child while the plan is being written. You should have frequent conversations with him about what he wants to do in the future and so forth, but much of the plan is more about you as a parent helping your child to move toward independent and successful functioning.

Even so, some parents may feel strange about setting goals, especially the long-term ones, without the direct involvement of the child whom it concerns. This is an individual choice, but before you involve your child in making this action plan, consider your child's maturity and stability level. Some children will be mature enough to understand the plan and give input. In fact, it may get them excited about moving toward the future and help you determine and focus on the areas that are the most important to your child. Other children may simply be too young to understand the plan, and still others may have a negative reaction. A very unstable child may even rip up the plan. If you perceive that your child is not able to be part of this process, there is certainly nothing wrong with going ahead without their direct involvement. You will most likely be able to show it to them someday, and they'll appreciate all your help.

Q. How can I teach my child to make a plan?

A. As you see the effectiveness and benefits of having your own plan, you may want to teach your child how to make an action plan of his own. Learning to make an action plan will be a skill that your child can carry with him into adulthood. A child's plan should center on his needs and desires, not yours. It must be simple and easy to follow. Help your child realize that not everything they try will work but that having a plan gives them a place to start and ideas for new things to try if one idea doesn't work out. Here is a sample of a young child's action plan:

My Action Plan
Justin

What I want to do:	*I want to be friends with James again.*
Why I want to do this:	*He was my best friend, but I yelled at him when I was angry and now he won't talk to me.*
Three things I want to try (if you can't think of three things, ask your parents or a friend to help with ideas):	1. *Send him a card to say I'm sorry.* 2. *Give him a week or two to calm down.* 3. *Invite him over to watch a movie and eat pizza.*

As your child grows, he will be able to set more goals and fill out a more detailed action plan. Go to Appendix F for both a young child's action plan template and an older child's action plan template.

Q. What if I'm too overwhelmed to make a plan?

A. Perhaps you have come to this chapter in the book at a time when you are feeling too overwhelmed to make any plan for your child. If this is the case, put the action plan aside for now and do one thing. Close your eyes and focus on breathing. Breathe in through your nose, filling your lungs completely, then breathe out through your mouth. Think only of your breathing and nothing else. Do this for five minutes, setting an alarm if you need one.

Once your five minutes are up, write down the most important thing you need to do for yourself. It may be scheduling an appointment with a therapist, or it may be taking care of yourself in some other way. Whatever it is, consistently follow up on this one thing for the next week. If you don't know what you should do for yourself, then do your breathing exercise every day. When you start to feel less stressed and overwhelmed, then begin making a plan by writing a parent self-care plan (see Chapter 14). You can do a shortened version of the plan if it is too much to think of the whole thing.

Don't start on any other plan yet; implement your self-care plan only. You can not make an effective action plan for your child if you are not well cared for yourself. If you continue to feel overwhelmed or hopeless, see a psychologist or psychiatrist. You need support on this journey.

Once you feel that you are in a better place emotionally, consider asking a trusted friend to assist you in making an action plan. Start by focusing on only one area of need with corresponding goals. Step by step this process will become easier.

Chapter 14

PARENTAL EMOTIONS

- Why do I have all these emotions?
- How can I keep my cool when my child loses his?
- Why do I have such strong negative emotions?
- How do I regain my parental warmth?
- When is it time for me to seek professional help?
- Will my children be taken away?
- How can I accept my child's illness?
- How can I stay off my child's roller coaster of emotions?
- What should I do if I'm at a breaking point?
- How do I deal with relatives who don't understand?
- Should I be scared to have another child?
- What are the positives of parenting a child with bipolar disorder?
- What if I feel very negative about parenting?
- How can I help others understand my child?
- How can abandoning preconceived notions help?
- How can I celebrate each day?
- What is a parent self-care plan?
- How can I make a parent self-care plan for myself?
- What is an example of a parent self-care plan?

Q. Why do I have all these emotions?

A. With the onset of bipolar disorder, a parent's life becomes filled with worries, doctor's appointments, medication trials, advocacy with the schools, and facing a society that still prefers to blame parents for a child who suffers from a brain disorder. In light of these difficulties, it is normal for parents of children with bipolar disorder to grieve. Some have compared this grieving to the process that people go through when a loved one dies. But this doesn't exactly fit what happens to parents of children with bipolar disorder. Instead of having grief that progresses through phases of emotions and then resolves, their grief becomes recurring. While the initial phase may be the most intense— feelings may range from fear to guilt, from anger to sorrow—these feelings may resurface when the illness worsens, a medical trial fails, or their child misses an important developmental milestone.

While it is normal to have these feelings, if a parent becomes stuck in the emotions of grief, it could immobilize him. While no one can tell you how to grieve, you may want to examine your own perceptions about bipolar disorder, which could be negatively impacting the grieving process. There are many views of illness, and how we react to a diagnosis is influenced by our preconceived notions about the disease. If you believe that your child has developed bipolar disorder as some type of punishment from a higher power or you're blaming yourself for it, it will be harder for you to deal with it.

Questioning your own view of illness may empower you, and realizing that you are not powerless can help you with the emotions of grief. While it is true that you may not be able to "cure" your child, you can have a significant positive influence over his future if you can control your emotions and help him control his.

Q. How can I keep my cool when my child loses his?

A. Keeping your cool with an unstable child may be one of the most difficult things you ever do. When your child is in a state of agitation, it is important not to throw fuel on the fire by being pulled into a yelling match. First, recognize that you didn't provoke the outburst and can't control this part of the disorder—your child is just going to have bad days. On the flip side, there are days when you have less ability to deal with your child. You are not Superman or Superwoman, and you don't have to be. If you do lose your cool and perhaps say or do something you regret, then regroup and start fresh for the next time.

Here are some things to help you keep a level head when you're child loses his cool:

- **De-escalate:** De-escalate the situation before it gets to the boiling point. Don't allow small issues to be blown out of proportion. Know which parenting mode you are in and stick to your goals.

- **Give yourself space:** If things are getting too heated, give yourself a time-out. Stop speaking and separate. Your child may be stuck on an idea or on a feeling. Trying to reason him out of this state is likely to just make things worse.

- **Listen to your inner voice:** Some parents find that an inner voice helps them keep things in perspective. For example, you might tell yourself, "His brain is stuck," or "I will stay calm." Say it over and over in your mind while saying nothing out loud.

- **Visualize:** Other parents find it helpful to picture a lighthouse or a strong tower with waves hitting the base but standing still, strong, and firm. Your child needs your strength.

Q. Why do I have such strong negative emotions?

A. When you are dealing with a very unstable child or even with low-grade instability over a lengthy period of time, your parental warmth may become taxed. It might become difficult to separate the child from the illness. Indeed, you may even begin to have strong negative emotions regarding your child. Some parents may even become afraid that they "hate" their own child. This strong negative reaction should not be mistaken for a lack of love, but it is a huge red flag that could indicate one of several closely related problems:

- **Caregiver burnout:** The effects of caring for a chronically ill child have long been recognized. There is a great degree of stress that inevitably accompanies this job, and when that stress overwhelms you to the point that you no longer have hope for the future, you feel helpless, and you become devoid of feeling, numb, detached, or depressed, you may be experiencing caregiver burnout.

- **Secondary trauma:** Some children with bipolar disorder may experience trauma as a byproduct of a severe episode, especially psychosis that leads to a hospitalization. As the primary caregiver, you may go through a type of secondary trauma while caring for your child, like a husband who develops a "sympathetic pregnancy" along with his wife. You may experience a type of emotional trauma, particularly if your child's illness has led to abusive behaviors toward you.

- **Compassion fatigue:** Showing compassion and understanding to your child is vitally important. However, if you repeatedly internalize your child's strong emotions, it could lead to compassion fatigue. This can make it difficult to show any compassion.

Q. How do I regain my parental warmth?

A. If you are experiencing caregiver burnout, secondary trauma, or compassion fatigue, you can recover the capacity to express parental warmth for your child. You may even be able to avoid these conditions altogether if you make adjustments prior to their onset. The key is to set up balanced guidelines ahead of time that will give you the ability to lower stress and recharge. Parents may feel guilty if they take time out to care for themselves—don't! You absolutely must care for yourself; it means that you will have ability to care for your child. Here are some ways to rejuvenate yourself to better care for your child:

- **Obtain support:** You must have adequate emotional support from friends or family as well as excellent medical support. If you are not yet taking advantage of the services that a therapist and a support group can offer, do so.

- **Pace yourself:** Get your rest every day, but also schedule respite times. If you don't have a family member who can give you a break, consider looking into more intensive services for chronically ill children, like an outpatient program that will take care of your child a few hours a day. You could also find trained caregivers to come to your home, but that might incur a large expense.

- **Get proper nutrition:** Pay attention to what goes in your body. Feed your body well and drink plenty of water.

- **Focus:** Be aware of your commitments. Practice saying "no" to friends or coworkers who zap your energy with extra tasks. Do say "yes" to your own hobbies or interests that help you recharge.

- **Practice spirituality:** For some people, fostering spirituality can give strength and an inner calm that cannot be obtained in any other way.

Q. When is it time for me to seek professional help?

A. Perhaps you have done all of the above and you are still seriously short-tempered, anxiety ridden, or depressed. Go seek professional help now. Get your own psychiatrist who can help you sort through your emotions. Some parents avoid seeing a psychiatrist, thinking that they can't allow themselves to be sick because they have to be there for their child. But if you are becoming sick yourself, not seeking the help you need will be detrimental to both you and your child. Think too of the type of example you want to set for your child. Do you want your child to seek help as an adult if his symptoms get out of control or are leading to personal suffering? Actively seeking help yourself can be the best way to teach your child this self-care skill.

You may not recognize the symptoms of burnout or compassion fatigue in yourself, but others may see them in you. It's easy to be insulted or offended if a partner or friend points out your symptoms. It's also easy to use your situation as an excuse not to seek help. One study revealed that even parents who were strong advocates of their young children with bipolar disorder suffered from "unrelenting fear, frustration, loneliness, and hurt." However, this is obviously not a reason to avoid help—it is an added reason to seek professional help. It is not beneficial to anyone, including your child, if you ignore symptoms and continue on an unhealthy path. You need and deserve to be healthy in all aspects and to have the strength to care for your child. If this means seeing a psychiatrist for your own symptoms—whether they are a result of caring for your child or totally independent from it—do it. You'll be a better parent for it.

Q. Will my children be taken away?

A. It can be terrifying for parents to seek help for symptoms of caregiver fatigue or even their own symptoms of an illness, because of the fear that such a visit could result in losing their children. However, while medical professionals are required to report abuse or neglect to Child Protective Services, they do not report routine psychiatric visits or even illness. Having symptoms of an illness certainly does not automatically mean that your child is at risk of being taken away from you. If psychiatrists routinely took children away from parents with caregiver fatigue or an illness, there would be millions of children without homes.

Indeed, it would be much more likely that a child would be removed from a home where parents are having uncontrolled symptoms that endanger the child or prevent them from adequately caring for the child than a home in which parents are caring for their own needs. There have been some instances in which a divorced parent has tried to use the other parent's illness to gain custody. This is a sad turn of events, but likely the same arguments could be made against a parent who has untreated symptoms.

If you have valid reason to be concerned because the home environment has become dangerous to your child, then you need help more than ever. It is not okay for your child to stay in a dangerous environment. You may wish to be proactive by arranging for your child to be cared for temporarily by a trusted family member while you get help so that you can safely care for your child once again. After all, if it were another illness interfering with your ability to care for your child, wouldn't you arrange temporary care? This is no different.

Q. How can I accept my child's illness?

A. If your child has bipolar disorder, it is important for you to accept the reality of the illness. Acceptance does not happen overnight but is a necessary part of healthy living for you and your child. First, let's understand what "acceptance" does not mean.

> **Acceptance does not mean helplessness.**
> **Acceptance does not mean giving up.**
> **Acceptance does not mean failure.**

Some people refuse to accept the illness, thinking that acceptance would mean defeat. But not accepting the illness when it is present absolutely means defeat—it gives you no basis for success, no avenue to get better. Full acceptance comes in stages, each of which has its own benefit.

The first step on the road to acceptance is recognition of the illness. Emotionally, this can be one of the most difficult stages. Recognition primarily comes from education and awareness and is vital to acceptance, but it's also just the beginning of the process. With time you can move into embracing the illness. Now you not only recognize the illness but also have made peace with its existence in your life. It also means that you have been able to identify both the negatives and positives about the illness. Some people use spirituality as a means to move through this phase. It is in this stage that you move beyond a type of "Why me?" mentality and onto "What now?"

The final stage of acceptance is empowerment. When you recognize the illness and embrace it, you are no longer held by the constraints of others or the idea that your child must be kept to a specific path to find success. Empowerment frees you to fully give your child what he needs to find success. It also lifts the shroud of shame and guilt. It allows you to fully advocate for your child despite the bias or prejudice of others.

Q. How can I stay off my child's roller coaster of emotions?

A. When your child's moods go up, down, and all around, it can be hard not to have your own emotions doing the same. It's important, however, that you as the parent maintain balance. You need to be a touchstone for your child; you are the steadying force. If your emotions are on the roller coaster with your child, how will he know what normal mood variation is? This is not to say that you will be unaffected or unmoved by your child's moods. You will be. But you don't have to be swept away by them. Here are some ways to help you stay off your child's emotional roller-coaster ride:

- **Let go of things you can't change:** Know your limitations as a parent. You can do a lot to help your child grow into a fine young adult, but you can't erase the illness and all its effects. Unreasonable expectations can lead to severe disappointment and plunge you into depression.

- **Define your life:** Your life should not be solely defined by your child's illness. You need to have outside interests and activities. Foster relationships and other interests. These will help keep you balanced during times of relapse.

- **Have an outlet:** Have your own touchstone or reality check. Have someone you can talk to and trust when things start going downhill. You may need to vent your frustration to an understanding source so you can be steady when dealing with your child's unstable emotions.

- **Seek help when needed:** If your child's strong emotions have sucked you in and taken you on a roller-coaster ride, it may be time to seek the help of a psychiatrist or therapist who can help you reach a better balance.

Q. What should I do if I'm at a breaking point?

A. Parenting a child with bipolar disorder is exceedingly difficult. At times, you may feel that you are at a point where you can no longer go on. This could be the result of a prolonged period of instability or a severely disappointing relapse. These circumstances are above and beyond the normal parental experience. Recognize that these feelings are a result of the extreme stress you are under and not due to a weakness in your character or your parental ability. Additionally, don't make any rash decisions while in this state. Feeling that you are at the breaking point may be a momentary emotional state, but there are things you can do if these feelings persist.

First, make sure that you are doing everything mentioned in this chapter to take care of yourself. Pay attention to your health, and know when to seek help. Neglecting these things is the fastest way to bring you to a breaking point. But you may be lacking one more important ingredient. To keep any object from breaking under extreme stress, one must apply reinforcement. One of the best reinforcements for your strength is *hope*. People have been known to endure extreme situations when they have the hope that the end is worth the struggle. Examine your beliefs and notions about your child's future. Do you see it as hopeful? You must, and there are many good reasons to believe it's true.

Start focusing on success stories. Your child can be one of them. Go to http://www.nostigma.org/speakers.php and look at these amazing young adults. Look at their faces, their hopes, and their future. They are living, breathing proof that your child has a future also. There will be dark hours, but there can be a bright light at the end of this tunnel.

Q. How do I deal with relatives who don't understand?

A. It can be disheartening when those close to you don't "get it" or even oppose your child receiving treatment, but unfortunately, this is not an uncommon situation. There is an old-fashioned stigma attached to psychiatric disorders, and sometimes the prejudice against people who suffer from them runs deep. If it is simply ignorance and lack of understanding, this may improve with time. Continued efforts to educate family members can pay off in the long run. But if your family doesn't understand your child's illness and is resistant to learning about it, you may need to look elsewhere for your major source of support. Realize that you are doing the best thing for your child, and focus on his needs; feel no pressure to accept misguided (though perhaps well-meaning) advice from family.

If, however, it is less a matter of understanding and more a matter of strong opposition in the form of antipsychiatry beliefs, this may change your relationship with that relative significantly. Strong opposition to psychiatry exists in some religious beliefs, and while every person has the right to exercise his belief, this may not be good for your family as you pursue medical treatment for your child. You may have to consider the toxic effect this negative belief could have on your family and your child's treatment.

At the least, you will want to make your child's treatment a taboo topic of conversation with this family member. If that relative still repeatedly makes you feel guilty for seeking help, undermines your efforts, or tears you down, you may have to consider minimizing contact with this individual despite the family relation.

Q. Should I be scared to have another child?

A. Many people already have all the children they planned on before they even realize that they have a child with bipolar disorder or that it's a genetic disease. By the time their child receives a diagnosis, they may be very glad they didn't know this information in advance. Children are a gift even when they come with medical problems. Also, while you may have one or two children with the disorder, it's very likely you'll also have healthy children.

Still, the toll that childhood bipolar disorder exacts on a family does make some people hesitant to have more children. This is true of all genetic disorders. People wrestle with these questions, and ultimately it will be up to you. Here are some factors that may weigh into your decision:

- **Stability of your child with bipolar disorder:** The severity of the illness and the stability level of your child with bipolar disorder may strongly influence your decision to have more children.

- **Time, energy, and finances:** You may want to consider your family resources and if they're plentiful enough to care for another child.

- **Genetic loading:** If both parents have bipolar disorder, the child has up to a 70 percent chance of having the illness. If neither parent has it but a sibling does, then the chances drop to somewhere between 15 and 25 percent. Obviously, not all risk factors are the same and not every child in the family will necessarily have the illness, but you can use these percentages as general guidelines.

- **Family desire:** What fits your family? Obviously, the desire for more children will factor strongly into this decision.

If your decision is to have another child, you will cherish and love that child whether he is healthy or ill. Every child can bring unexpected experiences and emotions. Life is about living through these experiences together, whether good or bad. All children are blessings who will enhance your life if you dare to see the positives in each person.

Q. What are the positives of parenting a child with bipolar disorder?

A. Having a child with special needs can totally change your perspective on life. It forces you to recognize positives that others may not see. You probably wish that your child did not have this illness above any other reasons because of the difficulties it brings to his life; however, there are some undeniable positives that come from raising a child with bipolar disorder:

- **Having the right focus:** In this fast-paced world, many families get lost in the world of work. Having a child with bipolar disorder forces a change in focus—you concentrate on your family, your children, and their needs.

- **Connecting with people:** Some of the most amazing friendships are formed over the common bond of raising children with bipolar disorder. These special friendships are a treasure.

- **Letting go:** Having children with bipolar disorder forces you to let go of preconceived ideas and notions about psychiatric illnesses.

- **Appreciating the small things:** You learn that small things can mean nothing and everything. You stop hyperfocusing on the small insignificant matters, but you also revel in the small joys of each moment.

- **Seeing the wider horizons:** You see the world in a new way. You understand people with disabilities and the unique gifts they bring to this world.

- **Learning with your child:** There is a special bond that forms when you embark on this journey with your child. It's not an easy road, but in the end your child knows how much effort you've put into getting them the best care and how loved they truly are.

- **Finding more compassion:** Your empathy, concern, and care for other people increases as you face the challenges of raising a child with special needs. You begin to understand that everyone has difficulties to face.

Q. What if I feel very negative about parenting?

A. Perhaps you have difficulty finding anything positive in your experience of parenting a child with bipolar disorder. You are not alone in feeling this way about your difficult task, but maintaining a negative mindset about your parenting responsibility could translate into negative feelings about your child as well. If you don't feel like you can relate to any of the positives in the list above, challenge yourself to find at least one thing you enjoy about parenting your child with bipolar disorder or something you have learned from it. When you find that positive—whether it is big or small—write it on a Post-It note and stick it on your bathroom mirror. Every time you think of another positive, post another note. When you actively start looking for positives, big or small, you may be amazed at the result.

Along with seeking out the positives, try to keep the negatives from overtaking your thoughts. It is certainly okay and healthy to have an outlet for the negative emotions provoked by raising a child with bipolar disorder. But if those negative emotions overtake everything, you can become disheartened in a way that makes it harder to fulfill your responsibilities. So, while you may acknowledge your negative feelings, don't foster and nurture them. One strong source of negatives is comparing your child to other more typical children. This is unhealthy to do, unfair to your child, and counterproductive. Remember too that you don't know what troubles are underneath the surface of another household. Many families have a false exterior that can hide some of the very troubles you deal with daily. To continue fostering a positive attitude, consider reading *The Feeling Good Handbook* by David Burns.

Q. How can I help others understand my child?

A. As a parent, you are keenly aware of both your child's struggle and his amazing spirit. You may even see more beauty in him because you know what a difficult road he has traveled. However, the outside world does not always share the same view of your child. Many times children with bipolar disorder are labeled as "troublemakers" or simply "bad." These labels could come from outbursts during a manic phase or from surliness during depression or from any other behavioral troubles that people may not understand are due to your child's illness.

As a parent, this can be painful. Of course you wish very much that outsiders could appreciate the many positive things about your child. However, keep in mind that not all opinions are worth changing—keep the focus on your family and their needs and don't worry about the misguided opinions of others. For those who need to understand, such as teachers or baby-sitters, share some information about your child and his illness. Emphasize the positives of your child's personality, and educate them on bipolar disorder.

Ironically, the opposite situation can exist—sometimes our children work hard to keep their emotions in check and then let loose when they arrive home. For this group of parents, the outside world may only see the beauty of your child and never see the symptoms that cause you so much worry and concern. This can be frustrating for parents because they may even receive criticism for seeking help for symptoms that others may doubt exist. Again, don't worry about opinions that don't matter. Only share information about your child's severe symptoms with those who really need to know. Close family will always know a child better than others. You will both appreciate the good and be acutely aware of the negative side of your child's illness more than anyone else. Only with time will your child define his role in the outside world.

Q. How can abandoning preconceived notions help?

A. Parents can be chained to preconceived notions about psychiatric disorders or proper childhood development that could be holding them back or making them unnecessarily upset. These ideas may have been molded by family experiences or perhaps by the images portrayed by the media, but regardless of where they came from, clinging to these ideas can actually prevent you from giving your child what he needs. Consider how abandoning these preconceived notions in the following areas can help move your family to a healthier place:

- **Time lines:** It's so easy to get caught up in the idea that if your child doesn't make a benchmark at a given time, he never will. This is not true. Children with bipolar disorder may be delayed in certain developmental areas. Letting go of constraining time lines helps you let your child grow and develop at his own pace.

- **Tradition:** Tradition can be an important supportive framework for family, but it can also be unnecessarily constraining. If adherence to a particular tradition is having a negative impact rather than a positive one, examine the importance of the tradition and ways it could be modified to result in a more positive family experience. For instance, if your family flies to your parents' house for the holidays every year but your child with bipolar disorder is terrified of airplanes, maybe you could host next year.

- **Competition:** You've probably met people whose children are perfect…or so they would have you believe. They walked earlier, were potty trained first, run faster, and of course they're smarter. Breaking free from this "one up" mentality helps you value your child based on his own uniqueness.

- **Opinions:** Opinions of others can be hurtful if they don't understand your child's illness. Don't let them mold the way you address your child's needs. Find what fits for your child and your family, and use it no matter what anyone else thinks about it.

Q. How can I celebrate each day?

A. You can only celebrate each day and each success if you are ready to recognize that every day your child is alive and fighting this illness is a success. And every day that you as a parent are tackling this job is a success. Find joy in the steps forward no matter how small. There will be plenty of setbacks and plenty of hard times, which will make finding joy and celebration in each day even more important. Even in the midst of difficulty, there are reasons to celebrate. Here are a few things in every mood state that you can celebrate:

- My child went to school today despite his anxieties.
- I was able to arrange emergency care for my critically ill child, which means we will have another day to celebrate.
- My child used a self-calming technique today.
- My child recognized his mood state.
- My child advocated for himself.
- I stood up for my child today despite the ignorance of another person.
- I kept my cool even though my child was unstable.
- My child was stable and enjoying the rewards of having a good wellness team.
- My child got a good report from school today.
- My child is on homebound studies and was able to do fifteen minutes of work.
- My relatives finally understood one aspect of this illness.
- I was able to help another family understand that they are not alone.
- My child was able to communicate scary feelings.
- I did something to take care of myself today.
- A new medication trial is working.
- A complementary treatment has enhanced my child's life.
- Today, I decided to get help for my child who may have bipolar disorder.

Q. What is a parent self-care plan?

A. You may be really good at knowing the needs of your children and taking care of them, but when was the last time you stopped to think about caring for yourself? For some people, this comes naturally, but others feel selfish if they care for their own needs. However, caring for yourself adequately is just another way of helping your children—if you don't, you might become burned out or ill and your children will be affected. If you truly want to take good care of them, you must take good care of yourself.

You may know in the back of your mind that you need to see a therapist or start an exercise program, but the parent self-care plan helps you put those thoughts into action. The first step of making your plan requires that you take an honest look at your life, your habits, and your needs. You may be shocked when you realize the personal issues that need your attention. Next, examine a few areas of your life and then put your goals for improving the deficits in writing. After you have your goals in writing, you will want to prioritize and to take care of any big issues first. But you may also be amazed at how small, daily changes can help you feel energized, refreshed, and back on track. By taking care of yourself, you are setting a wonderful example for your children.

Q. How can I make a parent self-care plan for myself?

A. Think about the following areas of your life. Is there an area that you are neglecting? Could you be taking better care of yourself so that you can be healthy enough to care for your child?

Health care:

Have I had a physical within the last year?	yes	no
Am I taking prescribed medications as directed?	yes	no
Do I have a healthy diet?	yes	no
Have I seen a therapist or psychiatrist for myself as needed?	yes	no
Am I getting regular exercise?	yes	no
Am I getting sufficient sleep?	yes	no
Am I staying hydrated?	yes	no

Respite:

Do I get any breaks from caregiving?	yes	no
Do I have someone I can call to help me if I am overwhelmed?	yes	no

Am I part of a support group?	yes	no
Do I feel strong and empowered to advocate?	yes	no
Do I feel defeated and hopeless?	yes	no

Marriage:

Do my partner and I operate as a parenting team?	yes	no
Do we go on dates together and rekindle our relationship?	yes	no
Can we talk about anything other than the children?	yes	no

Single parent:

Do I have an adequate support system?	yes	no
Have I reached out to other singles in similar circumstances?	yes	no
Have I explored resources for financial assistance if needed?	yes	no

Self:

Have I taken the time to do something special for myself?	yes	no
Do I have a hobby or interest outside of caretaking?	yes	no
Do I feel calm and at peace?	yes	no
Am I stressed to the max?	yes	no

Spirituality:

Do I pray or meditate?	yes	no
Am I angry with my situation in life?	yes	no
Do I feel that I have somewhere to draw strength from?	yes	no
Am I part of a supportive, caring faith community?	yes	no
Do I reach out to assist others?	yes	no

Q. What is an example of a parent self-care plan?

A. After answering the questions above and perhaps other questions that are unique to your situation, now it's time to put together a realistic plan that will fit your needs. Remember, the self-care plan should be updated as needed and always remains a work in progress. A self-care plan template can be found in Appendix E.

Self-Care Plan

Plan for: *Devoted but overwhelmed mom of three kids, two cats, one dog, a lizard, and one great but sometimes clueless hubby.*

Purpose of this plan: *To set up some healthy habits and goals so that I will feel good about myself and have enough energy to deal with the difficult issues surrounding bipolar disorder. I also want to stay healthy for myself and my family.*

What part of me needs better care?

1. *I haven't had a physical in three years because I know my cholesterol is high and I'm not in the shape I wish I was in.*
2. *I haven't had very good eating habits. I want chocolate when I'm stressed…which is a lot these days.*
3. *I have all but abandoned my hobbies and personal interests.*
4. *I don't get exercise except when I'm ducking flying objects.*
5. *My hubby and I haven't been on a date in…well, I don't remember.*
6. *I haven't had my hair done since my niece's wedding.*

Pick three of the above needs. Write three things you will do this week to move closer to meeting these needs.

1. *I will call Dr. Gyn and schedule my physical.*
2. *Since I don't have money to pay a sitter or go out, I will rent a movie for hubby and me to watch after the kids are in bed.*
3. *I will take a walk on my lunch break at least three days a week instead of sitting at my desk.*

Chapter 15

TEENS AND DIFFICULT BEHAVIORS

- What are the special needs of teens with bipolar disorder?
- What do I do if I suspect my teen is using drugs?
- How do I handle issues of hypersexuality?
- How should I handle the topic of pregnancy?
- What if my teen is skipping school?
- How do I prevent my teen from dropping out?
- What if my teen gets arrested?
- Can the juvenile justice system help my teen?
- What if my teen becomes verbally abusive?
- What if my teen keeps trying to run away?
- What if my teen starts cutting himself?
- Should I talk to my teen about suicide?
- What if my teen denies he has an illness?
- What if my teen uses his illness as an excuse?
- How do I deal with manipulation?

Q. What are the special needs of teens with bipolar disorder?

A. The teen years are never easy, and teens with bipolar disorder have the same needs, issues, and problems as any other teenager—and then some. Raising a teenager is challenging, and raising a teenager with bipolar disorder can be extremely difficult. Understanding your teen's areas of special concern will help you to adequately address his needs.

- **Social concerns:** Social ineptness, social anxiety, and stigma can make your teen feel like an outsider. Helping your teen feel accepted and find good friends is vital. Require your teenager to do things with the family. Invite others who are supportive and a good influence on your teen. Restrict your child's association with harmful friends.

- **Addictions:** Teens with bipolar disorder are especially susceptible to becoming substance abusers. Be open and up-front about alcohol and drugs. Have frequent conversations about this issue and why it is dangerous for your teen to experiment.

- **Balance:** There are some "normal" teen extremes that won't be healthy for a teen with bipolar disorder. For example, while other teens may be able to stay up all night studying or at a sleepover, this could destabilize a teen with bipolar disorder. Talk to your child about maintaining balance to stay healthy.

- **Symptoms:** Uncontrolled symptoms of the illness ranging from hypersexuality to anger combined with reckless teenage impulsiveness are a recipe for disaster. Your teen still needs you to be involved in monitoring his illness and his medication compliance.

- **Owning the illness:** While you are still there monitoring and helping, at some point, your teen has to want to take care of his health. Make sure you lead him to the resources that will move him toward this maturity. *Behind Happy Faces: Taking Charge of Your Mental Health* by Ross Szabo and Melanie Hall may help your teen begin to own his illness.

Q. What do I do if I suspect my teen is using drugs?

A. The erratic behavior associated with bipolar disorder can be made worse by drug use. As a parent, you may confuse the signs of drug use with symptoms of your teen's bipolar disorder. On the other hand, you may be so in tune with your teen's moods that it is quickly apparent when there is more going on. Here is what to do if you suspect your teen is using drugs:

- **Wait:** If you suspect your teen is using drugs, take a moment to collect yourself and to plan how you'll handle it if your suspicions are confirmed. You may feel angry and hurt and worried. Wait until the initial shock has passed before proceeding so that you don't act out of emotion.

- **Confirm:** You will want to confirm if your suspicions are correct. Talk to your teen when he is somewhat receptive and sober—if your teen is high or drunk, he may have limited reasoning ability. Let your teen know why you are concerned, and ask if he has been experimenting with drugs. Sometimes teens will admit to this if you ask the question outright.

- **Help:** If your concerns are confirmed, then his psychiatrist should be notified immediately. Hopefully your teen will want help. This will make the process easier. If he doesn't want help, work with your child's psychiatrist to find appropriate strategies.

- **Follow up:** Your teen's psychiatrist will recommend a course of action. What type of treatment is recommended will depend on a number of things, including how heavy the drug use, if your teen is already addicted, or if this was a one-time, isolated event. In some cases, your teen will require counseling. In more severe cases, your teen may need a residential drug rehabilitation program.

Q. How do I handle issues of hypersexuality?

A. Most teens with bipolar disorder will experience hypersexuality. Teens in general may have an awakened sexual desire due to changes in their hormones during this time of growth. When this awakened sexual desire meets up with mania, it is strongly intensified and very difficult to control. Your teen may dress provocatively and engage in risky sexual behavior. Unfortunately, many of your teen's peers and even adults might take advantage of this heightened sense of sexuality. Your child may do and say things against his own moral beliefs, which can produce lasting shame and guilt.

Hypersexuality can be extremely shocking and embarrassing for parents. It should be addressed as soon as it appears, because it can become extremely dangerous. It opens your teen to many risks, including pregnancy, sexual abuse, and sexually transmitted diseases. This symptom of mania generally lessens or disappears with an adjustment in treatment. Here are some things you can do:

- **Medication management:** Call your child's psychiatrist immediately so that medications can be adjusted.

- **Supervision:** Don't allow your teen to go out unsupervised when hypersexual. Insist that your child either stay home or be accompanied by an adult.

- **Education:** Educate your teen in advance regarding the dangers of risky sexual behavior. It will be difficult for your teen to think rationally during full-blown episodes of hypersexuality, but during mildly elevated times, this warning can help your teen make better choices.

- **Boundaries:** Establish personal boundaries within the home. If your teen does something shocking such as undress in front of others in the family, don't give the act undue attention. Firmly state the family's personal boundaries rule and ask your teen to go to his room for privacy.

Q. How should I handle the topic of pregnancy?

A. According to the National Center for Health Statistics, there were about 757,000 pregnancies among teenagers fifteen to nineteen years of age in 2002. With the hypersexuality, impulsiveness, and impaired judgment that accompany bipolar disorder, your child may be at risk for teenage pregnancy. What can you do?

- **Communication:** Have honest communication with your teen regarding the risks of teenage sexual activity, including emotional turmoil, unwanted pregnancy, and sexually transmitted diseases, some of which can lead to cancer.

- **Prevention:** If your teen is sexually active, birth control will need to be addressed. You should be aware that some medications, such as Tegretol, decrease the effectiveness of birth control pills. Additionally, your teen should know that condoms do not prevent all sexually transmitted diseases. If you have a daughter, ask her doctor about the vaccine for cervical cancer.

- **Reaction:** If your teen becomes pregnant, don't abruptly stop any medications. Schedule immediate appointments with the psychiatrist and obstetrician to determine if any changes in medication are advisable to minimize risk to the unborn baby. Ask about the use of folic acid to help prevent birth defects and the possibility of using any alternative approach to minimize medication use.

- **Outcome:** In 2002, about 43 percent of teen pregnancies ended in miscarriage or abortion. Twenty states now allow a minor to receive an abortion without the consent of parents. In these cases, you may not even be given the chance to influence outcome. You do not have to approve of your child's actions, but you do need to take care of her health. Focus less on what has occurred and more on the immediate physical and emotional needs of your child.

- **Support:** Recognize that your teenager is not yet fully grown, is currently at greater risk for episodes of the illness related to hormonal changes in her body, and really needs your direction and support now more than ever. Getting angry will not change the reality of the situation; do your best to support your child.

Q. What if my teen is skipping school?

A. If your teenager already struggles in school, skipping will compli-cate things even further. He is missing important instruction time and is likely hanging out where he shouldn't be or engaging in conduct that isn't acceptable. If your teen is skipping school, find out where he's been, what he's been up to, and if it was a one-time mess up or a chronic pattern. Let him know that this is a breach of trust and is not acceptable. Arrange for appropriate consequences and check in with his teachers for a time to make sure that he is attending classes. Some schools have call systems set up to report skipping. Others have websites where you can have access to your teenager's atten-dance records.

After taking care of the necessary steps to show your disapproval, do a little investigating to get to the root of the problem. While it could be just teen experimentation, it could also signify a deeper problem at school. It may be that skipping school is a way to avoid a difficult school environment. Find out if there is one particular class that is being skipped. Does it trigger manic or depressive episodes in your teen? Is this avoidance behavior? Is your teen being bullied? Is he having signif-icant anxiety or mood issues? Addressing the underlying concern is more likely to lead to compliance. It may be that changing classes or implementing new accommodations will help your teen avoid skipping.

Q. How do I prevent my teen from dropping out?

A. If your teen wants to drop out of school, he is not alone—according to the National Center for Educational Statistics for 2005, 3.5 million young people between sixteen to twenty-four years old were not enrolled in high school and did not have a diploma or GED. The reasons a student might not complete school are complicated. The Gates Foundation found that only a third of individuals who dropped out reported that they were failing their classes. Many left for jobs or family-related difficulties. Others felt disengaged and bored. Of those who dropped out, many had early warning signs, including repeated missed classes.

There is good reason to be concerned about your teen dropping out of school. Those who drop out are more likely to be unemployed, in poverty, on welfare, or in prison. For those who do work, the average income is $10,000 less per year than those who graduated or earned a graduate equivalency. Though the statistics are daunting, there are many things you can do to help keep your child in school:

- Be aware that skipping school could be a warning sign that your child might drop out.
- Know what is going on with your teen and school.
- Try to help your teen choose courses that will be relevant to him and his future work.
- Make sure appropriate accommodations are in place and implemented.
- Make sure your teen has a contact person at school who is involved in his school life.

If your teenager is beyond the early intervention phase and miserable in his school experience, consider choosing a new path. An alternate road doesn't have to be viewed as a failure; it's just a different way to succeed. A different school, online classes, or a GED program may be appropriate for your teenager. Check to see what local alternative programs are available.

Q. What if my teen gets arrested?

A. While any teen could make a poor choice and end up in legal troubles, teens with bipolar disorder often are impulsive, have poor judgment, and lack the cognitive skills needed to think through consequences. Add to that a manic state and you have a recipe for juvenile detention. Seeking treatment for your child or teen with bipolar disorder is the best way to reduce the chance that he will have trouble with the law.

If your teen is arrested, your actions will depend largely on the nature of the offense and the seriousness of the charges your teenager faces. If the offense is minor, it is likely that your teen will be remanded into your custody. The court may order a probationary time period and perhaps community service. However, if the offense is more serious, you have a few immediate concerns. If your teenager is not remanded into your custody, check with the detention center to arrange for him to have his medication. You will likely have to supply the prescription bottle with the original label stating the directions. It may also be helpful to have a letter from the prescribing doctor so that there is no dispute about the necessity of the medication.

Juvenile justice laws vary greatly from state to state. You may need legal counsel and help. To find out information regarding the laws in your state and where you can find legal help, check with the American Bar Association. You can find them on the Web at http://www.findlegalhelp.org.

Q. Can the juvenile justice system help my teen?

A. Some parents have felt so exasperated at trying to get their teen adequate help that they have resorted to using the juvenile justice system to get aid and maybe even a respite from caring for their child. It is true that some situations may necessitate a call to the police, especially if there is an imminent danger. But it would be a mistake to equate the juvenile justice system with a mental health facility. Relying on this system to obtain adequate care for your teen is a risky roll of the dice. For some families, things have turned out well with a judge mandating treatment for a teen who is otherwise noncompliant. Unfortunately, not all cases end up this way. Your child may be sentenced to a punitive boot camp or jail. Neither of these places is equipped to address the needs of teens with bipolar disorder.

Even if mental health services are ordered by a judge, there may be an extended waiting period before a teen is transferred to an appropriate treatment facility. According to a report commissioned by the House of Representative's Government Reform Committee, "Incarceration of Youth Who Are Waiting for Community Mental Health Services in the United States," one in every seven incarcerated youths is waiting for mental health treatment. A youth may, in fact, continue to be held in jail for more than three or four months while awaiting a transfer to an appropriate treatment facility. In the meantime, without adequate care, these teens may be exposed to harmful practices by fellow inmates who may be held for completely different reasons. They may become victims of sexual abuse or may even attempt suicide. Additionally, parents may be asked to relinquish custody for treatment to take place. While you might think that all of this sounds impossible, there are far too many families who have experienced these exact scenarios. Unless absolutely necessary, do not involve the juvenile justice system in your child's care.

Q. What if my teen becomes verbally abusive?

A. More than 60 percent of caregivers reported being verbally abused by their family member with a psychiatric illness. Relatives who experienced higher levels of abuse were more likely to have symptoms of emotional distress. Verbal abuse from a teen may be something that you are ashamed to talk about. But like so many other aspects of this illness, it is an experience commonly shared by families dealing with bipolar disorder. A pattern of verbal abuse is not healthy for you and not a healthy pattern for your teen. Verbal abuse may first occur during instability but if accepted as normal or okay may continue into periods of wellness. Here are some steps to take:

- **Assess your teen's stability:** Your teenager may need to visit his psychiatrist for a medication adjustment. If he repeats words consistently while yelling, make sure that he doesn't have a co-occurring disorder such as Tourette's syndrome. This may cause some unsavory repetitive language that is not the same as verbal abuse but can be disturbing nonetheless.

- **Have clear family rules:** Make sure your teenager is aware that if he is not stable enough to have control over what is coming out of his mouth, then he is not stable enough to participate in desired activities outside the home. This will both keep him safe if unstable and encourage him to exercise any control or restraint that is within his ability.

- **Set the example:** Don't engage in verbal abuse yourself. If your teen is on a verbal tirade, refuse to have a dialogue. State clearly that you cannot listen to him when he speaks that way. Then, if possible, remove yourself from the situation.

- **Create consequences:** Work with your teenager's therapist to develop a plan appropriate to your teen to address verbal abuse.

Q. What if my teen keeps trying to run away?

A. Your teen may have a strong tendency to run away, especially when in an agitated mixed state in which he is both manic and depressed. This state strongly pushes him to do something, and many times that something is to run. He may feel an extreme inner restlessness that doesn't seem to abate. These feelings can be so strong that he may feel he will die if he doesn't leave. If your teen has shown this tendency and you find yourself worried sick and chasing him down constantly, then consider developing a "safe run" spot. This is an agreed upon safe destination where he can go. It may not be that he wants to stay away; he may just need to get away or feel as though he needs to run. If he doesn't have a "safe run" spot, he could end up anywhere. This leaves you at home, terrified, wondering if he'll walk through the door or if he is in danger.

Decide together on a "safe run" destination. It could be a friend's house or a relative's house, but wherever the spot is, he should be able to get there safely on well-lit, secure roads. Make sure that the spot is agreed upon by all parties and that those living there will provide a safe atmosphere. Let your teen know that if he goes missing, you will give him a reasonable specified amount of time to either be home or be at his "safe run" spot. Make it clear that if he doesn't turn up there within this amount of time, you will call the police and report him as a missing person. The police may consider an unstable teen with bipolar disorder as a medium- or high-risk missing person because the teen needs to take medication and may be a risk to himself.

Q. What if my teen starts cutting himself?

A. Cutting is a type of self-injury. Your teen may use self-injury as a method to gain relief from intense emotional pain. Some researchers have suggested that an immediate release of pain-numbing endorphins may soothe a cutter's emotional distress. Self-injury may also be a way to exert control over something when everything else seems out of control. Severe self-injury, however, is likely to be accompanied by suicidal thoughts.

Your teenager may feel guilty or ashamed and hide the fact that he self-injures, so you need to be alert to this possibility. Be aware that cutting may be done with objects of all sorts, including ones you might not suspect, like safety pins and soda cans. Other types of self-injury include burning oneself, biting oneself, and hitting oneself. Cutting can become addictive or an obsession. Without intervention, self-injury could become more difficult to stop and could interfere with your teen practicing healthy coping skills.

Look for the signs. If your child starts wearing long sleeves and long pants even when it is hot outside, he may be hiding cuts or bruises. He may have unexplained or poorly explained scratches. He may also have many scars in well-concealed areas from previous self-injuries. If you discover that your teen is practicing self-injury, both his psychiatrist and therapist should be made aware of this activity so that they can work to stabilize him and replace these behaviors with better coping skills. Realize that your teen may have frequent setbacks as he attempts to stop self-injurious behavior. Keep an open and supportive dialogue with your teen during this time.

Q. Should I talk to my teen about suicide?

A. Suicide is the third leading cause of death among young people fifteen to twenty-four years old. You may talk to your teen about the dangers of drugs, abduction, or reckless driving, but what about the dangers of a suicide attempt? For some it is a very uncomfortable topic—but know that talking about suicide does not cause an attempt; it can actually prevent one. It is likely that your teen will not approach you if he is having thoughts of suicide. It's important for you to bring up the topic and to open a dialogue about it. Don't wait until you are in a crisis. Talk about suicide now.

Suicidal teens are generally not thinking rationally, so it may help your teen to have clearly written steps of what to do if he feels suicidal. Appendix B has an example of a no-suicide action plan; this plan involves more than your teen writing down phone numbers or making an arbitrary promise. It means you are signing a promise to help your teen. At least three other individuals should give their contact information; make it clear to your teen that he can call them anytime for help or just a sympathetic ear. This gives your teen hope and reassurance that it is okay to tell someone. Finally, it involves your teen agreeing to go through these steps for help if he feels this way. You may also want your teen to carry a yellow ribbon "Ask 4 Help" card. It can be printed or ordered from http://www.yellowribbon.org.

Remember too that while a no-suicide action plan is important, it is not a replacement for medical care. Don't be lulled into thinking that a teen won't attempt a suicide plan because he has a piece of paper with some friends' phone numbers on it. If your teen begins obsessing over death or has become increasingly withdrawn and despondent, seek immediate medical attention.

Q. What if my teen denies he has an illness?

A. Denial can be caused by many factors, including being afraid of treatment, not wanting to be different, not understanding the illness, or simply not wanting to be sick. In addition to these factors, there is a very serious condition called anosognosia that could be at work. The term literally means "without disease knowledge." It can be described as a lack of the ability to have insight into one's own illness. This phenomenon occurs in some stroke victims, Alzheimer's patients, and those with traumatic brain injury. It literally causes the patient to deny very obvious disease or illness symptoms. For instance, a paralysis patient may deny being paralyzed, or a blind patient may deny that he is blind if he is suffering from anosognosia.

Studies show that about half the people with bipolar disorder have this lack of insight. This is why your teen may deny that there is anything wrong, even when symptoms are apparent and out of control. In addition, he may refuse to take medication since he believes nothing is wrong. This can be extremely frustrating for parents who are desperate to encourage awareness of the illness and medication compliance.

You may want to begin encouraging your child to accept treatment by making it seem less tied to admitting that he needs help and more tied to something important to him, like special privileges or weekend activities. Your teen may not see the overall value of treatment but may understand its value on his immediate schedule. Start by trying to get him to agree to treatment for a period of time—sometimes once your teen is treated, some of the fear subsides and symptoms come under better control, allowing your teen to see the benefit. For more information on how to handle anosognosia, read Dr. Xavier Amador's book, *I Am Not Sick, I Don't Need Help!*

Q. What if my teen uses his illness as an excuse?

A. Bipolar disorder can be a hidden illness, in that other people don't always recognize its full impact and limiting nature. They may be unaware of its effects on learning, executive functioning, sensory processing, social interactions, energy levels, and moods (see Chapter 9, Learning and Development). Parents may spend a great deal of time educating themselves and others about these limiting factors. This is important because parents must understand the illness and the needs of their teen. At the same time, parents must be careful not to unwittingly give teenagers the idea that their illness makes them incapable. Parents of teenagers with any disability face this same issue.

Instead, teach your teenager that he is just as capable as the next person to achieve his goals. Think of a teenager in a wheelchair. Perhaps he can't enter a building the same way as a nondisabled peer. He has to use his wheelchair and perhaps travel all the way around to another side where there is an entrance ramp. Can he still go in the building? Yes. We don't expect him to stand up and walk in, but neither do we expect him to give up. He must recognize his realistic limitations while using appropriate compensations to reach his destination. Will it take more time and effort? Yes. The same is true of your teenager. Perhaps he can't take the same route as others, but with a bit more time and more effort, he can achieve his goals. Give him the tools and skills he needs to get there, but never give him reason to think that he won't achieve great things.

Your teen may test the waters from time to time by using his illness as an excuse. While it's good if your teenager recognizes his valid limitations, your job is to help him see a way around them and not self-impose additional limitations.

Q. How do I deal with manipulation?

A. Many parents and teachers report that children with bipolar disorder are masters of manipulation. These children must become skilled and artful in the management of their environment to survive with such a difficult illness, and that is a good form of manipulation. So the first important thing to recognize is that although manipulation is generally viewed very negatively, when it is used positively as a coping skill, it is an important element for survival. As in everything else, children will need direction to develop "skillful and artful management" in a healthy way and not in a negative way.

If you perceive that your child is manipulating a situation, don't react immediately as if the manipulation in and of itself is bad. Step back and analyze the situation. Ask yourself the following questions:

- Does this artful management of the child's environment (whether positive or negative) address a need for your child?
- Does it adequately address the need in a positive way?
- Is it harmful to others in any way?
- Is there a better way to help my child be comfortable in the situation?
- If this occurs at school, what accommodations could be put in place to address the same need?

You should not remove all control and power from your child. The goal is to empower your child with appropriate, positive coping mechanisms that are artful in the management of his illness without being hurtful to others.

Chapter 16 | THE PATH TO ADULTHOOD

Q. How do I help my teen advocate for himself?

A. While it is important for you to continue advocating for your child through high school, you will not always be available in this capacity throughout his life. It will serve your teenager well, both now in school and later in the workplace, if he learns to take on a role of self-advocacy. This will happen in stages. It should not be a sink or swim scenario.

The first step is to allow your teen to see you advocating. Be aware that your teen will imitate you, so make sure to set a good example by advocating in a professional manner. Have your teen sit in on IEP meetings. Ask for his opinions about his own needs. Whenever he is able to identify a need and suggest a solution, he has participated in the advocacy process—make sure to point out these instances to him. Also, taking your teen to support group meetings or even conferences on bipolar disorder will expose him to many positive role models for self-advocacy.

The next step will be for your teenager to speak up and begin asking for the things he needs. This can be a difficult transition—sometimes self-advocacy begins with speaking up but not in a way that is likely to get results. Don't be quick to criticize or be harsh with your teenager. He is taking steps in the right direction, and it will take time to learn the appropriate ways to ask. Praise his efforts while guiding him to a more effective approach. Emphasize that the way he advocates and the words he uses can make a difference in the result. There are several key factors for self-advocacy that you will want to emphasize to your child:

1. Avoid using blame.
2. State your concerns.
3. Recommend a course of action.
4. Stay open to other solutions.

Q. When do I know it's time for my teen to drive?

A. While it is always scary when a teen becomes of age to drive, it can be even scarier when that teen has bipolar disorder. Maturity, attentional abilities, and responsibility will all play a part in when your teen is ready to drive. If your teenager does not express a desire to drive, don't push it. Wait until he feels ready. If your teenager does want to drive, then make a list of requirements he must meet before he can get his driver's license. Requirements could include medication compliance, stability, demonstration of responsibility at home and in school, and compliance with household rules. You may want to use a learner's permit for longer than the required minimum time so there continues to be state enforced restrictions and supervision on driving until you are confident that your teenager is ready to have his license.

Consider developing a driving contract for your teenager to sign before getting his license. This should clearly outline his responsibilities and what will happen (that is, loss of driving privilege) if there is a breach in them or if there is concern over stability. This driving contract should be in effect as long as your teenager lives under your roof. Allowing a teenager to drive when very unstable could lead to fulfillment of a death wish or manic reckless driving that could result in the death of another driver. There is too much at stake here to become complacent. Additionally, keep in mind that when your teenager begins a new medication or there is a dosage increase, driving should be monitored until you know how your teenager will react to the change. Some medications are sedatives, which could increase the risk of falling asleep at the wheel.

Q. How can I teach my teen a good work ethic?

A. When an employer thinks of a good work ethic, generally he wants to see his employee show up on time, ready to work, and ready to give 110 percent every day of the week. A good work ethic is based on believing that work is beneficial, important, and good for building moral character. To evaluate your teenager's work ethic, ask your teen, is work important to you? What benefits do you see from work? Do you think working hard helps you improve qualities in yourself? Many teens are likely to focus more on the monetary value that work brings and less on the moral character that it builds. Help your teenager realize some of the ways that work can benefit him by talking about how work has rounded out your personality or has contributed to your personal growth. Give him opportunities to experience the benefits of working hard.

However, when considering your teenager's work ethic, don't be quick to assume the worst based on poor functioning during times of instability. Your teenager's illness can drastically impact his work performance. When your teenager is depressed, he may be giving 150 percent of himself to function at a level that is half of what others can accomplish. Whose work ethic is better—the teenager who gives 80 percent and can breeze through his shift or your teenager who gives 150 percent effort to make it through half his shift? His limiting factors should not cause you to look down on his efforts.

Recognize that his ability to perform can be inconsistent, just as the illness is inconsistent. This is worrisome for parents because employers may not be concerned with personal effort but only with output. With increased stability comes increased ability for consistent output, and hopefully your child will have acquired the maturity and sense of responsibility needed to foster a good work ethic by the time he enters the workforce.

Q. Will my teen grow out of bipolar disorder?

A. Certainly your teen will change in many ways as he crosses the threshold from adolescence to adulthood. No doubt some of those changes will be beneficial. Less volatile levels of hormones and increased development of the frontal lobes of the brain can give your teenager improved functioning. This may occur closer to the mid twenties than to late adolescence, so as with all of your child's developmental milestones, be patient.

Current studies indicate that children who are diagnosed with bipolar disorder do not grow out of the condition. Most studies show that the illness continues on the same course of chronic expression through adulthood. However, some individuals do report a change in how the symptoms manifest. Some people move into a state that's more like the adult-onset version of the disorder, with longer periods spent in each mood state, including wellness. It is uncertain if this coincides with a particular subtype or classification of the illness or if these cases are more about the specific individual.

Especially if your teen has had a very difficult road with many crises, it can be hard to imagine what adulthood will bring. At times, you may even fear that he won't reach adulthood. But even a teen with severe difficulties, including suicide attempts and hospitalizations, can go on to find success as an adult. These people typically say that finding the right medication combination made all the difference. They hold jobs, marry, participate in further education, and even become strong advocates for others. So no matter how rough the teen years are, keep them in perspective. This is one phase of your child's life and not necessarily the defining time period. Your love, direction, and support through this time will be well worth the effort spent.

Q. How can I help my teen with weight issues?

A. Young people with bipolar disorder frequently gain weight as a medication side effect. Additionally, they may crave carbohydrates and eat for comfort when depressed. This makes it difficult to fit into the already unrealistic body image that is popular today. It also makes it hard for parents, who want to help their teenager with weight issues while still promoting a healthy diet and exercise. What can you do?

- **Recognize the issue:** There are both health and social implications for those struggling with weight issues. Even if your teenager doesn't talk about his weight, you can be sure that he is acutely aware of it.

- **Promote health vs. weight:** Promote the need to be healthy and balanced and not "thin." Overall health and well-being must be considered, including management of their illness. A family membership to the local gym or another fitness program may help your teenager keep weight gain to a minimum.

- **Make family choices:** Focus less on diet and more on a healthy family lifestyle. Make healthy snacks available and make exercise a regular part of family activity. Taking walks together, swimming in the pool, and riding bikes are fun family activities that promote health and weight control.

- **Consult with a psychiatrist:** Be aware that some medications have a greater weight gain potential than others. Talk to your teenager's psychiatrist about the possibility of using a medication that has less risk of weight gain. If this is not possible, ask about using a secondary medication such as Topamax (topiramate) to help control weight gain. Avoid over-the-counter and herbal weight loss medications because these may induce mania.

Q. How can I identify mood shifts and symptoms?

A. People who have not raised children with bipolar disorder may make casual assumptions that the symptoms of the illness are part of "normal" childhood or teen behavior. If, however, you have lived through full-blown mood symptoms, you know that they are much more extreme and dangerous than what occurs with a "typical" teenager.

It gets tricky for parents after their teenager is treated and the worst full-blown symptoms are modified. You want to be aware of early warning signs that symptoms are returning. Giving too much room for a return of symptoms based on the idea that it is just teen behavior can spell trouble. At the same time, you don't want to overreact in case it's just a normal teen mood variation.

Two things can help you distinguish between regular teen behavior and a relapse of symptoms. First, observe your teenager's behavior in the context of other teens and talk to other parents. This may help you get a good handle on what is developmentally appropriate. You also need to know your teenager. If you see a specific pattern of mood recurrence that's reminiscent of pretreatment episodes, you are likely catching a relapse in the early stages. The fact is you are not raising a "typical" teen, and not everything can be neatly separated out. You are raising a teen with bipolar disorder, and that never leaves the equation. So even if a specific behavior is normal to a "typical" teen, it may spell trouble for your teenager if he lacks the ability to modify or have a normal range of control over it. There will definitely be some trial and error here. Give yourself room to make mistakes, and keep a record of any patterns you see to help you avoid them in the future.

Q. How can I help my teen establish friendships?

A. It's important for your teen to establish friendships, and some teens with bipolar disorder find this difficult. Helping your teenager make and maintain friendships can be challenging since most teens don't want their parents involved in their social life. But that doesn't mean you have to take a totally hands-off approach. While your teenager will want to form relationships himself, he needs a positive group of peers to choose from.

Arrange activities with a peer group that has values similar to your family's. You may look within your faith-based community or your neighborhood. If your teenager has established friends at school or through school clubs, invite them over. Get to know their families. Meeting other families through support groups can also afford opportunities for your teen to make friends. If your teenager has a special interest, participating in an activity related to that interest can also be a way to make friends. Close family such as cousins may become close friends. Also, realize that if your teenager has developmental delays, he may find it easier to make friends with those in a different age group.

If your teenager has made some poor friendship choices with people who are negatively impacting him, this may be difficult for him to see. Help your teen evaluate his friendships. Try to help him come to the conclusion on his own that a particular friend may not be a true friend who is concerned about his well-being. Talk about what makes a real friend. If you suspect that a friend is having a negative impact, don't be afraid to set boundaries so that interaction is supervised. Your teenager will not be happy about it, but he will eventually figure out that you're doing it because you care.

Q. How do I help my teen manage his illness?

A. As your teenager progresses and moves closer to adulthood, your role as parent begins to change. Eventually, the inevitable will happen, and your teen will grow up and become responsible for managing his illness. While there is no way to predict how your teenager will fare during this adjustment period, there are some things you can do now to give him the best shot at transitioning:

- **Help him take over:** Soon it will be time for your teen to become manager of his treatment team. Help him see the necessity of a support team. He might prefer to think of it as his pit crew.

Emphasize to your teen that these are not people robbing him of independence; they are supporting his success and helping him maintain his independence. Without this crew, it is likely he will crash and end up more reliant on others. Ask your teen to sign a release of information authorization which can be obtained from the doctor's office. This will allow the physician to share information with you as part of his support team.

- **Switch to a psychiatrist for adults:** If his current psychiatrist only sees children, then ask for a recommendation to a psychiatrist who can see him as an adult. Switching to a doctor who sees both teens and adults while your teen still has a year or two before adulthood may make this transition easier.

- **Fill out a psychiatric advanced directive:** The fastest way for a young adult to lose the control he wants is to become unstable and to have others making decisions for him. Help your older teen see the need to take control now by expressing his wishes ahead of time, including designating whom he wants to be his mental health care agent, the person who will make decisions about his mental care if he is unable to. He can do this by filling out a psychiatric advanced directive here: http://www.bazelon.org/issues/advance directives/index.htm.

Q. How can I use gradual transition techniques?

A. Your level of involvement in raising this special child has been high. It can be difficult to step out of that role. On the other hand, you might be so tired that you drop out suddenly. Either scenario can be negative. Transitioning responsibility and ownership of illness will need to happen gradually over the course of years. Additionally, put supports in place to help your child succeed in becoming independent. To find out more about programs that may assist in the transition to adulthood, read the Bazelon Center's pamphlet, "Moving On: Analysis of Federal Programs Funding Services for Transition-Age Youth with Serious Mental Health Conditions." Here are two transition steps:

1. **Doctor visits:** Initially, you were the main reporter of symptoms to your child's doctor. Start transitioning that role to your child by discussing symptoms with him ahead of time and letting him report them to the doctor, after which you give a follow-up report. Next, let your teen begin to give his report on his own, with no follow-up from you unless necessary. Once your teen is on the verge of adulthood, perhaps you can drive him to the office and wait in the waiting room. Eventually, your adult child will drive to his own appointments.

2. **Medication responsibility:** Initially, you will manage medication, arrange for refills, fill medication containers, remind your child when it is time to take his medication, and record any adverse side effects. The next step is for your child to know what time he takes his medication. As your teen gets older, you can supervise while he fills his medication container—don't just hand your teen a bottle of meds and expect him to be able to manage his medication. Next, teach your child how to call in refills when his meds are low or call the doctor's office when he needs a refill. Have him record any adverse effects. Eventually, your role will turn into one of supervision only.

Q. Will my teen grow up to find success?

A. People with bipolar disorder can lead full lives and accomplish great things; many already have. In fact, brilliance and creativity tend to run in families who also carry bipolar disorder. Artists, writers, and people in other creative professions are much more likely to have a mood disorder or to have a family member with a mood disorder. This creative link in childhood was recently confirmed by a study done on children who were at high risk for developing bipolar disorder due to the existence of the illness in their parents. Children in this group scored higher on tests of creativity than children in families without bipolar disorder. Even outside of the realm of creative professions, people with bipolar disorder can and have excelled in all walks of life.

As a parent, your greatest concern may be whether your child can be successful now. While this is important, it's not necessarily reflective of how your child will function throughout life. School, especially, is set up for the masses—if a child is outside of that mold, he may not excel in this atmosphere. This does not mean his life is doomed or he won't excel in another setting. In adult life, there is much more freedom to express oneself and find a niche. Even some children who had a very severe presentation of the illness and endured multiple hospitalizations have grown up to marry, have a career, and manage their illness. There is every reason to believe that with appropriate intervention and treatment your child can have a successful future.

Q. Are there programs to help my adult child at college?

A. There are many choices to make as your teen considers his options for postsecondary education. This is an exciting time, but it is also a time during which your teen may need extra support for a smooth transition. If your teen is on an IEP plan, the IEP should address considerations to make sure your teen is prepared for further education. Make sure this is being discussed and addressed.

If your teen attends a college close to home, it may be easier for him to transition. He may be able to keep his own psychiatrist, therapist, and support system. If, however, he attends a college away from home, this support will not be as readily available. Your teen will need to make visits back home to his regular psychiatrist or get a new, local psychiatrist. It may be worthwhile during the transition phase to schedule phone visits between your teenager and his regular therapist. This will give some continuity of care and will help the therapist monitor for symptoms of relapse. It will also be important to help your teenager understand the things in college that could trigger such a relapse. Losing sleep, partying, and experiencing excessive stress can all spell trouble. Your teen may want to start with a light class load, schedule classes later in the day, and live off campus to avoid the parties.

Most colleges now have counseling services available. These counseling services are not generally intensive but may be able to give your teen a little extra support. Don't be afraid to ask prospective colleges about their services for those with disabilities. Additionally, many campuses now have support groups on campus. Active Minds is a nonprofit association that has support groups in campuses across the

United States. To see if a prospective college has a chapter, go to http://www.activeminds.org.

Q. What is too much help to give to an adult child?

A. As a parent, you likely hope that your child will grow into an independent and successful adult. This process may take longer for children with bipolar disorder. Few eighteen-year-olds are fully ready to tackle the responsibilities of total independence, and delayed development or chronic mood instability can make this even truer of your teenager. In some cases, your adult child will always need a certain amount of assistance. It is okay for you to help out in the long term if this is what is warranted by the illness. In other cases, your child will become completely independent and need very little help from you. There is a varying degree of severity in this illness.

For many parents, though, it becomes a balancing act to know how much help to give. Rather than focus on how much, focus more on what kind of help you give. Try to direct your help in ways that assist your adult child while allowing as much independence as possible. For instance, if your adult child can't afford medication, you can buy it for a month or two. However, rather than paying for medication endlessly, help your child apply for assistance with medication through a patient assistance program.

Rather than focusing on what your adult child can't do, help him do what he can when he can and aim at getting him to be as independent as possible. For example, if holding a full-time job is not possible, maybe he could hold a part-time job or volunteer somewhere. Also, don't think that just because your adult child is not currently able to operate independently that he'll never be able to. Stability and ability may change over time. Most important, any time you are giving assistance to your adult child, it should be with the stipulation that he is receiving treatment.

Q. Should I always come to my adult child's rescue?

A. For some parents, stepping in to give care to an adult child comes after he repeatedly discontinues medications. You may feel that you're exerting constant energy to stabilize him only to see that stability thrown away when he stops taking his medication. And of course, if he discontinues his meds, the bipolar disorder might gain control of him. You may need to draw some clear lines regarding how you will help before any of these drastic situations occur:

- **Manic spending:** When manic, your adult child may go on extravagant spending sprees. It is a sad reality of the illness, but it is not your responsibility. If things have gotten well out of hand, you may want to help him go through the process necessary to declare bankruptcy.

- **Drug abuse:** If your adult child has become addicted to drugs, don't feed the habit. Help him get into a program for treatment. Also, see if the program has transition housing so that he is still in a monitored situation instead of back home where he could influence younger siblings.

- **Homelessness:** If your adult child has no place to live, you may wish to make treatment a condition of staying under your roof. However, if the behaviors of your adult child become a danger to younger siblings in the household, other living arrangements need to be made.

You can't force your adult child to be compliant or drug-free, but you can encourage it by limiting the ways in which you help him. Relapse is an inevitable part of this illness. When it does happen, you can be supportive and help your adult child recover. Focus should always stay on supporting and encouraging healthy behaviors and not on enabling unhealthy ones. You may want to have your own therapist who can help you work out necessary boundaries.

Q. What if I see symptoms in my grandchildren?

A. Now that your child is grown, he may have children of his own. These children will be at a higher risk of developing bipolar disorder. Though your adult child may have grown up with the illness, he may or may not be able to see the illness in his own offspring. This can be a touchy subject. It's difficult to walk the line between meddling and helping. At the same time, you may be keenly aware that your grandchildren are suffering with the same illness that has tormented generations of your family.

Make the possibility that the disease might be passed on a known issue long before grandchildren enter the picture. Let your adult child know that the illness is hereditary. If you do begin seeing symptoms in your grandkids, how you go about approaching the matter will depend on your relationship with your child. If he is open with you and you have a good relationship, bring up the matter frankly. You may be able to draw comparisons to him at that age.

Often adult children with bipolar disorder have a totally different perspective of their childhood than their parents have. Parents observe symptoms from the outside, while children feel them. Your adult child may not realize what the symptoms look like. Describing your observations of the illness in a kind manner may help your child see these symptoms in his own child. If your relationship is strained, it may be more beneficial for another family member to approach this subject. Perhaps giving your child a book such as this one or information printed from a support organization may be enough to set him in the right direction.

Q. How can I be a supportive grandparent?

A. By this stage in your life, you have had much experience being supportive. As a grandparent, you may enjoy your grandchildren in a very rewarding way, but there is a particularly special role you can play now. You can become your grandchild's safe person. Your grandchild may need space or time away from his ill parent. You can provide support and contact both on the phone and in person. Your grandchild may not understand why his parent has such extreme mood shifts and may blame himself. Be aware of the possibility of self-blame, and make sure to talk openly about the illness so this blame is not internalized. You may wish to read *Sometimes My Mommy Gets Angry* by Bebe Campbell with your grandchild.

There may be times when your adult child is too ill to care for your grandchild. In these instances, you may be able to provide stability and support by becoming a temporary guardian. Hopefully this will be a mutual decision and not a hostile one for either you or your child. When it does become a decision that is made not by mutual consent but by the courts, it may feel like you are being torn between your child and your grandchild. This can be very painful. But focus on whom you can help at this point and where your efforts will make a difference.

If you live far away from your grandchild, try to be supportive even in this removed position. Cards, phone calls, pictures, emails, and vacations can all provide a way to remain an active part of your grandchild's life.

READING LISTS

Reading List for Parents

The Bipolar Child by Dr. Demitri Papolos and Janice Papolos

The Explosive Child by Dr. Ross Greene

The Feeling Good Handbook by David Burns

Genius! Nurturing the Spirit of the Wild, Odd, and Oppositional Child by George T. Lynn and Joanne Barrie Lynn

Getting Past No by William Ury

Getting to Yes: Negotiating Agreement Without Giving In by Roger Fisher and William L. Ury

How to Talk So Kids Will Listen and Listen So Kids Will Talk by Adele Faber and Elaine Mazlish

I Am Not Sick, I Don't Need Help! by Xavier Amador

Intense Minds: Through the Eyes of Young People with Bipolar Disorder by Tracy Anglada

"Moving On: Analysis of Federal Programs Funding Services for Transition-Age Youth with Serious Mental Health Conditions" by the Bazelon Center for Mental Health Law

Raising a Moody Child: How to Cope with Depression and Bipolar Disorder by Mary A. Fristad and Jill S. Goldberg Arnold

Straight Talk about Psychiatric Medications for Kids by Timothy E. Wilens

The Ups and Downs of Raising a Bipolar Child by Judith Lederman and Dr. Candida Fink

Wrightslaw: From Emotions to Advocacy by Peter W. D. Wright, Esq., and Pamela Darr Wright

Reading List for Adolescents

Behind Happy Faces: Taking Charge of Your Mental Health—A Guide for Young Adults by Ross Szabo and Melanie Hall

Clinical Depression and Bipolar Illness: Frequently Asked Questions, A Handbook for Teens by Sallie P. Mink, R.N., B.S.

Everything You Need to Know about Bipolar Disorder and Manic Depressive Illness (Need to Know Library) by Michael A. Sommers

Mind Race: A Firsthand Account of One Teenager's Experience with Bipolar Disorder (Adolescent Mental Health Initiative) by Patrick E. Jamieson and Moira A. Rynn

Recovering from Depression: A Workbook for Teens by Mary Ellen Copeland and Stuart Copans

Reading List for Children

Anger Mountain by Bryna Hebert

Brandon and the Bipolar Bear: A Story for Children with Bipolar Disorder by Tracy Anglada

Darcy Daisy and the Firefly Festival: Learning about Bipolar Disorder and Community by Lisa M. Lewandowski, Ph.D., and Shannon Trost

Matt the Moody Hermit Crab by Caroline McGee

My Bipolar Roller Coaster Feelings Book and Workbook by Bryna Hebert

No One Is Perfect and You Are a Great Kid by Kim Hix

Sometimes My Mommy Gets Angry by Bebe Campbell

Turbo Max: A Story for Siblings and Friends of Children with Bipolar Disorder by Tracy Anglada

Reading List for Teachers

Educating the Child with Bipolar Disorder: A Brochure for Educators (brochure), available through the Child and Adolescent Bipolar Foundation (http//:www.bpkids.org)

The Student with Bipolar Disorder: An Educator's Guide (8-page brochure) by Tracy Anglada, available through BPChildren (http//:www.bpchildren.com)

Understanding and Educating Children and Adolescents with Bipolar Disorder: A Guide for Educators, available through the Josselyn Center (http://www.josselyn.org/)

Appendix B

NO-SUICIDE ACTION PLAN TEMPLATE

No-Suicide Action Plan

I won't let intense feelings trick me. I can feel better. I have other options. I can do this *now:*

1. I will tell this trusted adult: _____.
   I, _____, promise to help you if you ever feel suicidal.

   _____
   (Signature of trusted adult)
   Here is how to contact me:_____.

2. If for some reason I don't feel like I can tell this trusted adult, here are three other people who care about me and have agreed to help me. *Call now:*

   Name: _____ Home #: _____ Cell #: _____
   Name: _____ Home #: _____ Cell #: _____
   Name: _____ Home #: _____ Cell #: _____

3. If nobody is home, I will call the USA National suicide hotline at
   1–800–784–2433 or 1–800–273–8255

4. If I can't deal with this, I will call 911.
   I, _____, agree to follow these steps if I feel suicidal.

   _____
   (my signature)
   Date: _____

This template may be printed online at http://childhoodbipolaronline.com/templates.aspx

Appendix C

ACTION
PLAN
TEMPLATE

Action Plan for _____
dd/mm/yyyy

Current status	
Destination	
Area of need: _____	*Statement of need:*
Destination goal	
Midrange goal	
Midrange goal	
Short-term goal	
Short-term goal	
Area of need: _____	*Statement of need:*
Destination goal	
Midrange goal	
Midrange goal	
Short-term goal	
Short-term goal	
Area of Need: _____	*Statement of need:*
Destination goal	
Midrange goal	
Midrange goal	
Short-term goal	
Short-term goal	

This template may be printed online at http://childhoodbipolaronline.com/templates.aspx

Appendix D | CRISIS PLAN TEMPLATE

Crisis Plan

Child's name:_____ Child's date of birth: _____

Child's diagnosis: _____

In a crisis, my doctor has advised us to follow these steps (if crisis is severe, call 911):

1. _____
2. _____
3. _____

Current medications:_____

_____

Allergies to medication: no_____ yes _____
Bad reaction to these meds: _____

_____

Pediatrician: _____ Office number:_____
Psychiatrist: _____ Office number:_____
Emergency number: _____ Fax number:_____
Preferred hospital: _____
Insurance: _____ Primary insured:_____
Insurance ID#: _____ Group #:_____

The insurance requires prior authorization in these cases:

_____

Prior authorization needed by:

_____

Insurance phone number for authorizations: _____

This template may be printed online at http://childhoodbipolaronline.com/templates.aspx

Appendix E

SELF-CARE PLAN TEMPLATE

Self-Care Plan for _____

Purpose of this plan: _____

_____

_____

What part of you needs better care?

1. _____
2. _____
3. _____
4. _____
5. _____
6. _____

Pick three of the above needs. Write three things you will do this week to move closer to meeting these needs:

1. _____
2. _____
3. _____

This template may be printed online at http://childhoodbipolaronline.com/templates.aspx

Appendix F

CHILD'S ACTION PLAN TEMPLATE

Young child
My Action Plan

What I want to do:	
Why I want to do this:	
Three things I want to try (if you can't think of three things, ask your parents or a friend to help with ideas):	1. 2. 3.

Here is a picture of me trying one of my ideas.

This template may be printed online at http://childhoodbipolaronline.com/templates.aspx

Older child
My Action Plan

_____

What are three goals for my future?

1. _____
2. _____
3. _____

What goal do I want to work on first? _____

Why do I want to do this? _____

What are three things I can do to work toward my goal?

_____

_____

_____

What will I do first to work on my goal? _____
_____.

What or who might help me be successful at reaching my goal?
_____
_____

What is getting in the way of my goal? _____
_____

What will I do to get around this problem? _____
_____

Glossary

5–HTP (5–hydroxytryptophan) – an amino acid that boosts serotonin production.

Abilify – this antipsychotic medication, whose generic name is aripiprazole, helps balance dopamine in the brain and is FDA-approved to treat bipolar disorder in adults and children as young as ten.

action plan – a written plan based on your child's needs which incorporates both short term and long term goals to help move your child toward wellness.

acupuncture – the process of penetrating the skin with thin needles and manipulating the needles by hand or electrical impulse.

add-on treatment – a conventional or complimentary treatment used in addition to an already existing treatment.

agranulocytosis – an acute blood disorder which may be induced by a medication and marked by a severe reduction in white blood cells.

akathisia – a medication side effect that causes a feeling of inner restlessness.

American Psychiatric Association's Diagnostic and Statistical Manual of Mental Disorders (DSM-IV) – a manual published by the American Psychiatric Association for use by doctors in diagnosing bipolar disorder and other psychiatric conditions.

Americans with Disabilities Act – a civil rights law that prohibits discrimination against persons with a physical or mental impairment.

amygdala – an area of the brain located in the temporal lobes which plays a role in perceiving emotions in others and in emotional responses, especially those related to fear.

anosognosia – a condition which causes a lack of ability to have insight into one's own illness. A literal translation of the term could be rendered "without disease knowledge."

anterior cingulate cortex – a front outer region of the brain involved in cognitive function, decision making, and emotion.

anti-inflammatory – any product or medication whose action reduces inflammation.

antipsychotics – a class of medications which act on dopamine receptors in the brain, commonly used to treat bipolar disorder, schizophrenia, and aggressive behaviors related to autism.

aripiprazole – commonly known as abilify, this antipsychotic medication helps balance dopamine in the brain and is FDA-approved to treat bipolar disorder in adults and children as young as ten.

B12 – a vitamin known for its medicinal value and available both over the counter and by prescription.

bipolar I – a classification of bipolar disorder requiring a manic or mixed episode as outlined in the *Diagnostic and Statistical Manual of Mental Disorders*.

bipolar II – a classification of bipolar disorder requiring recurring episodes of depression and at least one hypomanic episode as outlined in the *Diagnostic and Statistical Manual of Mental Disorders*.

bipolar disorder NOS – a classification of bipolar disorder that does not qualify under bipolar I or bipolar II in the *Diagnostic and Statistical Manual of Mental Disorders*.

borderline personality disorder – a classification of personality disorder characterized by a pervasive pattern of instability as outlined in the *Diagnostic and Statistical Manual of Mental Disorders*.

BPChildren – an organization dedicated to helping young people and adults understand more about childhood bipolar disorder through their internet site and books.

bradykinesia – abnormally slow or sluggish movements.

bradyphrenia – abnormally slow or sluggish thoughts.

butterfly needle – a very small needle used to draw blood in young people or the elderly.

carbamazepine – commonly known as Equetro or Tegretol, this anticonvulsant medication is considered a mood stabilizer.

Child and Adolescent Bipolar Foundation (CABF) – a non-profit organization dedicated to improving the lives of families raising children and teens living with bipolar disorder and related conditions.

child and adolescent psychiatry – a specialty branch of psychiatry dealing specifically with the care of children and adolescents.

Child Protective Services – state-run U.S. government agencies that investigate allegations of child abuse or neglect.

childhood bipolar disorder – a descriptive term referring to bipolar disorder when symptom onset occurs prior to the age of eighteen.

cingulate gyrus – a brain region playing a role in emotional response to stimuli and aggression. It is part of the limbic system and located toward the middle on one of the crests of the many folds in the brain.

clozapine – commonly known as Clozaril, this potent antipsychotic medication is used for cases of schizophrenia or bipolar disorder that do not respond to other treatment.

Clozaril – this potent antipsychotic medication, whose generic name is clozapine, is used for cases of schizophrenia or bipolar disorder that do not respond to other treatment

co-occurring conditions – conditions that commonly exist along with another condition, having enough unique symptoms to be classified as a separate illness.

critical mode – a parenting mode that addresses the needs of a critically ill child with bipolar disorder.

cutting – the act of deliberately breaking the skin open by the use of a sharp object.

cyclothymia – a classification of bipolar disorder requiring chronically recurring episodes of hypomania and low-grade depression as outlined in the *Diagnostic and Statistical Manual of Mental Disorders*.

CYP2D6 – an enzyme produced by the body and involved in metabolizing medications.

Depakote – this anticonvulsant medication, whose generic name is valproic acid, is considered to have mood stabilizing properties.

Department of Education – a U.S. government agency existing at federal, state, and local levels that is responsible for ensuring a free and appropriate public education for children.

depression – a mood state marked by sadness, emptiness, loss of interest, and irritability. In bipolar disorder depression alternates with or mixes with mania or hypomania and causes marked impairment in a person's ability to function.

Depression and Bipolar Support Alliance (DBSA) – a non-profit organization with a grassroots base which provides hope, help, and support to improve the lives of people living with depression or bipolar disorder.

docosahexaenoic acid (DHA) – an omega 3 essential fatty acid considered important to neurological development and brain health. Commonly found in fish and seafood or as a nutritional supplement along with EPA.

dopamine – a neurotransmitter in the brain involved in the regulation of movement and emotion including pleasure and pain.

eicosapentaenoic acid (EPA) – an omega-3 essential fatty acid considered important to neurological development and brain health. Commonly found in fish and seafood or as a nutritional supplement along with DHA.

electroconvulsive therapy (ECT) – a process in which electrical currents are briefly sent into portions of the brain, causing a controlled seizure.

electroencephalogram (EEG) – a recording of the electrical activity of the brain.

emergency mode – a parenting mode that addresses the needs of a severely ill child with bipolar disorder.

EMLA cream – a topical analgesic cream.

emotional disturbance (ED) – one of thirteen classifications in the regulations of the Individuals with Disabilities Education Act that qualifies a student for special education and related services based on a disability due to emotional difficulties unrelated to a health problem.

EMPowerplus – a vitamin/mineral/herbal supplement distributed by Truehope Nutritional Support Ltd. being investigated in clinical trials for the treatment of bipolar disorder.

Equetro – an extended-release formulation of carbamazepine, which has been proven effective for acute mania and mixed states.

Equilib – a vitamin/mineral/herbal supplement which was marketed as Equilib after a split in the company that makes EMPower. The product has now been reformulated and is distributed by Evince International and Earth's Pharmacy Nutritionals.

equine-facilitated learning (EFL) – a type of animal-related therapy which seeks to improve attention, self-esteem, sequencing, and multi-tasking through leading and guiding the actions of a horse.

Eskalith – a brand name of the medication lithium which is FDA-approved to treat children as young as twelve with bipolar disorder.

euthymic – a stable or moderate mood.

extrapyramidal symptoms (EPS) – a medication side effect which has a negative impact on the part of the nervous system that controls muscle reflexes.

fetal alcohol syndrome – a condition caused by exposure to alcohol while in the womb, which causes abnormal development and can manifest in poor impulse control, short attention span, learning difficulties, hyperactivity, and poor judgment skills.

fluoxetine HCl – generic name for Prozac, an antidepressant medication used to treat depressive symptoms but considered high-risk in children with bipolar disorder due to its potential to activate mania and increase suicidal thoughts.

Food and Drug Administration (FDA) – a U.S. government agency responsible for protecting the public health in part by ensuring the safety of medications.

Free and Easy Wanderer Plus (FEWP) – an herbal supplement, also known as *jia wei xiao yao*, used in Chinese medicine and investigated as a potential complementary treatment.

full-spectrum light – light which incorporates a broad range of wavelengths to emulate natural sunlight.

fusiform gyrus – part of the temporal lobe of the brain responsible for processing stimuli related to social interaction, face recognition, and emotional context.

Geodon – this antipsychotic medication, whose generic name is ziprasidone, is used for manic and mixed episodes.

ginseng – a popular herb which may induce mania in patients with bipolar disorder.

Health Insurance Portability and Accountability Act of 1996 (HIPAA) – a U.S. law which establishes the privacy of medical records and requires medical centers to disclose their privacy policies to you.

high-risk – any medication, herbal supplement, or activity that has the potential to increase mood symptoms.

hippocampus – part of the temporal lobe which plays a role in the formation of memories and associations.

hypericum – also known as St. John's Wort, this herb may induce mania or psychosis in patients with bipolar disorder.

hypersexuality – an extremely heightened sexual desire associated with mania.

hyperthyroidism – excessive activity of the thyroid gland resulting in higher levels of thyroid hormone.

hypomania – a mood state marked by an elevation in mood similar to mania but less intense. In bipolar disorder hypomania alternates with or mixes with depression.

Independent Educational Consultants Association (IECA) – a not-for-profit association representing professional educational consultants who help families in making educational placement decisions.

independent educational evaluation (IEE) – an educational evaluation completed by a neutral party at public expense.

individual education plan (IEP) – a plan which outlines the specific needs, services, and goals for an individual child who qualifies for special education services. Parents or guardians are part of the team that writes this legally binding document.

Individuals with Disabilities Education Act of 2004 (IDEA) – the U.S. law that establishes the right of children with disabilities to receive a free and appropriate public education including specialized instruction and related services.

Invega – an extended-release version of risperidone, an antipsychotic medication.

jia wei xiao yao – an herbal supplement, also known as Free and Easy Wanderer Plus, used in Chinese medicine and investigated as a potential complementary treatment.

Joint Commission on Accreditation of Healthcare Organizations (JCAHO) – a not-for-profit organization which certifies and accredits health care organizations for meeting specific standards of performance.

Juvenile Bipolar Research Foundation (JBRF) – a charitable organization dedicated to the support of research for the study of early-onset bipolar disorder.

Katie Beckett waiver – a U.S. Medicaid waiver that allows children with severe medical conditions to be covered even when their family's income surpasses eligibility requirements.

lamotrigine – the generic name of Lamictal, an anticonvulsant medication which is used as a mood stabilizer in the treatment of bipolar disorder.

Lamictal – an anticonvulsant medication, whose generic name is lamotrigine, which is used as a mood stabilizer in the treatment of bipolar disorder.

limbic system – a group of interconnected structures in the brain involved in the regulation of emotional responses, the creation of memory, and the interpretation of sensory information.

lithium – a naturally occurring mineral which has been used as a medicinal treatment for bipolar disorder. The FDA-approved medical grade of lithium includes Lithobid and Eskalith.

Lithobid – a brand name of lithium which is FDA-approved to treat children as young as twelve with bipolar disorder .

lupus – an autoimmune disease which causes antibodies to attack the body, resulting in pain and inflammation.

***Ma-huang* (ephedra)** – an herbal supplement associated with inducing manic episodes and psychosis in patients with bipolar disorder.

mania – an unusually elevated mood state marked by euphoria or irritability. In bipolar disorder mania alternates with or mixes with depression and causes marked impairment in a person's ability to function.

Medicaid – a U.S. medical assistance program funded by state and federal government to assist eligible individuals.

megadoses – an unusually large dosage.

mindfulness-based cognitive therapy (MBCT) – a therapy that combines meditation practices and cognitive therapy.

mixed episode – a period of time during which a person experiences symptoms of both mania and depression together at the same time.

modified mode – a parenting mode that addresses the needs of a mildly ill or partially stable child with bipolar disorder.

monotherapy – treatment utilizing only one medication.

mood stabilizer – a common term referring to medication that equalizes a person's mood and helps to normalize the extreme fluctuations between depression and mania.

mood swings – the alternating of a person's mood between the low of depression and the high of mania.

motor cortex – brain region responsible for influencing motor movement.

multiple sclerosis – a degenerative disease of the central nervous system which can result in muscle weakness and loss of coordination.

N-acetylaspartate – a chemical that is only found in neurons and is considered a marker for the health of neurons.

National Alliance on Mental Illness (NAMI) – a non-profit grassroots organization for people with mental illness and their families.

National Center for Complementary and Alternative Medicine (NCCAM) – a U.S. federal agency for scientific research on complementary and alternative medicine.

National Institutes of Health (NIH) – the primary U.S. federal agency for conducting and supporting medical research.

National Library of Medicine - the world's largest medical library providing information and research services.

neurochemical – a chemical that affects the central nervous system.

neurofeedback – a process by which the brain is encouraged to change specific wave patterns by using feedback on brain wave activity provided by sensors on the scalp connected to a neurofeedback machine and specialized software.

neuroleptic dysphoria – a medication side effect from antipsychotics which causes an unusual feeling of unwellness and discontent.

neuroprotective – a mechanism or action that protects neurons from degeneration.

oculogyric crisis – side effect of a medication which causes movement of the eye into a fixed position, usually upward, for a few minutes or hours.

olanzapine – commonly known as Zyprexa this antipsychotic medication is used to control manic and mixed episodes and is FDA-approved for maintenance use in adults with bipolar disorder.

omega-3 – a group of essential fatty acids including DHA and EPA considered important to neurological development and brain health. Commonly found in fish and seafood or as a nutritional supplement.

oppositional defiant disorder – a behavioral disorder characterized by a pervasive pattern of negativistic, hostile, and defiant behavior as outlined in the *Diagnostic and Statistical Manual of Mental Disorders*.

orbitofrontal cortex – area of the brain located directly behind the eyes which plays a role in mood, motivation, responsibility, and addiction.

other health impairment (OHI) – one of thirteen classifications in the regulations of the Individuals with Disabilities Education Act that qualifies a student for special education and related services based on disability related to a health impairment.

out-of-pocket – being paid out of one's own money and not reimbursed by insurance.

outpatient – a patient receiving services from a hospital or other health care facility without being admitted for an overnight stay.

overtalkativeness – a symptom of mania that creates an intense need to talk. Speech is frequently louder and more rapid than normal.

oxcarbazepine – generic name for Trileptal, a mood stabilizer closely related to Tegretol. While frequently used to treat bipolar disorder, it is not FDA-approved for this purpose.

paliperidone – the generic name for Invega, which is an extended-release version of the antipsychotic medication Risperdal.

polypharmacology – the use of multiple medications to address the health care needs of a patient.

polypharmacy – the use of multiple medications to address the health care needs of a patient.

post-traumatic stress – an anxiety disorder characterized by severe emotional distress after a traumatic event, as outlined in the *Diagnostic and Statistical Manual of Mental Disorders*.

prefrontal cortex – a region of the brain located behind the forehead and involved in executive functions such as planning, sequencing, and working memory. This area of the brain is also involved in judgment and social control.

Prozac – the brand name for fluoxetine HCl, an antidepressant medication used to treat depressive symptoms but considered high-risk in children with bipolar disorder due to its potential to activate mania and increase suicidal thoughts.

putamen – an area of the brain involved in motor control and sensory motor integration.

quetiapine – the generic name of Seroquel which is an antipsychotic medication that works on both the manic and depressive states of bipolar disorder.

rapid cycling – switching between manic and depressive episodes more than four times in one year.

Rehabilitation Act of 1973 – a U.S. federal non-discrimination law which prevents discrimination on the basis of a person's disability by any agency receiving federal funds.

right nucleus Accumbens – an area of the brain that modulates desire, inhibition, and satisfaction.

Risperdal – the brand name for risperidone, an antipsychotic medication which is FDA-approved to treat children as young as ten with bipolar disorder.

risperidone – an antipsychotic, whose brand name is Risperdal, that is FDA-approved to treat children as young as ten with bipolar disorder.

SAMe (S-adenosyl-L-methionine) – a product derived from the essential amino acid L-methionine which can cause hypomania in some individuals with bipolar disorder.

schizoaffective disorder – a disorder which incorporates symptoms of both a mood disorder and schizophrenia, as outlined in the *Diagnostic and Statistical Manual of Mental Disorders*.

schizophrenia – a disorder which can include paranoid thinking, hallucinations, delusions, blunted emotions, and social withdrawal, as outlined in the *Diagnostic and Statistical Manual of Mental Disorders*.

section 504 – section of the Rehabilitation Act of 1973 which outlines the rights of individuals with disabilities and prevents discrimination in federally funded programs such as schools.

seizures – abnormal electrical activity in the brain which may cause an altered mental state.

self-medication – using prescription or nonprescription substances without the supervision of a medical practitioner to blunt emotional distress.

septum pellucidum – a cavity separating two membranes in the brain that would normally fuse together during infancy. These membranes are thought to be responsible for the modulation of emotional expression.

Seroquel – the brand name for quetiapine, an antipsychotic medication that works on both the manic and depressive states of bipolar disorder.

sleepwalking – engaging in activities such as walking without being in a state of wakefulness.

Social Security Administration – the U.S. government agency responsible for administering benefits to qualified disabled individuals.

soft bipolar – a term describing a milder symptom presentation than that found in the classical bipolar I disorder.

SPECT scans – Single Photon Emission Computed Tomography scans are nuclear imaging scans that create a 3-D image of the brain by tracing the blood flow through arteries and veins in the brain.

St. John's Wort – also known as hypericum, this herb may induce mania or psychosis in patients with bipolar disorder.

stand-alone treatment – a treatment, whether traditional or alternative, using one agent without additional pharmaceutical or complementary treatments.

STARFISH – a non-profit organization dedicated to helping children with various neurological conditions through support and advocacy training.

striatum – part of the basal ganglia which is located in the interior regions of the brain and responsible for motor activity, learning by habit, and cognitive function.

superior parietal lobule – region of the brain thought to be responsible for spatial orientation.

superior temporal gyrus – part of the temporal lobe thought to be involved in the areas of speech, music, insight, and information processing.

Symbyax – the brand name of a medication which combines the active ingredients of Zyprexa and Prozac. It is FDA-approved to treat depressive episodes in adults with bipolar disorder but the FDA has also issued a warning that it may increase suicidal thoughts in children and adolescents.

tardive dyskinesia – a side effect of antipsychotic medications that can cause involuntary movements, especially of the mouth, lips, and tongue. Movements may include facial tics, tongue rolling, and lip licking.

Tegretol – this anticonvulsant medication, whose generic name is carbamazepine, is considered a mood stabilizer.

temporal lobe seizures – abnormal electrical activity that occurs in the temporal lobe of the brain which may cause an altered mental state.

thalamus – located at the top of the brain stem this area of the brain helps process sensory information.

tic disorders – a group of disorders characterized by sudden, rapid, involuntary movements, as outlined in the *Diagnostic and Statistical Manual of Mental Disorders*.

transitional mode – a parenting mode that addresses the needs of a moderately ill child with bipolar disorder.

treatment plan – a comprehensive plan to significantly improve the patient's life by addressing all areas of need through medical, educational, and therapeutic intervention.

tricyclic antidepressants – a class of older antidepressant medications first used in the 1960s.

Trileptal – a mood stabilizer, whose generic name is oxcarbazepine, closely related to Tegretol. While frequently used to treat bipolar disorder, it is not FDA-approved for this purpose.

valproic acid – the generic name for Depakote, an anticonvulsant medication which is considered to have mood stabilizing properties.

vanadium – a trace mineral which is elevated in the blood, hair, and tissue of patients with bipolar disorder.

wellness mode – a parenting mode that addresses the needs of a stable child with bipolar disorder.

Wilson's disease – a rare disease that inhibits the body's ability to eliminate copper and can cause symptoms similar to bipolar disorder.

ziprasidone – the generic name for Geodon, an antipsychotic medication used for manic and mixed episodes.

Zyprexa – an antipsychotic medication, whose generic name is olanzapine, used to control manic and mixed episodes.

References

Ahn, M. S., J. L. Breeze, N. Makris, D. N. Kennedy, S. M. Hodge, M. R. Herbert, L. J. Seidman, J. Biederman, V. S. Caviness, and J. A. Frazier. 2007. Anatomic brain magnetic resonance imaging of the basal ganglia in pediatric bipolar disorder. *Journal of Affective Disorders* 104 (1–3): 147–54.

American Psychiatric Association: *Diagnostic and Statistical Manual of Mental Disorders*, Fourth Edition, Text Revision. Washington, DC: American Psychiatric Association, 2000.

Antun, F. T., G. B. Burnett, A. J. Cooper, R. J. Daly, J. R. Smythies, and A. K. Zealley. 1971. The effects of l-methionine (without MAOI) in schizophrenia. *Journal of Psychiatric Research* 8: 63–71.

Becerra, J., T. Fernández, T. Harmony, M. I. Caballero, F. García, A. Fernández-Bouzas, E. Santiago-Rodríguez, and R. A. Prado-Alcalá. 2006. Follow-up study of learning-disabled children treated with neurofeedback or placebo. *Clinical EEG and Neuroscience* 37 (3): 198–203.

Biederman, J., A. Kwon, J. Wozniak, E. Mick, S. Markowitz, V. Fazio, and S. V. Faraone. 2004. Absence of gender differences in pediatric bipolar disorder: Findings from a large sample of referred youth. *Journal of Affective Disorders* 83 (2–3): 207–14.

Blumberg, H. P., C. Fredericks, F. Wang, J. H. Kalmar, L. Spencer, X. Papademetris, B. Pittman, A. Martin, B. S. Peterson, R. K. Fulbright, et al. 2005. Preliminary evidence for persistent abnormalities in amygdala volumes in adolescents and young adults with bipolar disorder. *Bipolar Disorders* 7 (6): 570–76.

Blumberg, H. P., J. Kaufman, A. Martin, D. S. Charney, J. H. Krystal, and B. S. Peterson. 2004. Significance of adolescent neurodevelopment for the neural circuitry of bipolar disorder. *Annals of the New York Academy of Sciences* 1021:376–83.

Blumberg, H. P., J. Kaufman, A. Martin, R. Whiteman, J. H. Zhang, J. C. Gore, D. S. Charney, J. H. Krystal, and B. S. Peterson. 2003. Amygdala and hippocampal volumes in adolescents and adults with bipolar disorder. *Archives of General Psychiatry* 60 (12): 1201–8.

Botteron, K. N., M. W. Vannier, B. Geller, R. D. Todd, and B. C. Lee.1995. Preliminary study of magnetic resonance imaging characteristics in 8- to 16-year-olds with mania. *Journal of the American Academy of Child and Adolescent Psychiatry* 34 (6): 742–49.

Caetano, S. C., R. L. Olvera, D. Glahn, M. Fonseca, S. Pliszka, and J. C. Soares. 2005. Fronto-limbic brain abnormalities in juvenile onset bipolar disorder. *Biological Psychiatry* 58 (7): 525–31.

Centers for Disease Control and Prevention, National Center for Health Statistics. 2007. America's Children: Key National Indicators of Well-Being. http://www.childstats.gov/americaschildren/health3.asp (accessed October 15, 2007).

Chang, K., N. Adleman, K. Dienes, N. Barnea-Goraly, A. Reiss, and T. Ketter. 2003. Decreased n-acetylaspartate in children with familial bipolar disorder. *Biological Psychiatry* 53 (11): 1059–65.

Chang, K., N. E. Adleman, K. Dienes, D. I. Simeonova, V. Menon, and A. Reiss. 2004. Anomalous prefrontal-subcortical activation in familial pediatric bipolar disorder: A functional magnetic resonance imaging investigation. *Archives of General Psychiatry* 61 (8): 781–92.

Chang, K., A. Karchemskiy, N. Barnea-Goraly, A. Garrett, D. I. Simeonova, and A. Reiss. 2005. Reduced amygdalar gray matter volume in familial pediatric bipolar disorder. *Journal of the American Academy of Child and Adolescent Psychiatry* 44 (6): 565–73.

Chen, B. K., R. Sassi, D. Axelson, J. P. Hatch, M. Sanches, M. Nicoletti, P. Brambilla, M. S. Keshavan, N. D. Ryan, B. Birmaher, et al. 2004. Cross-sectional study of abnormal amygdala development in adolescents and young adults with bipolar disorder. *Biological Psychiatry* 56 (6): 399–405.

Chen, H. H., M. A. Nicoletti, J. P. Hatch, R. B. Sassi, D. Axelson, P. Brambilla, E. S. Monkul, M. S. Keshavan, N. D. Ryan, B. Birmaher, et al. 2004. Abnormal left superior temporal gyrus volumes in children and adolescents with bipolar disorder: A magnetic resonance imaging study. *Neuroscience Letters* 363 (1): 65–68.

DelBello, M. P., C. M. Adler, and S. M. Strakowski. 2006. The neurophysiology of childhood and adolescent bipolar disorder. *CNS Spectrums* 11 (4): 298–311.

DelBello, M. P., M. E. Zimmerman, N. P. Mills, G. E. Getz, and S. M. Strakowski. 2004. Magnetic resonance imaging analysis of amygdala and other subcortical brain regions in adolescents with bipolar disorder. *Bipolar Disorders* 6 (1): 43–52.

Dickstein, D. P., M. P. Milham, A. C. Nugent, W. C. Drevets, D. S. Charney, D. S. Pine, and E. Leibenluft. 2005. Frontotemporal alterations in pediatric bipolar disorder: Results of a voxel-based morphometry study. *Archives of General Psychiatry* 62 (7): 734–41.

Diego, M. A., T. Field, M. Hernandez-Reif, J. A. Shaw, E. M. Rothe, D. Castellanos, and L. Mesner. 2002. Aggressive adolescents benefit from massage therapy. *Adolescence* 37 (147): 597–607.

Dilsaver, S. C., F. Benazzi, Z. Rihmer, K. K. Akiskal, and H. S. Akiskal. 2005. Gender, suicidality and bipolar mixed states in adolescents. *Journal of Affective Disorders* 87 (1): 11–16.

Duax, J. M., E. A. Youngstrom, J. R. Calabrese, and R. L. Findling. 2007. Sex differences in pediatric bipolar disorder. *The Journal of Clinical Psychiatry* 68 (10): 1565–73.

El-Badri, S. M., D. A. Cousins, S. Parker, H. C. Ashton, V. L. McAllister, I. N. Ferrier, and P. B. Moore. 2006. Magnetic resonance imaging abnormalities in young euthymic patients with bipolar affective disorder. *The British Journal of Psychiatry* 189: 81–82.

Elster, E. L. 2004. Treatment of bipolar, seizure, and sleep disorders and migraine headaches utilizing a chiropractic technique. *Journal of Manipulative and Physiological Therapeutics* 27 (3): E5.

Frazier, J. A., M. S. Ahn, S. DeJong, E. K. Bent, J. L. Breeze, and A. J. Giuliano. 2005. Magnetic resonance imaging studies in early-onset bipolar disorder: A critical review. *Harvard Review of Psychiatry* 13 (3): 125–40.

Frazier, J. A., J. L. Breeze, G. Papadimitriou, D. N. Kennedy, S. M. Hodge, C. M. Moore, J. D. Howard, M. P. Rohan, V. S. Caviness, and N. Makris. 2007. White matter abnormalities in children with and at risk for bipolar disorder. *Bipolar Disorders* 9 (8): 799–809.

Frazier, J. A., S. Chiu, J. L. Breeze, N. Makris, N. Lange, D. N. Kennedy, M. R. Herbert, E. K. Bent, V. K. Koneru, M. E. Dieterich, et al. 2005. Structural brain magnetic resonance imaging of limbic and thalamic volumes in pediatric bipolar disorder. *The American Journal of Psychiatry* 162 (7): 1256–65.

Gates Foundation. 2006. The Silent Epidemic: Perspectives of High School Dropouts. http://www.gatesfoundation.org/nr/downloads/ed/TheSilentEpidemic3–06FINAL.pdf (accessed August, 2007).

Geller, B., and J. Luby. 1997. Child and adolescent bipolar disorder: A review of the past 10 years. *Journal of the American Academy of Child and Adolescent Psychiatry* 36: 1168–76.

Goldstein, T. R., B. Birmaher, D. Axelson, N. D. Ryan, M. A. Strober, M. K. Gill, S. Valeri, L. Chiappetta, H. Leonard, J. Hunt, et al. 2005. History of suicide attempts in pediatric bipolar disorder: Factors associated with increased risk. *Bipolar Disorders* 7 (6): 525–35.

Hajek, T., N. Carrey, and M. Alda. 2005. Neuroanatomical abnormalities as risk factors for bipolar disorder. *Bipolar Disorders* 7 (5): 393–403.

Haldane, M., and S. Frangou. 2004. New insights help define the pathophysiology of bipolar affective disorder: Neuroimaging and neuropathology findings. *Prog Neuropsychopharmacol Biological Psychiatry* 28 (6): 943–60.

Kaplan, B. J., J. E. Fisher, S. G. Crawford, C. J. Field, and B. Kolb. 2004. Improved mood and behavior during treatment with a mineral-vitamin supplement: An open-label case series of children. *Journal of Child and Adolescent Psychopharmacology* 14 (1): 115–22.

Kaur, S., R. B. Sassi, D. Axelson, M. Nicoletti, P. Brambilla, E. S. Monkul, J. P. Hatch, M. S. Keshavan, N. Ryan, B. Birmaher, et al. 2005. Cingulate cortex anatomical abnormalities in children and adolescents with bipolar disorder. *The American Journal of Psychiatry* 162 (9): 1637–43.

Kim, E. Y., and D.J. Miklowitz. 2004. Expressed emotion as a predictor of outcome among bipolar patients undergoing family therapy. *Journal of Affective Disorders* 82 (3): 343–52.

Kim, M. J., I. K. Lyoo, S. R. Dager, S. D. Friedman, J. Chey, J. Hwang, Y. J. Lee, D. L. Dunner, and P. F. Renshaw. 2007. The occurrence of cavum septi pellucidi enlargement is increased in bipolar disorder patients. *Bipolar Disorders* 9 (3): 274–80.

Leibenluft, E., B. A. Rich, D. T. Vinton, E. E. Nelson, S. J. Fromm, L. H. Berghorst, P. Joshi, A. Robb, R. J. Schachar, D. P. Dickstein, et al. 2007. Neural circuitry engaged during unsuccessful motor inhibition in pediatric bipolar disorder. *The American Journal of Psychiatry* 164 (1): 52–60.

Leverich, G. S., R. M. Post, P. E. Keck Jr., L. L. Altshuler, M. A. Frye, R. W. Kupka, W. A. Nolen, T. Suppes, S. L. McElroy, H. Grunze, et al. 2007. The poor prognosis of childhood-onset bipolar disorder. *The Journal of Pediatrics* 150 (5): 485–90.

Lyoo, I. K., H. K. Lee, J. H. Jung, G. G. Noam, and P. F. Renshaw. 2002. White matter hyperintensities on magnetic resonance imaging of the brain in children with psychiatric disorders. *Comprehensive Psychiatry* 43 (5): 361–68.

McClellan, J., R. Kowatch, R. L. Findling, and work group on quality issues. 2007. Practice parameter for the assessment and treatment of children and adolescents with bipolar disorder. *Journal of the American Academy of Child and Adolescent Psychiatry* 46 (1): 107–25.

McClure, E. B., J. E. Treland, J. Snow, M. Schmajuk, D. P. Dickstein, K. E. Towbin, D. S. Charney, D. S. Pine, and E. Leibenluft. 2005. Deficits in social cognition and response flexibility in pediatric bipolar disorder. *The American Journal of Psychiatry* 162 (9): 1644–51.

Merikangas, K. R., H. S. Akiskal, J. Angst, P. E. Greenberg, R. M. Hirschfeld, M. Petukhova, and R. C. Kessler. 2007. Lifetime and 12–month prevalence of bipolar spectrum disorder in the national comorbidity survey replication. *Archives of General Psychiatry* 64:543–52.

Miklowitz, D. J., M. W. Otto, E. Frank, N. A. Reilly-Harrington, S. R. Wisniewski, J. N. Kogan, A. A. Nierenberg, J. R. Calabrese, L. B. Marangell, L. Gyulai, et al. 2007. Psychosocial treatments for bipolar depression: A 1–year randomized trial from the systematic treatment enhancement program. *Archives of General Psychiatry* 64 (4): 419–26.

Monkul, E. S., K. Matsuo, M. A. Nicoletti, N. Dierschke, J. P. Hatch, M. Dalwani, P. Brambilla, S. Caetano, R. B. Sassi, A. G. Mallinger, et al. 2007. Prefrontal gray matter increases in healthy individuals after lithium treatment: A voxel-based morphometry study. *Neuroscience Letters* 429 (1): 7–11.

Moore, C. M., J. A. Frazier, C. A. Glod, J. L. Breeze, M. Dieterich, C. T. Finn, B. Frederick, and P. F. Renshaw. 2007. Glutamine and glutamate levels in children and adolescents with bipolar disorder. *Journal of the American Academy of Child and Adolescent Psychiatry* 46 (4): 524–34.

Moreno, C., G. Laje, C. Blanco, H. Jiang, A. B. Schmidt, M. Olfson. 2007. National trends in the outpatient diagnosis and treatment of bipolar disorder in youth. *Archives of General Psychiatry* 64 (9): 1032–39.

Najt, P., M. Nicoletti, H. H. Chen, J. P. Hatch, S. C. Caetano, R. B. Sassi, D. Axelson, P. Brambilla, M. S. Keshavan, N. D. Ryan, et al. 2007. Anatomical measurements of the orbitofrontal cortex in child and adolescent patients with bipolar disorder. *Neuroscience Letters* 413 (3): 183–86.

Papolos, J., and D. Papolos. Why Johnny and Jenny can't write: Disorders of written expression and children with bipolar disorder. *Bipolar Child Newsletter* (June 2004 Volume 17). http://bipolarchild.com/Newsletters/0406.html (accessed September 15, 2007).

Rich, B. A., D. T. Vinton, R. Roberson-Nay, R. E. Hommer, L. H. Berghorst, E. B. McClure, S. J. Fromm, D. S. Pine, and E. Leibenluft. 2006. Limbic hyperactivation during processing of neutral facial expressions in children with bipolar disorder. *Proceedings of the National Academy of Sciences of the United States of America* 103 (23): 8900–8905.

Sanches, M., R. L. Roberts, R. B. Sassi, D. Axelson, M. Nicoletti, P. Brambilla, J. P. Hatch, M. S. Keshavan, N. D. Ryan, B. Birmaher, et al. 2005. Developmental abnormalities in striatum in young bipolar patients: A preliminary study. *Bipolar Disorders* 7 (2): 153–58.

Sassi, R. B., M. Nicoletti, P. Brambilla, A. G. Mallinger, E. Frank, D. J. Kupfer, M. S. Keshavan, and J. C. Soares. 2002. Increased gray matter volume in lithium-treated bipolar disorder patients. *Neuroscience Letters* 329 (2): 243–45.

Stahl, L. A., D. P. Begg, R. S. Weisinger, and A. J. Sinclair. 2008. The role of omega-3 fatty acids in mood disorders. *Current Opinion in Investigational Drugs* 9 (1): 57–64.

U.S. Department of Education. 2006. Assistance to states for the education of children with disabilities and preschool grants for children with disabilities. http://idea.ed.gov/download/finalregulations.pdf. (accessed August 1, 2007).

U.S. House of Representatives Committee on Government Reform. 2004. Incarceration of youth who are waiting for community mental health services in the United States. http://oversight.house.gov/documents/20040817121901-25170.pdf (accessed July, 2007).

Wilke, M., R. A. Kowatch, M. P. DelBello, N. P. Mills, and S. K. Holland. 2004. Voxel-based morphometry in adolescents with bipolar disorder: First results. *Psychiatry Research* 131 (1): 57–69.

Wozniak, J., J. Biederman, E. Mick, J. Waxmonsky, L. Hantsoo, C. Best, J. E. Cluette-Brown, and M. Laposata. 2007. Omega-3 fatty acid monotherapy for pediatric bipolar disorder: A prospective open-label trial. *European Neuropsychopharmacology* 17 (6–7): 440–47.

Zhang, Z. J., W. H. Kang, Q. R. Tan, Q. Li, C. G. Gao, F. G. Zhang, H. H. Wang, X. C. Ma, C. Chen, W. Wang, et al. 2007. Adjunctive herbal medicine with carbamazepine for bipolar disorders: A double-blind, randomized, placebo-controlled study. *Journal of Psychiatric Research* 41 (3–4): 360–69.

Zubieta, J. K., J. A. Bueller, L. R. Jackson, D. J. Scott, Y. Xu, R. A. Koeppe, T. E. Nichols, and C. S. Stohler. 2005. Placebo effects mediated by endogenous opioid activity on mu-opioid receptors. *The Journal of Neuroscience* 25 (34): 7754–62.

Index

About the Authors

Tracy Anglada is the founder and president of BPChildren and the mother of two children with bipolar disorder. She has authored several works on bipolar disorder in children including *Brandon and the Bipolar Bear, Intense Minds: Through the Eyes of Young People with Bipolar Disorder, Questions Kids Have About Pediatric Bipolar Disorder, The Student with Bipolar Disorder: An Educator's Guide,* and *Turbo Max.*

Sheryl Hakala completed her medical degree, general adult psychiatric training, and child psychiatric fellowship serving as chief resident at the University of South Florida. Dr. Hakala is also active in organized psychiatry, has several scientific publications, and has made several television appearances. She provides both psychotherapy and pharmacotherapy in her private practice in Tampa, Florida.